T0366635

WOMEN
IN THE
MISSION
OF THE
CHURCH

WOMEN
IN THE
MISSION
OF THE
CHURCH

Their Opportunities and Obstacles
throughout Christian History

Leanne M. Dzubinski *and* Anneke H. Stasson

Baker Academic
a division of Baker Publishing Group
Grand Rapids, Michigan

Published by Baker Academic
a division of Baker Publishing Group
PO Box 6287, Grand Rapids, MI 49516-6287
www.bakeracademic.com

Printed in the United States of America

Library of Congress Cataloging-in-Publication Data
Names: Dzubinski, Leanne M., 1963– author. | Stasson, Anneke H., author.
Title: Women in the mission of the church : their opportunities and obstacles throughout
    Christian history / Leanne M. Dzubinski and Anneke H. Stasson.
Description: Grand Rapids, Michigan : Baker Academic, a division of Baker Publishing Group,
    [2021] | Includes bibliographical references and index.
Identifiers: LCCN 2020039069 | ISBN 9781540960726 (paperback) | ISBN 9781540964427
    (casebound)
Subjects: LCSH: Women in Christianity—History. | Women in church work—History. | Mission of
    the church—History.
Classification: LCC BV639.W7 D98 2021 | DDC 270.082—dc23
LC record available at https://lccn.loc.gov/2020039069

21 22 23 24 25 26 27   7 6 5 4 3 2 1

For my grandmothers, my mother,
my sisters, my daughters, and my nieces.
The world is better, and I am better,
because of you all.
—L. M. D.

For my mother, without whose love
I would never have written this book.
And for my daughters, with hope
for the world that will be theirs.
—A. H. S.

CONTENTS

PREFACE

As we wrote this book, we began to really understand John's exclamation in John 21:25: "Jesus did many other things as well. If every one of them were written down, I suppose that even the whole world would not have room for the books that would be written." Jesus's followers, over the last two thousand years, have also done "many other things." Library shelves are full of books recording those things.

For a number of years now, Leanne has been giving a presentation on women in the history of the church. She developed the presentation originally for a class on women in leadership at Philadelphia Biblical University, as it was then called. She chose to take a bird's-eye view, covering women's involvement in three eras of history in which their work was crucial to the spread of Christianity and was particularly visible: the early church orders of widows, virgins, and deacons; the medieval monastic movements; and the modern missionary movement. The goal of the presentation was to show that women have always—from the time of Jesus up to the present day—been crucial to God's work on earth. God has always had a place for women with a vocation to serve. She wanted to show that women in ministry was not a new idea of the twentieth century as part of 1960s second-wave feminism, as she often heard claimed, but was instead God's good plan from the beginning.

Next she started giving the presentation at retreats for women missionaries and for women in executive leadership in mission organizations. Pretty soon women began to ask, "Where's the book?" They wanted to read the stories of these amazing women for themselves. They wanted to see, in print, how women had been engaging in ministry throughout church history.

Keenly aware that she is not a historian, Leanne invited Anneke to join her in writing the book. Anneke had previously done historical work on women, sexual ethics, and marital practices in nineteenth- and twentieth-century Christian mission. She had long been interested in the church's teaching on gender roles, and she knew that while scholars have been doing tremendous work to reclaim the stories of women in church history, most of those stories have yet to make their way into our churches. This book aims to pass down this scholarship to students, parishioners, and pastors so as to enable them to better answer some of the questions about women and ministry.

We struggled to decide who and what to include in this book. For every story we did include, there are many others that we didn't and multitudes of stories beyond those that are completely lost to history. We also want to be transparent about our limitations. Although we have international experience and speak other languages, we are, first and foremost, English-speaking Americans. The material we can access is written in English; the perspectives we can obtain are primarily those of English-speaking Westerners. We have included some non-Western stories and perspectives in this book, but we are keenly aware of our limitations in that regard. We have not even scratched the surface of the contributions of women in Asia, Africa, and Latin America. Nor have we done an extensive, critical examination of racism, colonialism, and other -isms that have plagued the church. We are grateful that people around the world are also taking up their pens and writing the accounts of women in their societies, and we are eager for those stories to become more well known. We believe that women in every society need to be reminded that God loves them, values them as daughters, and calls them to kingdom service.

There are numerous people we would like to thank for their support and encouragement throughout this book-writing process. First of all, we thank our editor, Jim Kinney, who believed in us and offered us a book contract. Thank you! We are also grateful for our mentors, Alice Mathews and Dana Robert. Thank you for modeling the way and showing us how to look for women's contributions in church history. We also want to thank Lynn Cohick and Kristin Kobes Du Mez for offering helpful comments on early drafts of some of these chapters. And we want to thank Will Carpenter for conversing with us about the cover of this book and for painting the piece that is the current cover.

I (Leanne) received support and encouragement from many sources during the writing process. Wendy Wilson of Women's Development Track was the first to ask for a book and then continued to request the book until I finally agreed to write one. Biola University granted me a course release one semester. For years, Paul, Kate, and Anna Dzubinski have listened to me talk about the importance of women's stories and contributions to the church, and they have encouraged me every step of the way. Paul was unfailingly patient and supportive when I worked on the book at night and on weekends. Graduate student Stephanie Calley found sources, read drafts, and gave excellent feedback. Rob and Jackie Parke read early chapter drafts and also gave helpful feedback. Patricia Lantis read chapter drafts and described young women in ministry she knew who would "gobble this up like starved people." And Kate Dzubinski read the first draft of the chapter on women in the early church within hours of receiving it. Her response was that reading it "was balm to the soul." We pray this book will feed starved people and be balm to the soul for many more women!

I (Anneke) am grateful for a grant from the Lilly Endowment, which supported my research. I valued the input of students from my class on women in the mission of the church: Hannah Caringal, Cassie Olson, Kaylan Anderson, Hadley Wilson, Carolyn Logsdon, and Kailey Warner, who became my research assistant. Kailey's collaboration in researching, writing, and processing ideas about American and Chinese women evangelists was invaluable, as was her work on Hadewijch and Macrina. Alison Henry helped with research on deaconesses, Alison Johnson found sources for chapter 9, and Georgia Mamalakis introduced me to the three holy mothers of the three hierarchs. Amy Nelson, Rusty Hawkins, David Riggs, Ryan Dalrymple, Sandra Spee, and Fr. Shane Chellis gave helpful feedback on chapters. I want to thank Mary Lou, Ellie, Ruthie, and Joseph for their patience while their mother was busy working and for their interest when Mommy was ready to tell them a few stories about some of the awesome women in church history. Above all, I want to thank my husband, Steve, for his help in thinking through the tone and content of this book and for loving me in the way Christ loves the church.

We believe that one of the virtues of this book is its interpretive framework: opportunities *and obstacles* in ministry throughout Christian history. The book illuminates the gender-based obstacles women have faced throughout the history of the church and the common strategies they have used to overcome these obstacles: for example, turning constraints into assets. We hope this interpretive framework will be helpful even to readers whose particular faith tradition or geographical region does not appear in this book.

A note on the capitalization of "Black" and "White": we have chosen to follow the *Chicago Manual of Style* guidelines regarding the capitalization of these terms (in effect as of August 2020). Racism continues to plague the United States, and the summer was fraught with protests over the killing of Black Americans by police. Names like Breonna Taylor and George Floyd became household words, and the *Chicago Manual of Style* guidelines were updated to capitalize these terms. Since we followed *Chicago* guidelines for our book, we also chose to capitalize.

We hope this book will encourage, inspire, and perhaps also arouse some righteous indignation in our readers as we present some of the obstacles women have encountered throughout church history. The women we present here, like the men around them, were certainly not perfect. They loved God, they recognized God's call on their lives, and they sought to fulfill that call in obedience. They stumbled. They didn't always do it perfectly. But they persevered. In the words of the author of Hebrews 12, they serve now as our "great cloud of witnesses." The baton is now in our hands; let us run with endurance as well, without growing weary or losing heart (Heb. 12:1–3).

Leanne M. Dzubinski
La Mirada, CA

Anneke H. Stasson
Marion, IN

Feast of All Saints, 2020

INTRODUCTION

Women in Ministry Is Not
a Twentieth-Century Phenomenon

I (Anneke) am sitting in a guesthouse at a monastery in Michigan. I came for a writing retreat, for quiet, and for prayer. On the way here, I called a friend, and we reminisced about our freshman year of college, when both of us made our first visit to a monastery. The experience changed the course of both of our lives. It was for both of us the first time we had ever met a monk or a nun. I remember thinking that the chanted liturgy was incredibly beautiful. There were only a few monks in the chapel, but they filled the small space with their resonant chanting of the Psalms. On future trips to this same monastery, I rose in the middle of the night, pulled on a sweater, wrapped a scarf around my head, and silently crossed the courtyard to the chapel. I sat in the pew and basked in the beauty of the monks singing, a beauty that deeply connected me to God.

The book you have in your hands will lead you on a journey into monastic communities like the one I am currently visiting. You will visit the lands around the Mediterranean, where the early church grew, and the lands where African prophet-healers founded churches in the twentieth century. Parts of the story are beautiful, and parts of the story are uncomfortable. You might not feel drawn to the nuns you encounter on these pages. You might find their lives of poverty, chastity, and obedience hard to imagine today. That's okay. Church history is filled with a diverse array of women, and our hope is that some of their stories will connect with your own. You'll meet Anthusa, the fourth century's version of a "homeschool mom." Her son, John Chrysostom, became one of the most celebrated bishops of the early church. And Elleanor Knight, who persevered in her call to preach despite her husband's disapproval, expulsion from her beloved church, and ridicule from nineteenth-century American society. You'll meet Dora Yu, who led the revivalist movement that swept through China in the early twentieth century. And Ida B. Wells, the great African American crusader against lynching, who leaned heavily on the words and promises of Scripture to get her through difficult times.

We hope you will gain an appreciation for the roles these women and others played in the mission of the church. Through their prayers, activism, theology, art, preaching, teaching, patronage, mystical visions, and child-rearing, they ministered to God and to God's people. Their work has been central to the mission of the church in every generation.

We also hope you will come away from this book feeling troubled by the obstacles that women in church history have faced on account of their sex. Because of the doctrine of the *imago Dei* and the way in which Jesus interacted with women, Christians historically have affirmed women's humanity and value. Yet at the same time, Christianity has also been plagued with strands of thought that devalue women. The early church was born into the Greco-Roman world, and most people in that world saw women as irrational, cowardly, and more susceptible to temptation than men. This perspective is especially clear in the thought of Aristotle, a Greek philosopher from the fourth century BC, whose thought influenced not only Greek and Roman but also medieval European culture.[1] Aristotle considered men superior to women because men could produce seed, whereas women were only the receptacle for the seed. Aristotle developed an entire theory of gender from this starting point. He described baby girls in utero as "deformed men." He stated that while both women and men could reason, women lacked the ability to use that reason to control their emotions and desires.[2]

Many of the early leaders of the church were influenced by Aristotle and other Greek and Roman thinkers. The Greek and Roman classics were part of their education. Their world included myths, works of art, and everyday conversations that were peppered with commentary about women's fickleness and lack of self-control. They would have known the story of Pandora. According to this Greek myth, Pandora, the first woman, was given to humanity after Prometheus stole fire from the gods. Pandora had a jar that she should have kept closed. Of course, she opened it and, in so doing, introduced evil into the world.

1. Allen, *Concept of Woman*, 127, 251, 413.
2. Aristotle, *Politics* 1.13. See also Allen, *Concept of Woman*, 97.

Human beings are shaped by their cultural context. Just as twenty-first-century culture forms one of the lenses people today look through as they study Scripture, so Greco-Roman culture formed one of the lenses for the biblical exegetes in the first few centuries of the church. Thus, a strand of thought that depicted women as in some ways inferior to men was woven into some of the sermons preached and works of theology written at this time. And because the church has continued to form itself around these sermons and works of theology, that Greco-Roman perspective on women has continued to impact the church right up to the present day.

Of course, biblical passages about Jesus honoring women and passages about men and women being "one in Christ" also impacted how the early exegetes viewed women.[3] So too did their relationships with their mothers, sisters, and wives, many of whom showed a dedication to Christ, a level of self-control, and an inner strength that the church fathers found admirable. The early exegetes were also influenced by the courage of women who were martyred and the intellectual capacity of women who dedicated themselves to learning the ancient languages and studying the Scriptures. Therefore, the sermons and theology of the early church leaders present a highly inconsistent portrait of women. As Elizabeth Clark says, "The most fitting word with which to describe the Church Fathers' attitude toward women is ambivalence. Women were God's creation, his good gift to men—and the curse of the world. They were weak in both mind and character—and displayed dauntless courage, undertook prodigious feats of scholarship."[4]

This inconsistent view of women became an obstacle to the church's flourishing. It is true that some women in the early and medieval church were revered, even elevated above men. But their elevation did not change the fact that most women were still seen as inferior to men, as irrational and more susceptible to temptation. Not only did women have to carry this disparaging view of their sex with them as they lived their lives, but some of the specific obstacles they faced also flowed out of this underlying perspective. We will explore some of these specific obstacles in the chapters that follow.

Women Are Missing from the Historical Record

Another obstacle facing women is that the church collectively has tended to favor a certain type of church history, the type that focuses on major theologians,

3. See Luke 8:43–48; 10:39; Gal. 3:28. The doctrine of the bodily resurrection also cultivated greater respect for women. Allen, *Concept of Woman*, 213.
4. Clark, *Women in the Early Church*, 15.

bishops, and founders of new monastic movements and denominations. Telling the story in this way tends to leave out all but a few women. With the move toward social and cultural history and the entrance of numerous women historians into the field, the contributions of women are slowly making their way into mainstream church-history textbooks. However, some of women's most significant contributions to church history continue to be overlooked because the church has not deemed their work important enough to remember.

Women are also missing from the historical record because in some cultures it is considered inappropriate for women to take individual credit for their work. For example, the virtues of modesty and humility led many medieval nuns to leave their literary works anonymous.[5] Women have been socialized to be helpers, supporters of others. The result is that they may have downplayed their work with statements like "It wasn't a big deal" or "It just needed to be done." While it might be easy to blame women for this tendency not to acknowledge their own contributions, research has shown that there is a good reason for women to take this approach. Many societies have strong stereotypes about how men and women are expected to behave. Women who break those stereotypes by acting contrary to social expectations—for example, taking credit or drawing attention to their work—often suffer what's known as the backlash effect.[6] Backlash happens when women who behave in ways that don't fit the stereotypes suffer some kind of negative effect like disapproval or criticism. Girls learn quickly that calling attention to their achievements may be perceived as bragging and as inappropriate for well-behaved girls, and they may be puzzled when they see boys around them making similar statements but without the negative reactions. Still, they stop telling people about their accomplishments, focusing instead on just doing the work.

Yet another reason women are missing from the historical record is that often they lacked access to the tools needed in order to write. Education is a prime example. Anyone without an education can't write; women were—and in places continue to be—disproportionately impacted by a lack of education. People in many societies have argued that educating a woman is a waste of time because what she needs to do is get married, have children, and care for her family. The push for women's education in the United States came about because of the argument that a republic needed women to be able to educate their children, especially their sons, to become good citizens.[7] Thus,

5. Temple, "Mysticism and Identity," 649.
6. Rudman and Glick, "Prescriptive Gender Stereotypes"; Rudman and Phelan, "Backlash Effects."
7. The ideology became known as "republican motherhood." See Kerber, *Women of the Republic*, 235.

education for women was promoted as a means to an end rather than as a value for women themselves.

Women as a group have made massive contributions over two millennia to the mission of the church. Yet their story is hardly known. The efforts they have made to spread the Christian faith, the trials they have endured for the sake of that faith, the fidelity they have shown in the face of opposition, and the persistence with which they have obeyed God's call are all too often tragically overlooked.

Including Women in the Telling of Church History

Lack of knowledge about women in church history is problematic for many reasons. The old phrase "Those who don't know history are doomed to repeat it" persists. Generations of women preachers in America would have been much encouraged in their own pursuit of God's call had they known the stories of women who had gone before them. If they had known the stories, they wouldn't have had to start from scratch. They could have read the autobiographies of other women who had combed the Scriptures for support of women in ministry. But those stories had already been lost, so each generation of women had to repeat the angst-filled nights of crying out to God, feeling so alone.

The concept of women's work disappearing, or more accurately "get[ting] disappeared," from public view was named by Joyce Fletcher in 1999.[8] She discovered that organizations claimed to highly value certain behaviors among employees, and yet because those behaviors were not easily measured or reported and because they were viewed as feminine or "soft" skills, they tended to vanish from organizational memory, especially when performed by women. A careful look at the existing historical record shows that women's participation gets disappeared at an alarming rate. This disappearance matters because women matter.[9] What women see and how they reflect the image of God in humanity sometimes differ from what men see and reflect. Both perspectives matter to humanity's engagement with God's mandates to care for and build the kingdom. "Like facets of a diamond reflecting the divine image, we need to see and hear from one another in order to appreciate the fullness of the beauty of who God is."[10]

---

8. Fletcher, *Disappearing Acts*, 3.
9. Bryan Loritts makes a similar argument regarding people of color. He says, "When your name is never called—when you are never addressed by that name—you are being told you don't matter." Loritts, *Insider Outsider*, 41.
10. Turpin, "Whose Stories We Tell," 96.

The marginalization of women also sets an unfortunate precedent. Because people today do not know what women have done in the past, they may assume that what women do in the present is also unimportant. In effect, women are starting from a deficit position in relation to the men around them.[11] Thus, women themselves may struggle to believe that women have anything of significance to contribute to the kingdom. They may undervalue themselves and their work, believing that women have little to offer. Similarly, some men may struggle to see the value or importance of women's work and may treat women and women's concerns as irrelevant to the story of Christianity and their contributions as minimal.

Telling church history as a story predominantly about men suggests that women have not done much to extend the impact of the church, to deepen its thinking, or to contribute to its flourishing. Even when a few stories of women are included on the sidelines of the stories about men, the result is that people tend to see women's work as peripheral to the grand scheme of church history.

Nothing could be further from the truth. Women have been absolutely essential to the mission of the church historically. And they continue to be essential to mission today. As Dana Robert writes in her book *Christian Mission*, "The ratio of female to male Christians is approximately two to one. Within Catholicism, sisters outnumber brothers and priests by more than 50 percent."[12] As scholars, pastors, and parishioners tell the story of Christianity, we all need to find ways to include the stories of women so that women are not seen merely as token voices here or there but as coworkers in the kingdom of God.[13] We need to try to give equal weight to the ways in which men and women have shaped Christianity's history and been shaped by it.

Terminology and Assumptions

In this book, we use the word "mission" to mean anything that leads to the extension of the church or to the deepening of Christian commitment, such as teaching, preaching, evangelizing, prophesying, and founding churches. We also consider "mission" to encompass social justice work on behalf of disadvantaged members of society. We use the word "leadership" to signify

11. For a visual display of the impact of advantage and disadvantage, watch the video "Privilege/Class/Social Inequalities Explained" on YouTube. While privilege consists of many factors in addition to gender, gender is still a major factor cutting across all additional categories such as race, class, and socioeconomic status.

12. Robert, *Christian Mission*, 118.

13. The language of "coworker" is how Paul talks about several women in Rom. 16.

having authority and influence in society. This book will demonstrate that women have held positions of missional leadership throughout the history of the church.

At the same time, however, we want to challenge the assumption that the kingdom work of women and men in the public sphere is more important than their work in the domestic sphere. Women and men who raise their children to love the Lord and serve their neighbor are as important to the purposes of God as women and men who preach in public. This book will describe women in both public and domestic roles who were faithful to God's call on their lives.

Similarly, we want to state clearly our assumption that all vocations—married, celibate, active, and contemplative—are important to the work of God in the world. The medieval church saw priests, monks, and nuns as the most faithful followers of God. American evangelicals today tend to elevate pastors, married people, and cross-cultural missionaries. We prefer to approach church history with a perspective informed by the nineteenth-century French nun St. Thérèse of Lisieux. St. Thérèse describes the diversity of humanity as a field of flowers that God has created, each flower with its own purpose and beauty. "The splendor of the rose and the whiteness of the lily do not rob the little violet of its scent nor the daisy of its simple charm." Moreover, "if every tiny flower wanted to be a rose, spring would lose its loveliness."[14] Our survey of church history will therefore describe some of the diverse ways that women, with their different callings, have served the church. Ultimately, what matters in the kingdom of God is the extent to which people have been faithful to the particular callings that God has given them. Or as St. Thérèse says, "Perfection consists in doing His will, in being that which He wants us to be."[15]

Chapter Overview

Each chapter of this book describes opportunities that women have had for mission, obstacles that women have faced, and ways that women have navigated those obstacles. We want readers to recognize the historical precedent for women in leadership in the church. Women's leadership is not a twentieth-century phenomenon. On the contrary, women have played a leadership role in the mission of the church since the days of Jesus.

The first part of this book covers the early church from the time of Jesus to the fifth century. During much of this time, Christianity was not a legal

14. Thérèse of Lisieux, *Story of a Soul*, 2.
15. Thérèse of Lisieux, *Story of a Soul*, 2.

religion, and its followers were subject to persecution, imprisonment, torture, and death. Yet during this time, women followers of Jesus were exceedingly strong, both in numbers and in steadiness of commitment. Chapter 1 describes how the Virgin Mary, Mary Magdalene, and other women were involved in the ministry of Jesus and the early church. Nympha, Lydia, and Mary were patrons who hosted house churches and likely presided over the Eucharist. Junia was an apostle, Phoebe a deacon, Dorcas a widow, and Priscilla a missionary and gifted teacher. Blandina, Perpetua, and Felicitas were martyred for their faith. Chapter 2 discusses the ways in which virgins, ascetic scholars, desert mothers, and deacons contributed to the mission of the church. The chapter closes by addressing some of the reasons church leaders opposed the leadership of women, particularly women deacons.

The second part of the book looks at women's leadership in late antiquity and the Middle Ages. Chapter 3 discusses mothers, sisters, empresses, and queens who lived virtuous lives themselves and inspired their family members to do the same. Through their relationships with their influential male relatives, these women also shaped the theology, practices, and landscape of the developing church. Three Western queens, Clotilda, Bertha, and Ethelberga, played a major role in the Christianization of Europe by facilitating the conversion of their husbands and the wider population to the Christian faith. Chapter 4 describes how nuns contributed to the mission of the church by copying books, founding some of the first medieval hospitals, and providing support for their wider community through prayer and charitable work. Chapter 5 turns to the beguines, who crafted for themselves a more flexible form of religious life. Like nuns, they still lived in community, prayed together, and served poor people, but they did not take lifelong vows of poverty, chastity, and obedience. So many beguines and other women dedicated themselves to new forms of religious life in thirteenth-century Europe that scholars have referred to this movement as "the women's religious movement." Some beguines and nuns during this period also began to have mystical visions, which they shared with the church for its edification. Chapter 5 closes with a short discussion of the Reformation's impact on religious women. The Reformers' opposition to celibacy and monasticism dismantled the foundations for the leadership of medieval nuns. But even as they negatively impacted the ministries of nuns, they also positively impacted married women by elevating the missional significance of marriage and parenthood.

Part 3 describes opportunities women have had for leadership since the Reformation. We chose to devote an entire chapter, chapter 6, to the history of women preachers in America because this topic is so often treated as an issue that arose after the feminist movement of the 1960s. In actuality, hundreds of women preached during the First and Second Great Awakenings, and hundreds more preached throughout the nineteenth and twentieth centuries. Women around the world during this period were also active in numerous social justice causes, and chapter 7 tells the story of this "global sisterhood." Chapter 8 describes the work of the nineteenth-century women's missionary movement: evangelizing; planting churches; modeling Christian homes; providing medical care; founding schools, hospitals, and universities; and teaching. Chapter 9 describes how the faith mission movement provided new opportunities for women to serve as evangelists. This chapter also chronicles women's leadership in Chinese and African revivals and in African Initiated Churches, many of which were founded by women prophet-healers.

Final Thoughts

In choosing to write a history book that spans two millennia of church history, we were faced with some important choices. Perhaps the most obvious was the choice to "go wide" rather than "go deep." Furthermore, for every story told in this book, there are dozens or hundreds more that could have been told. For those who would like to "go deep," we have cited numerous sources throughout each chapter, and we invite interested readers to dig more deeply into any particular woman who is of interest to them.

The choice to present breadth rather than depth is an important one for us. It allows us to dispute the narrative that there are only a handful of important women in church history. A focus on only a "heroic few" can have the unintended effect of communicating to most women that they really don't matter. If the only stories available are the big-name ones, regular women may feel discouraged and believe that their everyday faithfulness is unimportant. We want to argue the contrary: everyday faithfulness is of primary importance.

We want to draw attention to a consistent, two-thousand-year history of faithful Christian service carried out by women. Women's contributions to the spread of Christianity have not been sporadic or insignificant. In every era, there have been Christian women who loved God and actively engaged in the spread of the Christian message. Their contributions have been incalculable. Taking a big-picture perspective and showing the persistent, faithful participation of women throughout history reveals that women are not marginal; we are central to God's story.

PART 1

WOMEN'S LEADERSHIP
IN THE
EARLY CHURCH

1

Patrons, Missionaries, Apostles, Widows, and Martyrs

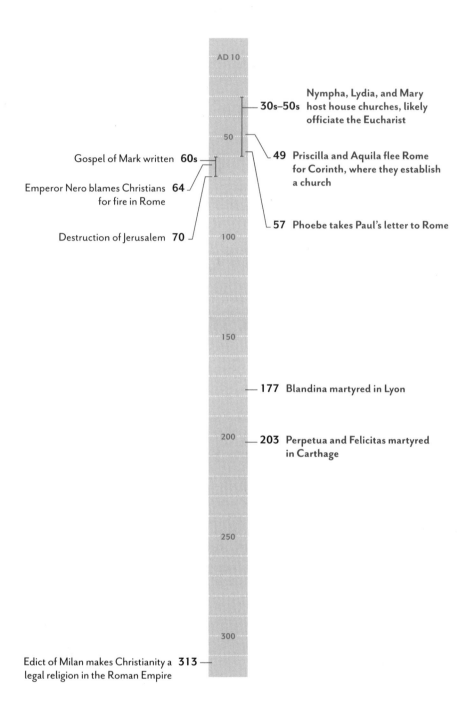

AD 10

30s–50s Nympha, Lydia, and Mary host house churches, likely officiate the Eucharist

50

Gospel of Mark written 60s

49 Priscilla and Aquila flee Rome for Corinth, where they establish a church

Emperor Nero blames Christians 64 for fire in Rome

57 Phoebe takes Paul's letter to Rome

Destruction of Jerusalem 70

100

150

177 Blandina martyred in Lyon

200

203 Perpetua and Felicitas martyred in Carthage

250

300

Edict of Milan makes Christianity a 313 legal religion in the Roman Empire

The New Testament shows that women were involved as leaders in the church from its earliest days. Women were disciples and supporters of Jesus. After Jesus's death, some women patrons hosted house churches, some served the church as widows, and some became important apostles, missionaries, and teachers of the faith. When persecution came, courageous martyrs held fast to their faith even to the point of physical death. This chapter describes some of these early Christian women. It shows how the ministry of women influenced the developing church and unpacks why their ministry was controversial in light of Roman social norms.

Women in the Life of Jesus

Jesus loved women, and women were an integral part of his ministry from the very beginning. God the Father could have sent his Son into the world in any number of ways, but God chose childbirth; God gave Mary the honor of being the *Theotokos*, the "Mother of God."[1] Mary carried the Son of God in her womb for nine months. She birthed him, nursed him, reared him, and urged him to do his first miracle. When so many deserted him, Mary stood by Jesus at the foot of the cross. She rejoiced when he rose again, she was in the upper room when he sent the Holy Spirit, and she was a revered leader of the early church.

Mary was Jesus's first teacher and first disciple. Jesus learned about devotion to God from his mother, and she in turn learned from him. At one point in Jesus's public ministry, a woman called out from the crowd, "Blessed is the womb that bore you and the breasts that nursed you!" Jesus responded, "Blessed rather are those who hear the word of God and obey it!" (Luke 11:27–28 NRSV). On first glance, this passage seems to depict Jesus as dismissive of his mother, but it actually makes more sense to read it as Jesus praising

---

1. At the Council of Ephesus in 431, the church used this title for Mary in order to say something about Jesus: that he was one person with two natures.

his mother's devotion to God.[2] During this time, women were valued for their capacity to bring forth children. They were especially valued when they bore children who turned out to be important figures. But Jesus says that Mary is not to be valued primarily for her ability to bring forth children but for her ability to "hear the word of God and obey it" (Luke 11:28).[3]

Tradition says that Mary's parents dedicated her to God from an early age.[4] Perhaps that is why she demonstrated such courage when the angel Gabriel visited her and told her she was going to bear the Son of God. Mary dared to ask the powerful, holy angel a question: "How will this be . . . , since I am a virgin?" (Luke 1:34). The angel told her that the Holy Spirit would come upon her, and Mary agreed to this amazing proposition. By saying yes, Mary became the "new Eve," just as Jesus would be the "new Adam." The first Eve had turned away from God and was told her husband would rule over her; this pattern of gender relations came to dominate history. Instead of letting this curse or her own fears rule over her, Mary courageously submitted herself to God and said, "I am the Lord's servant. . . . May your word to me be fulfilled" (1:38). In saying yes to God, she became part of God's plan of redemption. She birthed the savior of the world, trained him in the wisdom of God, and learned to follow him when he began his earthly ministry.

Other women followed Jesus too. Many people need to shift their mental picture a bit to accommodate them. Usually Jesus is pictured with the twelve disciples, but Luke states that as Jesus "traveled about from one town and village to another, proclaiming the good news of the kingdom of God," the Twelve were not the only ones with him. There were "also some women who had been cured of evil spirits and diseases: Mary (called Magdalene) from whom seven demons had come out; Joanna . . . ; Susanna; and many others" (Luke 8:1–3). When Jesus taught women, he did not speak in a way that differed from how he spoke with men. "It was no occasion of surprise to Him that woman could grasp His highest truths. He presented them as simply and naturally to women as He did to men, expecting the same response."[5] The Samaritan woman at the well discussed theology with Jesus and became a disciple and evangelist (John 4). Mary and Martha became his dear friends, and Martha, like Peter, confessed him as the Christ (John 11:27). Jesus affirmed Mary for sitting at his feet, making him the first rabbi

2. Part of the reason it makes more sense to view it this way is that it is essentially a restatement of what Elizabeth says in Luke 1:42, 45. Green, "Blessed Is She Who Believed," 11–13; R. Brown et al., *Mary in the New Testament*, 171–72.

3. Mbonu, *Handmaid*, 15–16.

4. *Protevangelium of James*, 55–66.

5. Southard, *Attitude of Jesus*, 36–37.

to accept a woman as a disciple in this manner.[6] And Mary demonstrated her love for Jesus by anointing his feet with perfume and wiping his feet with her hair. Even though the disciples chastised her for this act, Jesus made her an exemplar of faith.[7] According to New Testament scholar Ben Witherington, these "female disciples . . . were as loyal to Jesus as the male disciples, indeed more so at the end when the men abandoned, denied, or betrayed him."[8]

Women were also the first witnesses of the resurrection. The "Myrrh-Bearing Women" carried spices to the tomb, found it empty, and ran to tell the disciples. There is difference in the four Gospel accounts about exactly which women went to the tomb, but in each account Mary Magdalene is prominent. For her role in telling the male disciples about the empty tomb, she has been honored with the title "Apostle to the Apostles."

Women actively participated in the inauguration of the kingdom of God through Christ's life, death, and resurrection, and they were integral to the continued growth of the kingdom after he ascended into heaven. Paul chose a woman, Phoebe, to take his letter to Rome and proclaim it in the sanctuary, a task that required her to speak publicly in church. In Paul's letter to the Corinthian church, where he speaks of women being "silent," he also tells women that when they are speaking in church (prophesying), they should keep their heads covered—so it is clear that women were speaking in church (1 Cor. 11:5).[9] In the book of Acts, Luke tells the story of Lydia, the first convert to Christianity in Philippi. After listening to Paul and Silas preach the gospel, Lydia established the first church in Philippi. A wealthy merchant, Lydia supported the church financially and drew other people to it (Acts 16:13–15). The issue of women in ministry was debated in the early church; some in the church opposed the leadership of women, but not Paul. Time and again, Paul affirmed the women who were his coworkers in the mission of the church.

6. Witherington, *Women and the Genesis of Christianity*, 100. Paul himself describe his own training to become a rabbi as sitting "at the feet of" Gamaliel (Acts 22:3 ASV).

7. Matt. 26:6–13; Mark 14:3–9; Luke 7:36–50; John 12:1–8. Because of the different details in each telling of this story, there is discussion among scholars about whether this event happened once with Mary or another time with an unnamed "sinful" woman.

8. Witherington, *Priscilla*, 106.

9. The use of the word "silent" in 1 Cor. 14:34 in many translations is questionable. Paul uses the same word in v. 28 and v. 30. The NIV translates it as "keep quiet" in v. 28 and as "stop [speaking]" in v. 30. So the word clearly doesn't mean absolute silence at all times. Paul is concerned about order in the service, so a better explanation is that the reason he opposed women speaking in church in this instance was that they were uneducated women who were disrupting the service with their questions. See Keener, "Learning in the Assemblies," 162–63.

Women Were Patrons, Hosted House Churches, and Likely Officiated the Eucharist

The early church depended on patrons like Lydia, who is named in Acts 16. Patrons were people of means who used their wealth and influence for the mission of the church. In the early church, women as well as men were patrons, and some of these wealthy women opened up their homes so that communities of Christians could worship there. After all, there were no church buildings yet. Christians were a small sect within the Roman Empire, and these Christian communities depended on the generosity of wealthy believers to supply space for their meetings. Luke recorded the stories of some of these women in the book of Acts. For example, after an angel led Peter out of prison, "he went to the house of Mary the mother of John, also called Mark, where many people had gathered and were praying" (Acts 12:12). Scholars think they had gathered there to pray because Mary hosted a house church in her home. Several of Paul's letters mention other women who hosted house churches. In his letter to the Colossians, he says, "Give my greetings to the brothers and sisters at Laodicea, and to Nympha and the church in her house" (Col. 4:15). Lydia, Mary, and Nympha were patrons of the church, women who donated their resources to its mission and were regarded as leaders of the church.

Roman society had a complex and long-standing system of patronage that regulated the relationship between the upper class and the lower class. Members of the upper class were expected to patronize (support in exchange for service and loyalty) members of the lower class. People who grew up in the upper class learned that they had a responsibility to care for certain individuals from the lower class. These individuals were called "clients." The clients were bound to the upper-class "patron" in a mutually beneficial relationship. The patron would give funds or legal help, and the client would run errands or support the patron in running for office. Having many clients bestowed honor on a Roman patron, and honor was important in Roman society.

Both women and men in Roman society played the roles of patron and client. Wealthy Roman women, though they couldn't run for formal political office, still had influence, and so these women had clients.[10] Wealthy women patrons could decide to fund a temple project or erect a statue. If they became a follower of Jesus, they could decide to host a church. Wealthy women were sometimes independent and headed their own household. According to Christine Schenk, "The Christian Scriptures provide the best literary evidence available that independent women such as Lydia the purple-dye merchant

10. Osiek and MacDonald, *Woman's Place*, 209.

(Acts 16:14–40), Mary in Jerusalem (Acts 12:12–17), and Nympha of Laodicea (Col. 4:15) were heads of their own household without reference to any male relative."[11]

Lydia, Mary, and Nympha were independent patrons who hosted churches in their homes.[12] They also introduced Paul to people in their social circles, thereby facilitating the continued spread of the gospel into the upper echelons of society. Some patrons gave of their resources to support the social services carried out by members of the Christian community: caring for sick people, visiting those in prison, helping poor people. Jesus had benefited from women's patronage (Luke 8:1–3), and women patrons continued to be essential to the mission of the church. In fact, there may have been more wealthy women than wealthy men who supported the mission of the church during this early period. Schenk says, "There is good reason to surmise that over half of Rome's early house churches were founded and hosted by female patrons."[13]

There was significantly more openness to the ecclesial leadership of women in the earliest days of the church than there was later. It was common practice for the head of a household to officiate the Eucharist, and since Lydia, Mary, and Nympha were hosts of the churches that met in their homes, they likely led the Communion (or Eucharist) service that was part of early church worship.[14]

Women Were Missionary Evangelists, Teachers, and Apostles

One of the best places to see acclaim given to women in the mission of the church is chapter 16 of Paul's letter to the Romans.

> I commend to you our sister Phoebe, a deacon of the church in Cenchreae. I ask you to receive her in the Lord in a way worthy of his people and to give her any help she may need from you, for she has been the benefactor of many people, including me. Greet Priscilla and Aquila, my co-workers in Christ Jesus. They risked their lives for me. Not only I but all the churches of the Gentiles are grateful to them. Greet also the church that meets at their house. . . . Greet Mary, who worked very hard for you. Greet Andronicus and Junia, my fellow Jews who have been in prison with me. They are outstanding among the apostles, and they were in Christ before I was. . . . Greet Tryphena and Tryphosa, those

11. C. Schenk, *Crispina and Her Sisters*, 19.
12. Phoebe from Rom. 16:1 and Euodia and Syntyche from Phil. 4:2 may have also hosted house churches. Osiek and MacDonald, *Woman's Place*, 158–59.
13. C. Schenk, *Crispina and Her Sisters*, 35, 230.
14. Osiek and MacDonald, *Woman's Place*, 209.

women who work hard in the Lord. Greet my dear friend Persis, another woman who has worked very hard in the Lord. (vv. 1–7, 12)

Some of the women Paul names in this list were missionary evangelists and teachers. Priscilla is one of the most interesting, in part because her name is mentioned before that of her husband, Aquila. Mentioning her first may suggest that she married beneath her social class or that Paul considered her a more prominent church leader than her husband.[15] Or she may simply have been the more memorable character of the two.[16] Priscilla and Aquila were Jews who followed Jesus as Messiah and were part of the growing band of his followers. When Emperor Claudius expelled Jews from Rome in AD 49, Priscilla and Aquila moved to Corinth, where they founded a church.[17] As tentmakers, they were able to "offer Paul, who was also a tentmaker, both lodging and steady work" when he came to Corinth a few years later.[18] They later went with Paul as missionaries to Ephesus to found another church (Acts 18:18–19).[19] It was there that they met Apollos, another Jewish follower of Jesus and a gifted preacher. The book of Acts tells us that Apollos was already "a learned man, with a thorough knowledge of the Scriptures" (18:24), but Priscilla and Aquila "invited him to their home and explained to him the way of God more adequately" (18:26).[20]

The two couples Paul affirms in Romans 16—Priscilla and Aquila and Andronicus and Junia—took risks for the sake of the gospel. Paul says of the former, "They risked their lives for me" (v. 4); the latter were imprisoned with Paul. Both missionary couples were clearly proclaiming the gospel with great courage and conviction. And "there is no indication of the female partner's having a different or diminished role in relation to the male partner."[21]

Notice that in Romans 16:7, Paul calls Junia an "apostle." Sometimes Paul uses the word "apostle" (*apostolos*) to signify "a messenger or emissary of the

<hr>

15. Priscilla is named seven times in the New Testament; in five of them, her name precedes Aquila's.

16. This idea is suggested by Paula Gooder, who has written a fictional but historically informed account of the interactions of Priscilla, Aquila, Phoebe, Junia, Andronicus, and other church leaders in Rome at the time of Paul's letter to the Romans. See Gooder, *Phoebe*, 8.

17. Witherington, *Acts of the Apostles*, 541.

18. C. Schenk, *Crispina and Her Sisters*, 36. See also Acts 18:1–4.

19. Paul likely wrote his first letter to the Corinthians from the home of Priscilla and Aquila in Ephesus. At the end of his letter, Paul puts in a little "hello" from Priscilla and Aquila: "The churches in the province of Asia send you greetings. Aquila and Priscilla greet you warmly in the Lord, and so does the church that meets at their house" (1 Cor. 16:19).

20. In particular, Apollos didn't know about the need to be baptized in the name of Jesus. Witherington, *Priscilla*, 71–72.

21. Osiek and MacDonald, *Woman's Place*, 229.

church (for example, 2 Cor. 8:23). But Paul frequently uses the term to refer to itinerant preachers of the gospel (2 Cor. 11:4–6, 13; 12:11–12)."[22] The description of Junia's work in Romans 16:7 suggests that both she and Andronicus were itinerant preachers, just like Paul. Some scholars think Junia may have even known Jesus, which would have made her a particularly important leader in the early church.[23] Sadly, Junia's name has been mistranslated as "Junius" (a male name) in many versions of the Bible.

Paul counted many women among his coworkers. In his letter to the Philippians, he names two women, Euodia and Syntyche, who "contended at my side in the cause of the gospel" (Phil. 4:3). In his letter to the Romans, he highlights three more women—Tryphena, Tryphosa, and Persis, who "worked very hard in the Lord" (Rom. 16:12). According to Peter Lampe, Paul's use of the word *kopiaō* (work) in the book of Romans demonstrates that women in Rome were very active in mission and evangelism. Often, *kopiaō* is translated merely as "to work," but *kopiaō* actually was "a technical term in missionary language." Significantly, Paul uses this word to describe himself in Galatians 4:11 and 1 Corinthians 15:10 and to describe four women in Rome (Rom. 16:6, 12).[24]

Women's Leadership Curtailed

Women who held leadership positions in the church gradually saw their opportunities for leadership curtailed. Increasingly, church documents specified that only ordained men should officiate the Eucharist, baptize, and preach.[25] This shift was due in part to the doctrine of the priesthood that was unfolding over time as church leaders consulted biblical texts, held councils, and solidified doctrine, but it was also in part an accommodation to Roman culture. Women's leadership made Christianity subject to attack from Roman critics. In fact, it was common for all kinds of new religious movements in Rome to be "attacked by highlighting their attraction for women."[26] Most Romans thought women were more susceptible to being deceived. They believed that

22. Osiek and MacDonald, *Woman's Place*, 226.

23. Scholars think this because when "Junia" is translated into Hebrew, it becomes "Joanna," and Luke tells us about a Joanna who was among the women who went to the tomb to anoint Jesus (Luke 24:9–12). Paul tells us that Junia was a Jew and that she was a Christian before he was (Rom. 16:7). Furthermore, the word "apostle" suggests that the person actually saw the risen Lord. See Witherington, *Priscilla*, 98–98.

24. Lampe, *From Paul to Valentinus*, 166.

25. Tucker and Liefeld, *Daughters of the Church*, 122.

26. Osiek and MacDonald, *Woman's Place*, 222.

women were intellectually inferior to men. Celsus, a pagan who criticized Christianity in the second century, made fun of Christianity by saying that it attracted only "the silly, and the mean, and the stupid" women and children.[27] In short, the wider society viewed women's leadership as potentially dangerous and suspect. Interestingly, Celsus's critique helps to prove that women *were* integral to church leadership during this period. Another document from the period—a letter from a Roman governor named Pliny to the emperor—also highlights women's leadership in the church. After a series of investigations into the Christian sect, Pliny wrote, "I judged it all the more necessary to find out what the truth was by torturing two female slaves who were called deaconesses."[28] That Pliny chose these two women suggests that they held a particularly prominent place in the church community.

As the doctrine of the priesthood developed and as the Christian sect began to grow into a larger movement, some in the church likely viewed curtailing women's leadership as a pragmatic and missiological step, which would aid in the growth of the church. In the earliest days of Christianity, "tension between the church and the world was much less pronounced."[29] Fairly quickly, however, Christians began to be accused of incest because they called their gatherings "love feasts" and called each other "brother" and "sister."[30] They were accused of being cannibals because of the words they used in administering the Eucharist—"This is my body; this is my blood"—and because they were known to rescue babies that had been abandoned. Some people thought Christians were eating these babies at their love feasts. Despite criticism, the Christian movement continued to grow, but some in the movement felt that it was incumbent upon them "to present an appropriate male and female division of labor."[31] They viewed this move as a way to avoid the hostility that was being directed at them by people like Celsus.

In addition, some in the early church opposed the leadership of women because they saw limiting women as a way of distinguishing Christianity from pagan cults that gave women leadership roles. Similarly, the church struggled to distinguish itself from Montanist and Gnostic sects, many of which placed women in positions of high leadership. In an attempt to appear as dissimilar to these sects as possible, some churches hesitated to place women in positions of leadership.[32]

27. Origen, *Contra Celsum* 3.44.
28. Pliny, "Pliny to the Emperor Trajan" (AD 113).
29. Osiek and MacDonald, *Woman's Place*, 229.
30. Minucius Felix, *Octavius* 9; Tertullian, *Apology* 7.
31. Osiek and MacDonald, *Woman's Place*, 229.
32. Fitzgerald, *Women Deacons*, 136, 139.

Last, some of the church fathers held a perspective on women that was informed not only by Scripture but also by Aristotle and other Greek philosophers who considered women rationally and morally unfit to lead. Some of them believed that women were more prone to sin than men and that they suffered from "weak intellects."[33] Even though Jesus had welcomed women to participate in his ministry, some of the church fathers persisted in seeing women as "the devil's gateway."[34] Some saw limiting women's leadership as a fitting response to what happened in the garden of Eden. "[Eve] taught the man once, upset everything, and made him liable to disobedience. Therefore God subjected her, since she used her rule, or rather, her equality of honor, badly," writes Chrysostom.[35] Thus, even though Chrysostom revered his own mother (see chap. 3) and had many wonderful things to say about family life and women's spiritual significance as mothers, here in his sermon on 1 Timothy, it is the curse rather than redemption in Christ that characterizes his vision of women.[36] Additionally, as Elizabeth Clark points out, many of the fathers were not particularly adept with the Hebrew language. Thus, when it came to explicating how Eve was Adam's "helper" (Gen. 2:18), the fathers tended to talk about women's "help" in childbearing. However, they "failed to mention that the word *'ezer* is sometimes used in Scripture to designate God as the gracious helper of his Chosen People."[37]

But we are getting ahead of ourselves in telling the story. Before we talk any more about obstacles to women's leadership, we will take time to appreciate the wealth of leadership opportunities that women did have in the earliest days of the church.

Widows Had a Vocation in the Church

When the apostle Paul wrote letters to the various churches he had helped to found, he discussed different aspects of church order. Embedded in these discussions were comments about ministries that would eventually become full-blown vocations for women. It is common today to talk about a person being "called" to be a pastor or missionary. In the early church, a woman

33. Clark, *Women in the Early Church*, 163.
34. This phrase comes from Tertullian, *On the Dress of Women* I.1.2, quoted in Clark, *Women in the Early Church*, 39.
35. John Chrysostom, *Homily 9 on 1 Timothy 1*, quoted in Clark, *Women in the Early Church*, 157.
36. See Frost, *Maternal Body*, 13, for a claim about Chrysostom's esteem for families and mothers.
37. Clark, *Women in the Early Church*, 15–16.

could be called to be a widow or a virgin or a deacon. Each of these vocations was a way of serving God and the church. And just as we talk today about "the order [or office] of the priesthood," the early church had an order of widows, an order of virgins, and an order of deaconesses. There was overlap between the work of widows, virgins, and deaconesses, but the orders were also seen as having distinct features and requirements. The order of widow as a vocational ministry is described in 1 Timothy 5:9–10: "Let none be enrolled as a widow under threescore years old, having been the wife of one man, well reported of for good works; if she hath brought up children, if she hath used hospitality to strangers, if she hath washed the saints' feet, if she hath relieved the afflicted, if she hath diligently followed every good work" (ASV). Modern English translations of the Bible, such as the TNIV, the NIV, and the NASB, translate Paul's instructions as saying that a widow is to be "put on the list." Older translations say "be enrolled" (ASV) or "be taken into the number" (KJV). These earlier translations have a more active feel to them. A widow was choosing to participate in something, and the following verses described the qualifications for participation. She must be over sixty years old, have been the wife of one man (married once, according to some translations), have raised children, have been hospitable, and have done a number of good works. The widows who met these qualifications were enrolled as ministers for the early church and were paid a stipend in exchange for service to the church.[38] The arrangement was meant to benefit both the women and the church they served. Only widows who did not have family members available to help care for them were eligible (see 5:4, 16).

The Gospel of Luke tells the story of Anna, a prophet and widow who spent her time in the temple, who met the parents of Jesus when they brought him to be dedicated as the firstborn son. "There was also a prophet, Anna, the daughter of Penuel, of the tribe of Asher. She was very old; she had lived with her husband seven years after her marriage, and then was a widow until she was eighty-four. She never left the temple but worshiped night and day, fasting and praying. Coming up to them at that very moment, she gave thanks to God and spoke about the child to all who were looking forward to the redemption of Jerusalem" (Luke 2:36–38). Anna, according to Luke, had been married for seven years and then had lived as a widow to the age of eighty-four. Despite her advanced years, she spent her time in the temple, worshiping, fasting, and praying. When Jesus's parents brought him in to be dedicated, she recognized Jesus and, according to the text, "spoke about the child" to everyone she could. Perhaps she had heard Simeon's pronouncement

38. Belleville, *Women Leaders*, 66.

(2:25–35), or perhaps the Holy Spirit had spoken directly to her as to Simeon. However she had learned that Jesus was the promised one, she told all who would listen. Anna is an example of a widow who dedicated herself to ministry after her husband's death.

Acts 9:36–41 contains another good example of a ministering widow. The story goes like this:

> In Joppa there was a disciple named Tabitha (in Greek her name is Dorcas); she was always doing good and helping the poor. About that time she became sick and died, and her body was washed and placed in an upstairs room. Lydda was near Joppa; so when the disciples heard that Peter was in Lydda, they sent two men to him and urged him, "Please come at once!" Peter went with them, and when he arrived he was taken upstairs to the room. All the widows stood around him, crying and showing him the robes and other clothing that Dorcas had made while she was still with them. Peter sent them all out of the room; then he got down on his knees and prayed. Turning toward the dead woman, he said, "Tabitha, get up." She opened her eyes, and seeing Peter she sat up. He took her by the hand and helped her to her feet. Then he called for the believers, especially the widows, and presented her to them alive.

Dorcas, or Tabitha, appears to have been a well-loved woman in her community. When she died, her fellow widows were devastated. They knew that Peter was nearby, so they sent for him. Dorcas had been a diligent seamstress, and they were quick to show Peter how many garments she had made. Presumably, these were garments for donation to poor people, not simply clothes for herself. In one of only a few recorded resurrection miracles in the New Testament, Peter prays for Dorcas, and God brings her back to life. The unspoken assumption is that she continued with her ministry of making clothing as part of the widows' circle in Joppa. The text does not specifically state that she was receiving support from the church in exchange for her ministry of sewing. But it is not hard to think that this was the case, since it was only a little earlier, in Acts 6, that the "problem" of widows had first been addressed. In that story, seven godly men were chosen to oversee some practical concerns in the church in Jerusalem, including the care of widows in the church. It's quite possible that the tradition of financial and practical provision for widows in exchange for their service to the church began in Jerusalem and spread to other cities.

However, as with any ministry, it seems some people might have been abusing the system. When Paul wrote to Timothy, who was leading the church in Ephesus, after describing how to enroll widows over sixty on the list of church ministers, Paul then comments about some younger women who might have been taking advantage of the system. In 1 Timothy 5:11–14, Paul tells Timothy,

> As for younger widows, do not put them on such a list. For when their sensual desires overcome their dedication to Christ, they want to marry. Thus they bring judgment on themselves, because they have broken their first pledge. Besides, they get into the habit of being idle and going about from house to house. And not only do they become idlers, but also busybodies who talk nonsense, saying things they ought not to. So I counsel younger widows to marry, to have children, to manage their homes and to give the enemy no opportunity for slander.

Paul had three basic concerns when he talked about younger widows: their normal human desires for marriage and motherhood, their faith commitment, and the reputation of the church. On the basis of these concerns, he concluded that widows who were not yet sixty should not be enrolled in the ministering order. Instead, they should marry again and have children, if possible. He was worried that their commitment to ministry would wane in the face of normal desires for a husband and family and that their desire might lead them away from their commitment to the church (1 Tim. 5:11–12). His very warning against enrolling younger women adds strength to the argument that what older widows were joining was indeed a ministry order. Paul comments that younger women might forget or violate their pledge (5:12). What pledge? Apparently, a pledge to celibacy and service to the church.

The early church certainly understood that older widows were taking a pledge of service to the church in exchange for support. Linda Belleville explains, "Ministering widows flourished in the postapostolic period. Polycarp calls them 'God's altar' and Clement of Alexandria ranks them after elders, bishops, and deacons. There was some variation from church to church, but recurring responsibilities included praying for the church, teaching the rudiments of the faith, hospitality, caring for the sick, fasting, prophecy, and caring for the needs of destitute widows and orphans. . . . By and large what we have here is a distinctly pastoral position."[39] Widows were ordained and often sat in the front of the church.[40] Because of their self-disciplined life without husband or children, widows and virgins were thought to be particularly effective in prayer.[41]

The *Apostolic Constitutions*, compiled in Syria around 380, functioned as a kind of handbook for the church, describing how to carry out worship

39. Belleville, *Women Leaders*, 67.
40. Cohick and Hughes, *Christian Women*, 78.
41. Cohick and Hughes, *Christian Women*, 78.

practices and the responsibilities of various church members. Duties of widows were described several times: "Let the widow mind nothing but to pray for those that give, and for the whole church; and if she is asked any thing . . . let her [only] answer questions concerning the faith, and righteousness, and hope in God."[42] The *Apostolic Constitutions* relied on Paul's instructions in 1 Timothy for the behavior expected of widows and also laid out precisely which doctrines were the responsibility of widows and which they were not to teach.

Women Martyrs Were Witnesses for the Faith

Before Christianity became recognized as a legal religion in 313, it was often seen as a threat to the empire. Some followers of Jesus were killed, and some of the most prominent of these martyrs were women. A second-century text called *The Acts of Paul and Thecla* tells of Thecla, a virgin who faced martyrdom twice and escaped both times unharmed. Although most scholars think Thecla's story is largely apocryphal, she "inspired generations of men and women to forgo their ordinary life" and to be willing to follow Christ even unto death.[43] *The Acts of Paul and Thecla* describes how Thecla, who lived in Iconium (now Konya, Turkey), was captivated by the apostle Paul's preaching. Even though she was engaged to be married, she decided to become a Christian and embrace a virginal lifestyle. She informed her family that she was breaking off her engagement. Her fiancé and her mother were outraged but unable to change her mind. In the meantime, Paul had been arrested on charges of turning wives against their husbands. Thecla snuck into the jail to visit Paul and keep learning from him.

Soon afterward, Thecla was summoned to the governor's presence and asked about her refusal to marry. She persisted, at which point her mother demanded she be executed. Thecla was sentenced to death by fire in the arena, but when she entered the pyre, she wasn't burned. When the governor realized that the fire hadn't harmed her, he released her. Then Thecla met a child buying bread for Paul, who was in hiding, and the child took her to the apostle. From that point on, she accompanied Paul on his travels.

When they arrived in Antioch, a local nobleman named Alexander noticed Thecla's beauty and tried to embrace her, but she fought him off. He had her sentenced to death by wild beasts in the arena. Once again, Thecla was protected. Through a series of miraculous events, neither the lions nor the

42. *Apostolic Constitutions* 3.1.5; MacHaffie, *Readings in Her Story*, 19.
43. Cohick and Hughes, *Christian Women*, xix.

other beasts harmed her. By this point, the governor and Alexander were terrified because of her apparent power and stopped the attempts to kill her. She proclaimed God as her protector and was released. Once more she was reunited with Paul, who commissioned her to return to Iconium and continue preaching the gospel. Thecla died in nearby Seleucia, where she had traveled to continue her preaching ministry.[44]

According to Lynn Cohick and Amy Hughes, the story of Thecla may have been inspired by a real follower of Jesus from the first or second century, but her story "has been enhanced, changed, and remixed such that only the barest outline of historicity can be discerned."[45] However, readers of Thecla's story saw it as an example of "what could happen," and they looked to Thecla for inspiration.[46] Her courage in the face of danger and her willingness to sacrifice family, wealth, security, and status for a life of virginity and preaching continued to inspire Christians after her.

The fourth-century church historian Eusebius tells the story of Blandina, an enslaved woman who converted to Christianity and became the leader of a group of martyrs killed in Lyon (France) in 177. Blandina entered the arena with a young man, age fifteen. Blandina took it upon herself to act as the man's mother and encouraged him to stand firm in the faith all the way to their deaths. The most striking feature of Blandina's account, however, is what happened prior to her death in the arena. The Roman authorities had tried to kill her in various other ways. She was described as a "noble athlete," refusing to die despite her suffering. At one point, Blandina hung on a stake in a way that evoked Christ on the cross. According to Eusebius, "She seemed to be hanging in the shape of a cross, and by her continuous prayer gave great zeal to the combatants, while they looked on during the contest, and with their outward eyes saw in the form of their sister him who was crucified for them, so that she persuaded those who believe on him that all who suffer for the glory of Christ have for ever fellowship with the living God."[47] The thought is striking: Blandina hanging in the posture of Christ on the cross, her body evoking Christ, her soul united with him, sustained by him so that she might sustain others of his church body who were suffering.

Twenty-five years after Blandina was martyred, an upper-class Roman citizen named Perpetua became the leader of a group of martyrs in Carthage, North Africa. In this group was an enslaved woman named Felicitas, who was pregnant when she was thrown into prison. Perpetua had an infant son,

44. Cohick and Hughes, *Christian Women*, 1–7.
45. Cohick and Hughes, *Christian Women*, 8.
46. Cohick and Hughes, *Christian Women*, 9.
47. Eusebius, *Ecclesiastical History* 5.1, quoted in Cohick and Hughes, *Christian Women*, 96.

who was still nursing. At first, Perpetua's family brought the infant to her to nurse, but then Perpetua decided to keep the baby with her in prison. We know about Perpetua and Felicitas because Perpetua kept a diary while in prison. She wrote about her anxiety for her son and about the visions that God sent her to transform her anxiety into trust. In one vision, she saw herself climbing a ladder. A shepherd was at the top of the ladder. When she reached the top, the shepherd fed her a little bit of cheese. When she awoke from the vision, she still tasted the cheese on her tongue. She interpreted the vision to be God feeding her the Eucharist. Significantly, it was cheese, rather than the customary bread and wine, that he fed her. The cheese served to remind her of the milk that she herself was feeding to her infant son. A few days later, she wrote in her diary, "As God willed, the baby no longer desired my breasts, nor did they ache and become inflamed, so that I might not be tormented by worry for my child or by the pain in my breasts."[48] Buoyed by her vision, she knew that God would take care of her in the arena and that he would take care of her child after her death.

The experience of motherhood also gave Felicitas comfort and inspiration for her approaching martyrdom. Because the group of imprisoned Christians wanted to be able to die in the arena together, they prayed that Felicitas, who was eight months pregnant, would go into labor early. Their prayer was answered. As Felicitas labored to bring forth a daughter, the nearby prison guard taunted her: "If you are suffering so much now, what will you do when you are thrown to the beasts which you scorned when you refused to sacrifice?"[49] She replied, "Now I alone suffer what I am suffering, but then there will be another inside me, who will suffer for me, because I am going to suffer for him." Felicitas links the suffering of childbirth with the suffering of the cross and the suffering of martyrdom.[50] "While the guard sees only a suffering slave, who will endure greater pain a few days hence, Felicitas sees her childbirth experience as representative of Christ's passion. One might even suggest that her successful birth of a baby girl is a metaphor for her own success in the arena."[51] Felicitas expressed her confidence that Christ would be with her in the arena. Just as she suffered to bring forth a child in the prison cell, she believed Christ would suffer for her in the arena. And because Christ laid down his life for her, she looked forward to laying down her life for him.

After giving birth, Felicitas turned over the care of her daughter to another "sister" in the church. Her milk supply, unlike Perpetua's, did not dry up. She

---

48. Heffernan, *Passion of Perpetua and Felicity*, 128.
49. Heffernan, *Passion of Perpetua and Felicity*, 132.
50. Cohick and Hughes, *Christian Women*, 59.
51. Cohick, "Motherhood and Martyrdom."

went to the arena with milk still dripping from her breasts. The narrator of her account said that she went "from blood to blood"; she went from the blood of giving birth to the blood of martyrdom. The narrator also described her death as "a second baptism."[52] Thus, Felicitas's recent experience of childbirth continued to give meaning to her martyrdom. In baptism, a person is lowered into the water (to symbolize dying with Christ) and lifted up out of the water (to symbolize rising with Christ). After baptism, a person is said to be "born again." We don't often stop to think about this metaphor, but it is about childbirth, the experience Felicitas just had. When she went into the arena for her "second baptism," it was a baptism of literally dying and literally rising again. Martyrdom was for her being "born again." It was a second baptism, a second childbirth. Her suffering in childbirth led to new birth, a baby girl. Her suffering in the arena led to her own new birth. "As a mother, Felicitas can reflect Christ, the one who gives life and the one who births his followers. And Felicitas as a martyr resembles her child who receives life from her 'mother' Christ."[53]

The early church called women like Blandina, Perpetua, and Felicitas martyrs because the Greek word *martys* meant "witness." These women were witnesses for Jesus. They demonstrated what it looked like to "take up [their] cross and follow" him (Matt. 16:24; Mark 8:34; cf. Luke 9:23). These women and the male martyrs imprisoned with them also demonstrated the truth of the gospel that "there is neither Jew nor Gentile, neither slave nor free, nor is there male and female, for you are all one in Christ Jesus" (Gal. 3:28). Blandina's status as an enslaved woman did not keep the group in Lyon from looking to her as their leader. In the Carthage prison, Perpetua and Felicitas met together with the other believers—slaves and free, men and women—to pray. Social class and gender were not obstacles in this family of God. There is a particularly poignant illustration of equality in the narrative of their martyrdom. At one point in the arena, with the beasts running around, Felicitas fell down. When Perpetua saw her, "she went over to her, gave her her hand and helped her up. *And the two stood side by side.*"[54] In icons of Perpetua and Felicitas, the two continue to stand "side by side," illustrating that in Christ there is "neither slave nor free." The two are also often depicted with different colors of skin, one with darker skin and one with lighter skin. The varying skin tones offer further commentary on the capacity for people from different ethnic backgrounds to become "one in Christ Jesus."

52. Cohick and Hughes, *Christian Women*, 61.
53. Cohick, "Motherhood and Martyrdom."
54. Heffernan, *Passion of Perpetua and Felicity*, 134 (emphasis added).

Women Martyrs Shaped Theology and Church Practices

Through their actions, women like Blandina, Perpetua, and Felicitas helped to shape the developing theology and practices of the church. First of all, they shaped a theology of suffering. Paul told the Corinthian church, "Follow my example, as I follow the example of Christ" (1 Cor. 11:1). Martyrs showed what imitating Christ looked like. They helped people reflect on the role of suffering in the Christian life. Every year Blandina, Perpetua, and Felicitas were celebrated on the anniversaries of their deaths. On that day, pastors preached sermons about them, and people looked to them as exemplars of the faith.

The experiences of childbirth and breastfeeding figured heavily in the narratives of Perpetua and Felicitas, and it is clear that these women derived inspiration from God's communication to them through their experiences as women. However, their words and actions were seen as instructive for both women and men. People considered them heroes of the faith and journeyed on pilgrimage to the sites associated with their deaths. As people visited these sites and prayed to God at these sites, they began to believe that such heroes of the faith could intercede with God on their behalf.[55]

Many of the early martyrs were women, so it is important to see that even as the church was solidifying its preference for male priests and bishops, women's leadership was still central to the identity of the church. The stories of women were just as present in the minds of believers as the stories of men. As the stories of women martyrs were told every year on the anniversaries of their deaths, the stories inspired other Christians to pick up the baton of religious leadership. Just as the authority to lead the church was handed down through a process of apostolic succession (the apostles laid their hands on leaders to pass on their authority for leadership, and those leaders laid their hands on other leaders, etc.), in a similar way women martyrs and other women leaders handed down their power and authority. These women leaders passed the baton of religious leadership to the next generation every time people were inspired by their stories to live more faithfully.[56]

---

55. The idea of asking a saint to intercede with God on our behalf is strange to many Protestants today, but in the context of the developing church, it made a lot of sense. People knew that Perpetua had lived an extremely faithful earthly life. She had prayed for her sisters and brothers while on earth. Since people believed she was alive and with Christ, they had every reason to believe that she could still take up their case with God (i.e., pray for them). People who felt a special affinity with her, perhaps because they too were mothers, began to talk to her as they would talk to a friend.

56. Cohick and Hughes, *Christian Women*, 94.

Women Martyrs Transformed Cultural Notions of Womanhood

In addition to shaping Christian theology and church practices, women martyrs also challenged their culture's notion of femininity. We get a sense of how that happened when we read Perpetua's account of her interactions with her father. Three times Perpetua's father pleaded with her to give up her faith, and three times she refused to do so. Any Roman reading this account would have been shocked. A highborn Roman woman disobeying her father was unthinkable. And doing so publicly was shameful. We know from other aspects of her account that Perpetua was otherwise considered a very respectable woman. After all, she chose to nurse her baby—the ultimate sign of a woman's dedication to her family. But when Perpetua met Jesus, the gendered norms of her culture fell flat. She simply could not obey her father if it meant disobeying Jesus. She owed primary loyalty to Jesus, not to her father—and ultimately not even to her son. Her decision to die rather than live to take care of her son would have been seen by her community as a selfish and dishonorable thing to do. And certainly she herself must have questioned whether it was the right thing to do. She had been raised to see familial loyalty as her primary commitment. This is likely why God sent her such a powerful vision. The vision of his provision assured her that she was making the right choice and that he would take care of her son.

Nevertheless, others in her culture would still have seen her as being completely in the wrong. It begins to make sense why Christians were considered rather dangerous and immoral. What might happen if countless women started standing up to their fathers, started insisting on doing what they thought was right rather than what their fathers thought was right? Such attitudes help explain why the state decided to kill women like Perpetua. It would be impossible to run a stable empire with high-class women, let alone slave women like Felicitas, making their own decisions. In Roman thought, women were to obey their husbands and fathers, and slaves were to obey their masters. But in the kingdom of God, everyone obeys God. Husbands, fathers, sisters, mothers, slaves, and masters all become family, all become one in Christ. These are the truths that Perpetua, Felicitas, and Blandina died to proclaim.

In Roman culture, women were not known for being strong and courageous, but women like Perpetua, Felicitas, Blandina, and Thecla demonstrated profound strength and courage. They drew this strength from Christ, and they pushed people in their culture to begin to think differently about women. An interesting linguistic problem arose, however, as people tried to communicate the stories of strong women. Many languages use grammatical gender, meaning they have masculine and feminine endings for words. Some nouns are considered masculine and others feminine, grammatically. For example, in Spanish, "window" (*la ventana*) is feminine, and "boat" (*el barco*) is masculine. In the Roman world, the Latin words for "strong" and "courageous" were masculine words. There simply was no way of using these words to talk about women. So in one of Perpetua's visions, she said, "I became a man." According to Lynn Cohick and Amy Hughes, "The phrase 'becoming a man' is another way of saying, 'I am courageous.'"[57]

We know from the rest of Perpetua's account that she clearly did not think of herself as a man. God communicated to her and Felicitas through female imagery and experiences. These experiences communicated to them that they were not less in the kingdom of God by virtue of being women. Not all women, however, received that message. Rather than allowing God to widen their cultural conception of womanhood, many people in the early church chose instead to widen the cultural conception of manhood to include women. One church father, Palladius, said of some intelligent, holy women that they were "more like men than nature would seem to allow."[58] The only way Palladius knew how to affirm women as devout, rational, and self-controlled was to say they were like men.

And so women martyrs and other holy women of this time were described with the Latin word *vir*, "manly." This was considered a compliment. Unfortunately, it also did women a disservice. The goal in calling women *vir* was to emphasize their full humanity with men, but this move did not ultimately challenge the notion that men were the model human beings. Many people in the Roman Empire followed Aristotle in thinking that women lacked the ability to use reason to control their emotions and desires.[59] Thus, when women like Perpetua, Felicitas, and Blandina clearly demonstrated the ability to use reason to control their emotions (thereby being able to give themselves over willingly to death), people said they were *vir*, "manly." Also visible in the word *vir* is the root of the word "virtue." This masculine language shows once again what virtuous women were up against. It was essentially impossible for them to be both women and virtuous.[60]

57. Cohick and Hughes, *Christian Women*, 42.
58. Cohick and Hughes, *Christian Women*, 43.
59. Aristotle, *Politics* 1.13.
60. When church people wanted to revere a virtuous woman, they described the woman as "this female man of God" (Swan, *Forgotten Desert Mothers*, 39). John Chrysostom said of the deaconess Olympias, "Do not say 'woman,' but rather 'manly creature,' for she is a man in everything except body. . . . In her way of life, her works, her knowledge, and courage in misfortune" (Palladius, *Dialogue on the Life*, 105). Gregory of Nazianzus, wanting to describe his pious mother, wrote, "Though in her body she was but a woman, in her spirit she was above all men." Sanidopoulos, "Saint Nonna of Nazianzus."

Yet women did help the church to develop a vision of womanhood that departed from Roman ideals. Think about Blandina in the posture of Christ on the cross. Think about the fact that Eusebius, a powerful male leader of the church and member of Constantine's inner circle, chose to include the story of Blandina in his account of church history. In choosing to include this account, he communicated approval of Blandina's version of femininity. Of all the people killed with Blandina, she was the one whose body most fully demonstrated the image of Christ. She also showed courage, strength, and the capacity to conquer emotion with reason. Romans celebrated women for being faithful to their husbands and to the state, but Christians celebrated Blandina, Perpetua, Felicitas, and Thecla for being faithful to Christ. Romans saw these women as bringing shame upon their families, but Christians saw these women as the most honorable of human beings.

Conclusion

Women in the earliest days of the church had clear leadership roles. Starting with Jesus's mother, Mary, and the other women disciples, this chapter has presented women who served in all kinds of capacities. Lydia, Mary, and Nympha were independent heads of households who hosted house churches, likely served Communion, and spread the gospel to their neighbors through word and deed. Priscilla was an evangelist, a teacher of men, and a missionary who, with her husband, Aquila, established churches in Rome, Corinth, and Ephesus. Mary Magdalene and Junia were apostles. Dorcas belonged to the developing order of widows, who distributed aid to needy members of the church. These women had responsibilities for the mission of the church and commanded the respect and authority that accompanied their roles as leaders. They and their contributions to the mission of the church were lifted up by Paul when he wrote letters to the various churches.

Other women, like Blandina, Perpetua, and Felicitas, were martyred for their faith. Their lives not only testified to the power of Christ but also challenged some of the dominant thinking about women at the time. They showed the capacity of women to demonstrate courage, strength, and self-control. These woman were called *vir*, "manly," but their experiences of motherhood, breastfeeding, and childbirth nurtured their dependence on God and encouraged the faithful around them. Every year as the faithful celebrated these women on the anniversaries of their deaths, they continued to exert influence on individuals and on the church's developing theology.

2

Virgins, Scholars, Desert Mothers, and Deacons

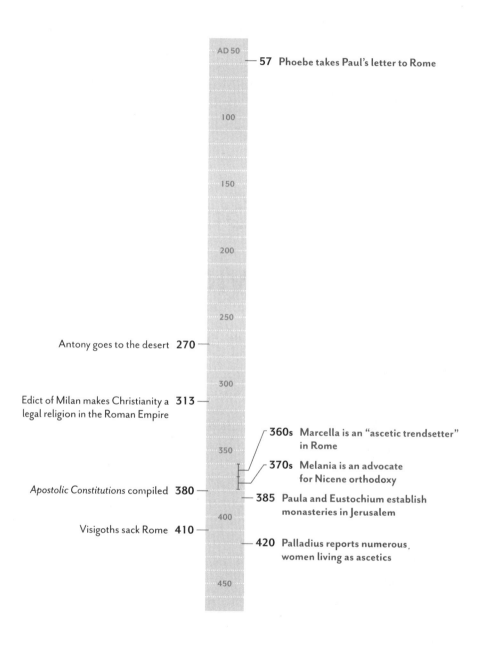

AD 50

— **57** Phoebe takes Paul's letter to Rome

100

150

200

250

Antony goes to the desert **270** —

300

Edict of Milan makes Christianity a **313** —
legal religion in the Roman Empire

⌐ **360s** Marcella is an "ascetic trendsetter"
            in Rome

350

⌐ **370s** Melania is an advocate
            for Nicene orthodoxy

Apostolic Constitutions compiled **380** —

— **385** Paula and Eustochium establish
           monasteries in Jerusalem

400

Visigoths sack Rome **410** —

— **420** Palladius reports numerous
           women living as ascetics

450

The previous chapter introduced several types of vocations for Christian women in the early church: disciple, patron, missionary, evangelist, apostle, teacher, widow, and martyr. This chapter continues the discussion of vocations for women in the early church by discussing virgins, scholars, desert mothers, and deacons. These vocations enabled women to minister to God and to God's people and to play an important role in shaping the development of monasticism and the diaconate.

Virgins and Celibacy: A Compelling Vocation for Women

Jesus never married; he lived his life as a celibate man in a culture that expected men and women to marry. One of the ways that people in the early church imitated Christ was through dedicating themselves to a life of celibacy. Such a choice, however, put them in opposition to Roman cultural norms. Choosing to stay single was essentially refusing to carry on the family line. A woman who aspired to be a virgin was seen as selfish for putting her own desires before those of her family.

In light of Roman social norms, being a virgin was truly countercultural. Such a lifestyle made sense only in the context of a different understanding of reality. Christian virgins did not think of themselves primarily as citizens of the Roman Empire; they thought of themselves primarily as citizens of the kingdom of God. They looked to God—rather than nation, family, or master—as the ultimate source of authority in their lives. And they were inspired by the vision of celibacy described by the apostle Paul in his letter to the church in Corinth.

First Corinthians is often thought of as one of Paul's most corrective letters because he spends a good portion of it discussing problems in the Corinthian church. Topics he addresses at some length are marriage and singleness. In particular, he discusses the value of being single and the capacity it offers for serving God. Singleness is his first preference: "Now to the unmarried and the widows I say: It is good for them to stay unmarried, as I do" (1 Cor. 7:8). He goes on to explain the various advantages of being single:

Now about virgins: I have no command from the Lord, but I give a judgment as one who by the Lord's mercy is trustworthy. Because of the present crisis, I think that it is good for a man to remain as he is. Are you pledged to a woman? Do not seek to be released. Are you free from such a commitment? Do not look for a wife. But if you do marry, you have not sinned; and if a virgin marries, she has not sinned. But those who marry will face many troubles in this life, and I want to spare you this. . . .

I would like you to be free from concern. An unmarried man is concerned about the Lord's affairs—how he can please the Lord. But a married man is concerned about the affairs of this world—how he can please his wife—and his interests are divided. An unmarried woman or virgin is concerned about the Lord's affairs: Her aim is to be devoted to the Lord in both body and spirit. But a married woman is concerned about the affairs of this world—how she can please her husband. I am saying this for your own good, not to restrict you, but that you may live in a right way in undivided devotion to the Lord. (7:25–28, 32–35)

In this section, Paul speaks about the way married people need to focus on their spouses and families while those who are not married have more freedom to focus on service to God. He makes it clear that neither choice is morally wrong and that each one offers different opportunities. From his perspective, though, there are definite advantages to being single and free to serve God.

Then Paul moves into an interesting discussion about men's and women's choices regarding singleness and marriage. He shows that he is aware of the different cultural constraints and requirements for men and women. There-fore, he phrases his instructions to men differently than his instructions to women. To men, he says this:

If anyone is worried that he might not be acting honorably toward the virgin he is engaged to, and if his passions are too strong and he feels he ought to marry, he should do as he wants. He is not sinning. They should get married. But the man who has settled the matter in his own mind, who is under no compulsion but has control over his own will, and who has made up his mind not to marry the virgin—this man also does the right thing. So then, he who marries the virgin does right, but he who does not marry her does better. (1 Cor. 7:36–38)

Culturally, men had greater freedom than women to choose marriage or singleness. In the first part of his discussion, Paul encourages men who are not pledged to be married to stay that way. He also says that those who are pledged to a woman should not break it off. In this section, Paul continues to encourage men to stay single, with two exceptions. The first is concern for the woman to whom a man is pledged, and the second is concern for the man's own sexual passions. If a man is pledged to a woman and is worried about her well-being and the need to commit to caring for her, then he should go ahead and get married. Even in the twenty-first century, this relegating of one's sexual drive to second place sounds somewhat odd. In the early Roman Empire, putting a woman's good first and a man's sexual drive second would have sounded ridiculous. Women in the Roman Empire could be citizens, could own property, and could be educated, but otherwise women had almost no rights. They couldn't hold political office or serve in the military, and even though society celebrated their childbearing capacity, they didn't have legal custody of their children. Their husbands or owners (in the case of enslaved mothers) could decide to expose a newborn child (a euphemism for killing it), and as mothers, they could do nothing about it. Thus, Paul's suggestion that a man's primary responsibility was to care for a woman was completely countercultural.

Paul's instructions to women make it clear that he is well aware of the different status held by women. To women, he says, "A woman is bound to her husband as long as he lives. But if her husband dies, she is free to marry anyone she wishes, but he must belong to the Lord. In my judgment, she is happier if she stays as she is—and I think that I too have the Spirit of God" (1 Cor. 7:39–40). Paul is aware that a woman was passed from her father's authority to her husband's at marriage. In some cases, even after marriage, she remained under her father's guardianship so that her finances would stay in her father's family. But in either case, she did not have the ability to choose singleness on her own. However, if she became a widow, she had more options. She might then have the freedom to choose to remain unmarried and thus to dedicate herself to God's service, as was explained in the discussion of widows in chapter 1. So Paul's preference is for a widow to stay single. However, if she wants to remarry, his only requirement is that she marry a Christian. As a widow, the woman would have had the ability to choose a second husband in a way that virgins under their father's care would not have had. In the early church, whether a woman never married or remained unmarried, once she became a widow, her singleness was crucial for her vocation in ministry.

Even if Paul wasn't targeting unmarried women with his call to lifelong celibacy, that call reached them nonetheless. Several of the early church martyrs were virgins—young women who chose death rather than marrying someone of their parents' choosing. Such young women felt deeply compelled by the vision of celibacy that Paul presented. They wanted to be concerned only about the Lord's affairs. They wanted "to be devoted to the Lord in both body and spirit" (1 Cor. 7:34). They didn't want to wait until they were widows to be able to choose this life for themselves. They wanted to choose this life as young women. Not much is known about many of these virgins, but the early church celebrated them, called them saints, and commemorated them on the anniversaries of their deaths. Thecla, in the previous chapter, was one of them. Agnes was another. In paintings of Agnes, she always has a lamb with her, both to symbolize her purity and because her name in Latin means lamb. Paintings of the virgin martyr Lucy always portray her with her eyes on a platter because her torturers gouged them out as part of her martyrdom. Even more disturbing is another account of Lucy that alleges she gouged out her own eyes so that her fiancé would not find her attractive anymore. Significantly, in both accounts, God restores her eyes. Thecla, Agnes, and Lucy shaped the developing theology of virginity, and their stories inspired other women to choose celibacy. Over time a liturgical service developed that allowed young women to be consecrated by a priest to a life of celibacy. These consecrated virgins were part of the line of succession discussed in the last chapter, whereby women passed the baton of religious leadership to the next generation.

Gradually, people committed to a celibate life began to live in community with one another. Women were involved in the development of monasticism from its beginning, but the history of monasticism is usually told as a history of men. For example, the desert monk Antony (251–356) is usually credited with being the founder of monasticism, but Antony's sister joined a convent when he went out to the desert. Clearly, women before Antony had begun to gather in monastic communities or she would have had no place to go. Around this time, cenobitic (communal rather than solitary) monasticism was being shaped by Pachomius (292–348), an Egyptian convert to Christianity.[1] Pachomius required his monks to be completely obedient to their superior and to give up all their worldly goods. His sister Mary founded similar communities for women.[2] She was responsible for teaching them the community rules observed by the men in Pachomius's houses, and she led the sisters in the burial processions when any of them died.[3]

After Christianity was legalized under Constantine, the number of people choosing a life of celibacy increased. Many Christians during Constantine's era worried that as Christians were welcomed into positions of power, the church would be corrupted by that power and the gospel would be watered down. People began to think of celibacy as part of the "new martyrdom." Christians no longer needed to literally die for the faith, but self-denial was itself a kind of death. People who were compelled by this vision chose to

1. González, *Story of Christianity*, 165.
2. González, *Story of Christianity*, 145.
3. Forman, *Praying with the Desert Mothers*, 7.

abstain not only from sex but also from rich food. Some of them gave up their wealth and, with it, the honor and status they held in society. They were called ascetics, and their dedication to self-denial was called asceticism. Their sacrifices were a way of "dying daily" and carrying on the tradition of the martyrs.

But celibacy was more than a form of death; it was also a way of living the resurrection life now. It was a way of anticipating what life in heaven will be like, for as Jesus said, "At the resurrection people will neither marry nor be given in marriage; they will be like the angels in heaven" (Matt. 22:30). The virgins of the church saw themselves as living like the angels here on earth.

Patrons and Scholars: Marcella, Paula, and Melania

Some women patrons of the church dedicated themselves to the ascetic life and allocated funds for others to live this kind of life as well. These patrons were just as essential to the developing communities of virgins as they had been to house churches. For example, Marcella (325–410) was a wealthy Roman woman whose husband died after only seven months of marriage. Since her father was also dead, Marcella had an unusual amount of control over her own finances and decided to turn her estate into a monastery. And then she became an "ascetic trendsetter."[4] When she turned her estate into a monastery, others were inspired to do likewise. When she stopped wearing jewelry, others did too. A wealthy widow named Paula (347–404) and her daughter Eustochium were two ascetics who were initially inspired by Marcella and went on to become recognized figures in their own right. All three of these women were part of the ascetic circle of the theologian Jerome in Rome and dedicated themselves to an intense study of Scripture and asceticism. In fact, Marcella was so knowledgeable about Scripture that when Jerome "left Rome, Marcella became the point person to resolve disputes over Scripture." Paula, also a keen student of the Scriptures, was fluent "in both Greek and Hebrew." Unlike Marcella, who stayed in Rome, Paula followed Jerome to the Holy Land and used her wealth to establish monasteries there.[5]

Melania the Elder (341–410) was another wealthy widow in the fourth century who became an ascetic and used her wealth to found monasteries in the Holy Land. She also used her power and biblical knowledge to shape theological discussions. During Melania's time, the church was debating Arianism (the belief that God the Father created God the Son at a particular moment in time). Melania was among those considered orthodox, who argued that

4. Cohick and Hughes, *Christian Women*, 196.
5. Cohick and Hughes, *Christian Women*, 195, 202.

the Son of God had always existed. Theological debates of that day were heated. People didn't just debate; they also hurled insults at one another, and sometimes the losers of a debate were thrown in prison or forced to flee for their lives. At one point, Melania was thrown in prison. The authorities didn't know she was a member of the upper class because she dressed in shabby clothes like the other ascetics of her time. After being thrown in prison, she finally declared her upper-class status and threatened her captors with reprisals. Her tirade worked, and they let her go. On another occasion, she was brought before the authorities for hiding some orthodox monks from the Arian emperor. Melania again defended herself brilliantly. She also "fearlessly accepted whatever punishment they might mete out. . . . Apparently the judge was so impressed with her that his rage cooled."[6] Rather than press charges, he let her go. One way to view Melania throwing her wealth around and invoking her power and connections is to say that her behavior was not very Christlike. But another perspective is also possible: she was a woman who—through her wealth, power, courage, connections, and obedience to Christ—shaped theology. The church today is orthodox rather than Arian partly due to Melania's influence.

Desert Mothers

During the fourth and fifth centuries, several thousand ascetics lived in the deserts of Egypt and Syria. Just as Jesus had gone into the desert, these desert mothers and fathers went into the desert to be tempted and, through Christ's power, to overcome temptation. Desert mothers were called *ammas*. They lived in solitary caves or remote monasteries, survived on hardly any food, prayed and studied Scripture throughout the day, and wove baskets to keep from being idle. Ammas "favored dark or natural colored clothing like that of the poor, and concealed or cropped their hair."[7] Some of them dressed like men in order to avoid drawing attention to themselves.[8]

Some people may criticize the desert mothers and fathers, believing they failed to live out Jesus's call to serve others because they spent so much time focusing on their own spiritual growth. But a better way to understand the path of the desert is to see that these ascetics withdrew from society to

6. Cohick and Hughes, *Christian Women*, 208.
7. Swan, *Forgotten Desert Mothers*, 10.
8. According to legend, some saints disguised themselves as men in order to escape an unwanted suitor or to demonstrate their union with Christ and renunciation of a past life. Others did so to join a male monastery or live as a hermit in the desert. Anson, "Female Transvestite," 11–16; B. Ward, *Harlots of the Desert*, 59–62.

become better disciples of Jesus who could, in turn, better serve the church. Pilgrims would often journey to visit the desert mothers and fathers, converse with them, and learn from them. The desert mothers and fathers helped visitors to see how "hurry, crowds, and noise" made it difficult to hear the voice of God.[9] They encouraged people to cultivate silence, calmness, and slowness in order to hear the still, small voice of God. The pilgrims then took the wisdom of the desert back to their communities and churches. Although the desert mothers and fathers might have preferred silence and solitude, they knew that they needed to be gracious and hospitable to visitors: "With the guest, Christ was received. Hence, [the amma's] fast might be set aside to join the guest in a light meal. Silence would be broken for heart-to-heart conversation."[10] Another way the ammas loved their neighbor was by weaving baskets, which they could give to poor people.[11] Some ammas also served as deaconesses.[12]

When church father Palladius wrote about the desert ascetics in his *Lausiac History*, he noted that many women excelled at the ascetic life. It seems he thought that people might be surprised by this news, so he wrote, "It is necessary also to mention in my book certain women with manly qualities, to whom God apportioned labours equal to those of men, lest any should pretend that women are too feeble to practise virtue perfectly. Now I have seen many such and met many distinguished virgins and widows."[13] He mentioned Theodora, "who reached such a depth of poverty that she became a recipient of alms," Basianilla, "who practiced virtue ardently and scrupulously," and Avita, "who was worthy of God."[14] He described Alexandra, who lived her entire life in a tomb, and Piamoun, an ascetic prophet who lived with her mother.[15] He described a "nun who feigned madness" as an ascetic discipline and a beloved abbess, Amma Talis, "who had spent eighty years in asceticism."[16] He told of Magna, who "provided for the needs . . . of hospitals, the poor and bishops on tour."[17] In the town of Ancyra, where Magna lived, there were "some 2000 or more" ascetic women. In the town of Antinoe, there were twelve convents, with probably around sixty women in each, and there were four hundred

---

9. Swan, *Forgotten Desert Mothers*, 15.
10. Swan, *Forgotten Desert Mothers*, 26.
11. Swan, *Forgotten Desert Mothers*, 40.
12. Swan, *Forgotten Desert Mothers*, 16.
13. Palladius, *Lausiac History* 41.
14. Palladius, *Lausiac History* 41.
15. Palladius, *Lausiac History* 5.
16. Palladius, *Lausiac History* 34, 59.
17. Palladius, *Lausiac History* 67.

nuns in Tabennisi.[18] Given numbers like these, it is clear that Palladius was just scratching the surface of women's prominence within the early Christian monastic movement.

Despite the prominence of women in the ascetic movement, the church for the most part chose to record and preserve the stories of the fathers. The desert mothers would probably be pleased that their stories have been forgotten. After all, they tried to disappear from view in order to devote themselves more fully to Jesus. That was why the nun described in Palladius's *Lausiac History* feigned madness—so that no one would revere her.[19]

Despite their efforts to disappear from view, the ascetics were heroes of the church. People believed a virgin lifestyle to be holier than a married lifestyle. In much of the world today, the value of singleness and celibacy has declined.[20] In many Christian communities, marriage is valued more than celibacy. In these communities, the stories being passed on to the next generation are stories of married men and women who lived out their Christian faith in the world rather than stories of celibate men and women who withdrew from the world in order to live out their Christian faith. Each kind of life has its merits, but the contemporary church could learn a great deal from the ascetics. The desert mothers and fathers show us how to "take up our cross" in the midst of a culture that has no place for the cross. They demonstrate how to set one's sights on eternal rather than temporal goods and to eliminate distractions so as to hear the voice of God in prayer, Scripture, and creation.

How Desert Mothers Overcame Obstacles

The previous chapter discussed some of the obstacles martyrs faced, particularly how it was difficult for women martyrs to demonstrate that they were both virtuous and women. Their culture thought that women were irrational and sinful and that men were rational and virtuous. Desert mothers faced this same cultural obstacle. It is interesting how Amma Sarah, who "lived alone by

18. Palladius, *Lausiac History* 59, 33.
19. Palladius, *Lausiac History* 34.
20. The number of monks and nuns in Roman Catholicism has also declined. According to the Center for Applied Research in the Apostolate, from 1970 to 2018, the number of religious brothers decreased from 11,623 to 3,897, and the number of religious sisters decreased from 160,931 to 44,117 ("Frequently Requested Church Statistics"). Two things are interesting about these numbers: first, how many more women than men commit to the vocation, and second, proportionately, the sisters have declined faster than the brothers. This decline aligns with research done by the Barna Group showing that women leave church at a higher rate than men in the twenty-first century ("Five Factors"). However, there is also evidence that the number of nuns is beginning to increase again. See Fairbanks, "Behold, the Millennial Nuns."

the Nile for sixty years," overcame it.[21] Here is how the story has come down to us: "Two old men, great anchorites [who lived in seclusion, often in a cell attached to a church], came to the district of Pelusia to visit her. When they arrived, one said to the other, 'Let us humiliate this old woman.' So they said to her, 'Be careful not to become conceited thinking to yourself: Look how anchorites are coming to see me, a mere woman.' But Amma Sarah said to them, 'According to nature I am a woman, but not according to my thoughts.'"[22]

This story is disturbing. First, two men who were supposed to be model Christians came with the intention of humiliating Amma Sarah. Next, in order to defend herself, Amma Sarah had to distance herself from her body. Her strategy made sense. Her culture viewed the female body as less than the male body, so distancing herself from her body was a way to assert her spiritual equality with men. Still, it is sad that she had to take that approach. And it is sad that these men were trying to humiliate her in the first place. But the best part of the story is what she said next: "Amma Sarah said, 'If I prayed God that all people should approve of my conduct, I should find myself a penitent at the door of each one, but I shall rather pray that my heart may be pure toward all.'"[23] Amma Sarah realized that her culture had a negative view of women, a view that had also unfortunately infiltrated the church. But she knew that God accepted her as a woman and that it was only God's opinion of her that truly mattered. She saw that the insult the men hurled at her had the capacity to enslave her to the desire to please every person. She prayed that God would help her to have only pure thoughts toward the men. She prayed that God would help her not to care what other people said of her. Such a prayer offered grace to the men and kept her own heart free from the burdens of anger and trying to please all people.

Ascetics like Amma Sarah were often described as "athletes." The Greek word askēsis (from which English gets the word "asceticism") was originally used in regard to the training athletes did. Ascetics like Amma Sarah trained themselves in virtue and devotion to Jesus. As "great athletes," they dedicated themselves to "longer fasts, more difficult prayer vigils, and greater experiences of solitude" in order to grow deeper in their relationship with Jesus.[24] Amma Syncletica said that "those who are great athletes must contend against stronger enemies."[25] It may well have been that "stronger enemies" came in unexpected forms, like the men who visited Amma Sarah. But ultimately the

21. B. Ward, "Apophthegmata Matrem," 65.
22. Swan, Forgotten Desert Mothers, 38–39.
23. Swan, Forgotten Desert Mothers, 39.
24. Swan, Forgotten Desert Mothers, 54.
25. Swan, Forgotten Desert Mothers, 54.

ammas understood that spiritual growth occurred as one contended against enemies, storms, and trials. "Amma Theodora said, 'Let us strive to enter by the narrow gate. Just as the trees, if they have not stood before the winter's storms cannot bear fruit, so it is with us; this present age is a storm and it is only through many trials and temptations that we can obtain an inheritance in the kingdom of heaven.'"[26]

Women Deacons

The role of deacon (later, deaconess) was another way women contributed to the mission of the church and passed the baton of religious leadership from generation to generation. The order of deacons was open to both married and single women and offered a strong vocation for women in the early years of the church. The first letter from Paul to Timothy spells out qualifications for deacons:

> In the same way [as elders], deacons are to be worthy of respect, sincere, not indulging in much wine, and not pursuing dishonest gain. They must keep hold of the deep truths of the faith with a clear conscience. They must first be tested; and then if there is nothing against them, let them serve as deacons.
> In the same way [as male deacons], the women are to be worthy of respect, not malicious talkers but temperate and trustworthy in everything.
> A deacon must be faithful to his wife and must manage his children and his household well. Those who have served well gain an excellent standing and great assurance in their faith in Christ Jesus. (1 Tim. 3:8–13)

In this section of 1 Timothy, Paul sets out qualifications for elders, deacons, and women deacons in the church in Ephesus. The church there badly needed a reliable group of overseers because they had been struggling with so many false teachers. The church was in trouble and the people were suffering, just as Paul had warned would happen in Acts 20:29. Close monitoring of the believers and those who wished to teach was needed to guard against heresies. After describing the qualifications for elders, Paul next spelled out the responsibilities of male and female deacons.

Some people think that the women in verse 11 are the wives of deacons, but that doesn't make as much sense in the context as women deacons. The phrase "in the same way" in verse 8 compares deacons to elders, which were previously mentioned; the same phrase repeated in verse 11 connects the

26. Swan, *Forgotten Desert Mothers*, 64–65.

women to male deacons and possibly back to elders. The parallel structure of each section and the similar types of requirements show that Paul had three groups of leaders in mind for the church. At the time, there was no word for "deaconess," so he simply used the word "women."[27] If Paul had meant deacons' wives, he could have used the pronoun "their" to make the meaning clear. If a qualification for office were a certain kind of wife, then a discussion of elders' wives would also be needed, but there is none. For all these reasons, it makes more sense that Paul was talking about women deacons.[28]

Another reason to think that Paul meant women deacons is that he had previously written about a particular woman, Phoebe, and had used a word that could be translated as "deacon" to describe her role in the church in Cenchreae. Toward the end of his letter to the church in Rome, Paul says, "I commend to you our sister Phoebe, a deacon of the church in Cenchreae. I ask you to receive her in the Lord in a way worthy of his people and to give her any help she may need from you, for she has been the benefactor of many people, including me" (Rom. 16:1–2). Most Bible scholars agree that Phoebe was the person carrying Paul's letter from Corinth to the believers in Rome. His request that they "receive her in the Lord" suggests strongly that she was the messenger and that he gave them his endorsement of her as a fellow believer and leader in the church.

Translating Terms for Phoebe's Leadership in a Gender-Specific Way

Paul uses two crucial words to describe Phoebe: "deacon" and "benefactor." The word "deacon" is used in the NIV and the NRSV translations of the Bible, but other translations use the word "servant."[29] Similarly, the word "benefactor" is used in the NIV and the NRSV, but other translations use the word "helper" or "patron."

Every language is unique, and sometimes it is difficult to find the right word to express an idea from one language in another language. Bible translators have to make a choice about which English word will best express the Greek word Paul used when he wrote the letter. In the case of the choice between "deacon" and "servant," Greek scholars have pointed out that most occurrences of the Greek word *diakonos* are translated as "minister" in the New

27. The term can be translated either as "women" or "wives," just as the term for men can be translated either as "men" or "husbands."
28. See Belleville, *Women Leaders*, 62–63.
29. See Belleville, *Women Leaders*, for a fuller discussion of translation choices.

Testament; only in relation to Phoebe do some translators choose to translate the word as "servant."

The following table shows the verses in Paul's letters where he uses the Greek word with regard to a specific person and how the different versions of the Bible have translated that word.

Verse	NKJV	NASB	ESV	NRSV	NIV
Romans 16:1 (Phoebe)	servant	servant	servant	deacon	deacon
Romans 13:4 (a ruler)	minister	minister	servant	servant	servant
Romans 15:16 (Paul)	minister	minister	minister	minister	minister
Ephesians 3:7 (Paul)	minister	minister	minister	servant	servant
Ephesians 6:21 (Tychicus)	minister	minister	minister	minister	servant
Colossians 1:23 (Paul)	minister	minister	minister	servant	servant

It is interesting that the NKJV, the NASB, and the ESV translate the Greek word into English as "minister" when the reference is to a man and as "servant" when the word refers to a woman. The NIV and the NRSV are less consistent, with no obvious pattern for their translation choice. Still, only for Phoebe do they use the word "deacon"; other uses are translated either as "servant" or "minister." What is it about Phoebe that makes translators reluctant to call her a minister? The most likely answer is her gender. Translators may be influenced by assumptions about what work is appropriate for men and for women. The apostle Paul did not make a distinction between Phoebe's work and that of the men; had he wanted to call her "servant" (*doulos*), there was a perfectly good, everyday word with that meaning that he could have used. Instead, he chose to call her "minister" along with the men. In fact, Paul uses the same word five times in the New Testament to refer to himself and his work.[30] Apparently he saw Phoebe's work as similar to his own.

Something similar happens with the word translated "helper" or "benefactor," but it's a little harder to see because the word used in verse 2 for Phoebe is used only this one time in the New Testament. It's a feminine noun form, and the masculine form isn't used in the New Testament either. What is used several times is the verb form of the same word, and it's often translated "to manage," "to rule," or even "to lead." When a word occurs only once in the New Testament, the standard approach to understanding its meaning is to look at its cognates, or closely related words. In English, some examples of

30. McCabe, "Reexamination of Phoebe."

cognates would be ruler / to rule, leader / to lead, and manager / to manage. This table displays the translation choices made for Phoebe's work:

Verse	NKJV	NASB	ESV	NRSV	NIV
Romans 16:2 (church leadership)	helper	helper	patron	benefactor	benefactor
Romans 12:8 (church leadership)	leads	leads	leads	the leader	to lead
1 Thessalonians 5:12 (church leadership)	are over you	have charge over you	are over you	have charge of you	care for you
1 Timothy 5:17 (church leadership)	rule	rule	rule	rule	direct
1 Timothy 3:4 (house-hold organization)	rules	manages	manage	manage	manage
1 Timothy 3:5 (house-hold organization)	rule	manage	manage	manage	manage
1 Timothy 3:12 (house-hold organization)	ruling	managers	managing	manage	manage

Based on the use of the verb form in the New Testament, calling Phoebe a "helper" is a very poor description of what she actually did. If Paul had wanted to call her a helper, there were Greek words available with that meaning. But the word he chose is closely connected to a verb form that clearly indicates a position of leadership and authority.[31]

Romans 12:8, 1 Thessalonians 5:12, and 1 Timothy 5:17 are about church leadership, so they are the closest to what Paul is talking about with Phoebe. In all three of these verses, every translation uses a word that clearly implies authority over and responsibility for people. But the translations chosen for Phoebe don't convey either of those ideas. While a "patron" in the ancient world was definitely a person with authority over other people, in modern English in the United States, a "patron" or a "benefactor" is someone who donates time or resources to a cause, not someone with authority over or responsibility for people. A "helper" is even weaker, someone who assists rather than someone having authority and responsibility.

Similarly, in the verses about household management in 1 Timothy, the English words chosen convey authority and responsibility—to rule or manage

---

31. Dunn, *Romans 9–16*, 888; Bray, *Romans*, 355–56. James D. G. Dunn states, "The un-willingness of commentators to give προστάτις its most natural and obvious sense of 'patron' is most striking." Dunn, *Romans 9–16*, 888.

resources and people. Again, neither "patron" nor "benefactor" in modern English conveys the idea of ruling or managing. Once again, the question becomes why translators chose English words that don't convey authority and responsibility when talking about Phoebe. The most likely answer is her gender. Truly, the best way to understand Phoebe based on Paul's language in Romans 16:1–2 is that she was a recognized leader of the church in Cenchreae with a role that included authority and responsibility.[32]

The Development of the Female Diaconate

Although many English translations make it difficult to see, the early church had no trouble with the idea of women deacons. Initially, both men and women who served in this role were called deacons. In order to distinguish between male and female deacons, the term "deaconess" began to be used during the late third century, but the term did not "become popular in usage [until] at least a century later."[33]

Information about the female diaconate comes from two main sources: writings of the time and burial inscriptions. For example, as mentioned in the last chapter, the second-century governor Pliny the Younger interrogated two Christian women and called them *ministrae*, which is usually translated as "deaconesses."[34] Clement of Alexandria in the second century said that the verses in 1 Timothy meant women deacons. Origen wrote a commentary on Romans in which he argued that the verses about Phoebe justified women serving as deacons.[35]

The *Didascalia Apostolorum* (Teaching of the Apostles) was a book of instructions for the church compiled in the early third century.[36] It describes liturgies for worship and rules for choosing and ordaining leaders. Women deacons are described in some detail. Women chosen to be deacons were to be righteous; they were to assist in the baptisms of women and to teach the women "how to live a holy and pure life" after baptism.[37] They were to care for sick women and to visit pagan women to share the gospel with them. The reason for having women deacons assist the bishop was Jesus's example: "For

32. For an entertaining and informative account of Phoebe, see Gooder, *Phoebe*. Although this is a fictional story, Gooder is a Pauline scholar, and her book offers a plausible account of the kind of leadership and authority Phoebe likely had in the early church.

33. Fitzgerald, *Women Deacons*, xiv.

34. Olson, *Deacons and Deaconesses*, 29.

35. Belleville, *Women Leaders*, 62–63.

36. Gibson, *Didascalia apostolorum*.

37. Fitzgerald, *Women Deacons*, 23.

our Lord and Savior was ministered to by women ministers, 'Mary Magdalene, and Mary the daughter of James and mother of Jose, and the mother of
the sons of Zebedee' [Matt 27:56], and other women besides. And you [the
bishop] also need the ministry of a deaconess for many things."[38]

A century later, the *Apostolic Constitutions* also spelled out the duties
of deaconesses and included instructions for their ordination: "O bishop,
do thou ordain thy fellow-workers. . . . Ordain also a deaconess who is
faithful and holy, for the ministrations towards women. For sometimes he
cannot send a deacon, who is a man, to the women, on account of unbeliev-
ers. Thou shalt therefore send a woman, a deaconess. . . . For we stand in
need of a woman, a deaconess, for many necessities. First in the baptism
of women, the deacon shall anoint only their forehead with oil and after
him the deaconess shall anoint them."[39] Once the baptism was completed,
the *Apostolic Constitutions* instructed, "Let a deacon receive the men, and
a deaconess the woman."[40] Additional instructions for deaconesses were
these: "Let the deaconess be diligent in taking care of the women; but both
of them [men and women deacons] ready to carry messages, to travel about,
to minister, and to serve. . . . So therefore ought they also to do, and not
to scruple it, if they should be obliged to lay down their life."[41] Both the
Didascalia Apostolorum and the *Apostolic Constitutions* show the parallel
responsibilities of deacons and deaconesses. The expectations of service,
assisting in baptism, and even perhaps martyrdom were the same for both
men and women.

In the fifth century, the Council of Chalcedon proclaimed, "A woman shall
not receive the laying on of hands as a deaconess under forty years of age,
and then only after searching examination."[42] This statement shows that there
was both an ordination process ("receive the laying on of hands") and some
requirements (age and qualifications) for a woman to become a deaconess.

An eighth-century manuscript from the Eastern church gives a detailed
account of the ordination service for deaconesses. At the beginning of the
service, the woman "bows her head. He [the archbishop] imposes his hand
on her forehead, makes the sign of the cross on it three times," and then says
the following prayer: "Holy and Omnipotent Lord, through the birth of your
Only Son our God from a Virgin according to the flesh, you have sanctified
the female sex. You grant not only to men, but also to women the grace and

38. P. Miller, *Women in Early Christianity*, 63.
39. *Constitutions of the Holy Apostles*, sec. 2.
40. *Constitutions of the Holy Apostles*, sec. 2.16.
41. *Constitutions of the Holy Apostles*, sec. 2.19.
42. "Canons of the Council of Chalcedon," canon 15.

coming of the Holy Spirit."[43] Later in the service, the bishop prays, "Lord, Master, you do not reject women who dedicate themselves to you and who are willing, in a becoming way, to serve your Holy House, but admit them to the order of your ministers. Grant the gift of your Holy Spirit also to this your maidservant who wants to dedicate herself to you, and fulfil in her the grace of the diaconate, as you have granted to Phoebe the grace of your diaconate, whom you had called to the work of the ministry." When he finishes his prayer, the bishop puts "the stole of the diaconate round her neck, under her veil, arranging the two extremities of the stole towards the front." After taking Communion, the now ordained and consecrated deaconess would begin to assist at the Communion table.[44]

Some tombstone inscriptions offer additional evidence for the prevalence of deaconesses in the church. For example, a tombstone from the Mount of Olives says, "Here lies the slave and bride of Christ, Sophia, the deacon, the second Phoebe."[45] A later inscription from the sixth century reads, "Here lies the deacon Maria of pious and blessed memory, who according to the words of the apostle raised children, sheltered guests, washed the feet of the saints, and shared her bread with the needy. Remember her, Lord, when she comes into your kingdom."[46]

Olympias was a particularly prominent deaconess in fourth-century Constantinople. When her husband died, her relatives (including Emperor Theodosius II) tried to get her to remarry, but Olympias refused and said, "If my King, the Lord Jesus Christ, wanted me to be joined with a man, he would not have taken away my first husband immediately."[47] Olympias built a monastery for herself next to the Cathedral of Hagia Sophia. She brought two of her sisters and a cousin to join her, and the bishop ordained all four of them as deaconesses even though the normal age for deaconesses was over sixty and Olympias was half that age.[48] Olympias had a sharp mind, and her theological debate partners included Macrina and the Cappadocian fathers.[49] John Chrysostom was her dear friend and consulted with her about

43. "Codex Barberini gr. 336, Italy (780)," quoted in Wijngaards, *Ordained Women Deacons*, 191–92.
44. "Codex Barberini gr. 336, Italy (780)," quoted in Wijngaards, *Ordained Women Deacons*, 191–92.
45. Eisen, *Women Officeholders*, 159. Interestingly, the inscription shows the early church did regard Phoebe as a deacon.
46. Eisen, *Women Officeholders*, 165.
47. *Life of Olympias, Deaconess* 3, quoted in Clark, *Women in the Early Church*, 225.
48. Zahirsky, "Deaconess Olympias," 48. The minimum age for deaconesses was lowered to forty at the Council of Chalcedon in 451.
49. Swan, *Forgotten Desert Mothers*, 121.

everything from delicate church matters to indigestion. Even after he was exiled from Constantinople, he continued to correspond with and confide in Olympias.

The role of deaconess was an established and accepted vocation for women in the early church. Linda Belleville sums up the importance of women deacons:

> In many ways women deacons were a very practical development. Women could gain entry into places that were forbidden to the average male and perform activities that would be deemed inappropriate for the opposite sex. The duties of female deacons in the postapostolic period were quite extensive. They taught children and youth. They discipled new female believers. They went to the homes of believers and evangelized unbelieving women of the household. They visited the sick, cared for the ailing, administered communion to the shut-ins, and distributed charitable donations to women in need in the congregation. In the worship service they served as doorkeepers, assisted with the baptism of women, and administered communion in times of need.[50]

Women deacons were considered members of the clergy and played an essential role in the mission of the church.[51]

Obstacles Faced by Deaconesses

The office of deaconess spread more slowly in the West than it had in the East, and several theologians and synods explicitly forbade women in ministry.[52] In 396, the Synod of Nîmes argued that deaconesses had inappropriately taken on ministry that was "against apostolic discipline" and that their ordination should be revoked.[53] In 441, the First Council of Orange ordered churches to stop ordaining women as deaconesses. In 517, the Council of Epaone ruled to "abrogate totally within the entire kingdom the consecration of widows who are named deaconesses."[54] In 533, the Second Synod of Orleans again tried to abolish the order of deaconesses by declaring, "No woman shall henceforth receive the *benedictio diaconalis*, on account of the weakness of this sex."[55] Interestingly, the fact that so many councils had to keep abolishing the ordination of deaconesses suggests that local bishops kept ordaining deaconesses

---

50. Belleville, *Women Leaders*, 64.
51. Karras, "Female Deacons," 272–316.
52. Marucci, "History and Value," 41.
53. Hefele, *History of the Councils of the Church*, 2:404.
54. Council of Epaone, canon 21 (Landon, *Manual of the Councils*, 1:253).
55. Tucker and Liefeld, *Daughters of the Church*, 133.

even though synods had ruled against doing so. Perhaps this was because deaconesses played such an important role in the mission of the church. There is also evidence that at least three popes supported the ordination of deaconesses.[56] However, the latest evidence of a deaconess in the West is from 1054.[57]

The office of deaconess lasted until the twelfth century in the East, but deaconesses did face obstacles during this time. As the church moved toward infant baptism, the need for women deacons to help baptize women converts disappeared. Other duties, which likely could have been assigned to deaconesses, were instead given to men, particularly during the Middle Ages.[58] When no new responsibilities within the church were allocated to deaconesses, the diaconate atrophied from neglect. The role of deaconess became more of an honorary title than a set of functional responsibilities within the church. For example, the ninth-century saint Irene of Chrysobalanton "was ordained deaconess . . . immediately before her election as abbess. Subsequently, she never left her monastery to fulfill the public role of deaconess."[59] Women's menstruation was also invoked throughout the Middle Ages as a reason against ordaining women to the diaconate.[60]

The office of deaconess had been mostly eliminated by the twelfth century, but there were still some ordained deaconesses in Eastern monasteries.[61] Also, "the *Armenian Apostolic Church* revived the feminine diaconate in the seventeenth century," and some Protestants reinstated the role of deaconess in the nineteenth century.[62] In the Orthodox church today, deaconesses are not canonically outlawed, but few are ordained. There is a movement to reawaken the role of the deaconess, although it is widely accepted that the diaconal roles of the past may not be the diaconal roles of the future.

Conclusion

Women influenced the development of monasticism and the diaconate. Wealthy women scholars like Marcella, Melania, and Olympias used their

56. Marucci, "History and Value," 43.
57. Marucci, "History and Value," 42.
58. Fitzgerald, *Women Deacons*, 135.
59. Herrin, *Unrivalled Influence*, 145.
60. Fitzgerald, *Women Deacons*, 144.
61. Marucci, "History and Value," 40.
62. Marucci, "History and Value," 41. See chap. 8 of this book for Protestants. See Olson, *Deacons and Deaconesses*, chaps. 7 and 8, for a description of how Lutherans, Methodists, Anglicans, and other Christians still ordain deaconesses today. See the website of the Diakonia World Federation for international gatherings of deaconesses and deacons: http://www .diakonia-world.org/.

wealth and prestige to establish monasteries and inspire the growing ascetic and diaconal communities. They used their extensive biblical knowledge and theological expertise to shape theological conversations.

The roles of virgin, desert mother, and deacon offered meaningful ways for women in the early centuries of the church to live out a Christian vocation. These vocations were similar in their focus on asceticism, charitable deeds, prayer, and fasting. The position of deaconess was an ordained ministry within the church, with the accompanying responsibility and authority that a recognized office brings. Deaconesses were expected to evangelize, disciple, assist with the baptism and training of women converts, and be theologically equipped to engage in such ministries. Deaconesses were "examined" or "tested" before being admitted to their office and were expected to remain faithful in living out their vocation for the rest of their lives. The diaconate flourished in the early church but faded by the twelfth century.

PART 2

WOMEN'S LEADERSHIP IN LATE ANTIQUITY AND THE MIDDLE AGES

3

Mothers, Sisters, Empresses, and Queens

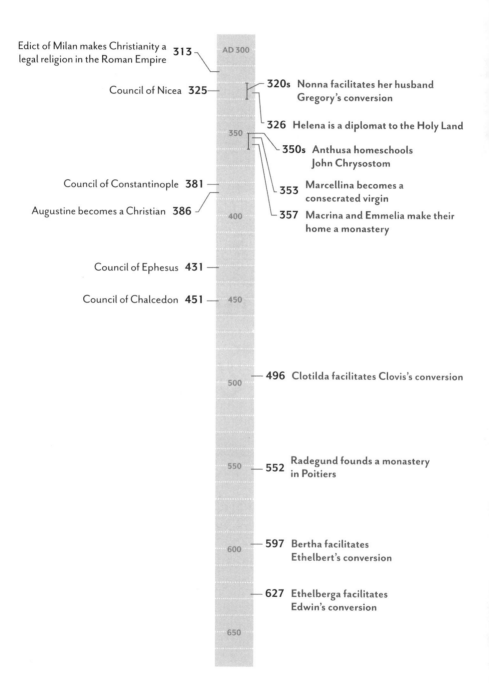

Edict of Milan makes Christianity a **313**
legal religion in the Roman Empire

AD 300

320s Nonna facilitates her husband
Gregory's conversion

Council of Nicea **325**

326 Helena is a diplomat to the Holy Land

350

350s Anthusa homeschools
John Chrysostom

353 Marcellina becomes a
consecrated virgin

Council of Constantinople **381**

Augustine becomes a Christian **386**

400

357 Macrina and Emmelia make their
home a monastery

Council of Ephesus **431**

Council of Chalcedon **451**

450

496 Clotilda facilitates Clovis's conversion

500

552 Radegund founds a monastery
in Poitiers

550

597 Bertha facilitates
Ethelbert's conversion

600

627 Ethelberga facilitates
Edwin's conversion

650

The previous chapters showed that women contributed to the mission of the church as patrons, missionaries, apostles, widows, martyrs, virgins, scholars, desert mothers, and deacons. This chapter looks at women who were influential in spreading the gospel through their roles as mothers, sisters, empresses, and queens. These women of strong faith were instrumental in bringing their husbands, sons, and brothers into the Christian faith. Through their relationships with their influential male relatives, these women also shaped the theology, practices, and landscape of the developing church.

The chapter starts off by describing Nonna, Emmelia, Anthusa, and Monica, who were the mothers of Gregory of Nazianzus, Basil of Caesarea, John Chrysostom, and Augustine. Next it looks at Macrina and Marcellina, sisters of Gregory of Nyssa and Ambrose. Then it turns to empresses. Constantine's mother, Helena, played a role in the Christianization of the Roman Empire, and Pulcheria was called the "new Helena" for her role in the Council of Chalcedon. Finally, the chapter examines several queens who influenced the Christianization of Europe. Significantly, three Western queens—Clotilda, Bertha, and Ethelberga—married pagan kings and facilitated the conversion of these kings and their kingdoms to Christianity. Queen Radegund founded two monasteries, and Queen Margaret reformed the church of Scotland.

Mothers

Nonna

Nonna (305?–374), a Christian of Greek descent who lived in the Roman province of Cappadocia, is remembered for her virtuous life and for converting her husband to Christianity. Her son, Gregory of Nazianzus, wrote, "She who was given by God to my father became not only a helper . . . but also a leader, personally guiding him by deed and word to what was most excellent."[1] At this time, "mixed marriage between Christian and pagan tended to move in a Christian direction," and Nonna's marriage exemplified this trend.[2] Nonna's

1. Gregory of Nazianzus, "Funeral Oration for His Father," 124.
2. Frend, *Rise of Christianity*, 561.

husband was baptized at the Council of Nicea. Three years later, he became bishop of Nazianzus (in modern-day Turkey), and Nonna was ordained a deaconess. Their daughter, Gorgonia, also became a deaconess after she married and had children. Nonna's younger son, Caesarius, trained in medicine and became the emperor's doctor.

Nonna's son Gregory had a special place in his mother's heart. When he was born, she dedicated him to the Lord, expecting him to grow up to be a monk or a priest. In fact, he became both. He also became Patriarch of Constantinople.

According to Gregory, the first thing Nonna did every morning was pray. "What time or place for prayer escaped her? This was the first thought of her day."[3] In a sermon he preached at his father's funeral, Gregory praised Nonna's piety, generosity, and discipline:

> She recognized only one true nobility, that of piety, and the knowledge of our origin and final destiny. The only wealth she considered secure and inviolate was to strip one's self of wealth for God and the poor, and especially for kinsfolk whose fortunes had declined. . . . Who subdued her flesh more by fastings and watchings, or stood like a pillar during the nightlong or daily singing of the psalms? Who had greater admiration for virginity, although she herself was under the bond of matrimony? Who was a better champion of widows and orphans?[4]

Nonna was a model Christian, a leader in her family and in her community. By prayer and example, she led her husband to Christian faith and raised three children who became saints. And when her son, daughter, and husband died in close succession, she became the caregiver to her daughter's orphaned children.[5] Nonna's life is celebrated every year in the Eastern Orthodox Church on the Sunday following the Feast of the Presentation of Christ in the Temple.

Emmelia

Emmelia (d. 375) was born into a deeply Christian family. Her father had died as a martyr during the Diocletian persecution.[6] Like Nonna, Emmelia lived her married life in the Roman province of Cappadocia (modern-day Turkey). She gave birth to ten children, five of whom became saints.[7] Emmelia's

---

3. Gregory of Nazianzus, "Funeral Oration for His Father," 125.
4. Gregory of Nazianzus, "Funeral Oration for His Father," 125–27.
5. Vasilopoulos, "Inheritance of Holiness."
6. Cohick and Hughes, *Christian Women*, 163.
7. Sanidopoulos, "Saint Emmelia."

son Basil, looking back on his childhood, said, "I received the knowledge [*ennoia*] of God from my blessed mother from my early childhood."[8] Georgia Vasilopoulos, reflecting on this passage in Greek, notes just how significant Basil's statement is. She explains that the Greek word *ennoia* means something much deeper than knowledge. "*Ennoia* comes from *en* and *nous*, so when we say I have the *ennoia* of God, it means I am thinking like God, I feel like God, I am one with God."[9] Thus, Basil was saying that his mother helped him develop the ability to align his desires with the desires of God.[10]

Three of Emmelia's sons became bishops (Basil of Caesarea, Gregory of Nyssa, and Peter of Sabaste), and her son Naucratis became a monk. Emmelia also experienced great sorrow in her life. In the span of about a year, her husband died, she gave birth to her tenth child, Peter, and her second oldest son, Naucratius, died. It was in this environment that her daughter Macrina (whose story comes later in this chapter) stepped in as a leader of the family.

Anthusa

Anthusa (324/334–?), a Christian of Greek descent living in Antioch (modern-day Turkey), was the mother of John Chrysostom. Her husband died when John was born, leaving her a widow at age twenty. She could have remarried easily, but she chose not to, largely because she believed that staying single was the decision that was best for John and because the church frowned on remarriage.

Anthusa was the fourth-century version of a homeschool mom. Although half of the people in Antioch were Christian, "and although she had the means to give her son a good education, she dreaded bringing him up amid the corruptions of Antioch and decided to teach him at home for a time."[11] She herself was well educated. She taught John classical literature, the Bible, and virtue. Looking back on his homeschool education, John remarked that his mother gave him his "enthusiasm for the good, his moral energy, his aversion to ostentation, his zeal for justice and truth and his steadfast faith."[12] He said, "My mother was the protecting wing for my salvation."[13]

When John got older, Anthusa sent him to study with the greatest speech and theology teachers of the day. He became a master of rhetoric (the art of argument) and the best orator in the school. John imagined himself becoming

8. Vasilopoulos, "Inheritance of Holiness."
9. Vasilopoulos, "Inheritance of Holiness."
10. Vasilopoulos, "Inheritance of Holiness."
11. Sanidopoulos, "Saints Emmelia, Nonna and Anthousa."
12. Morgan, "Anthusa."
13. Vasilopoulos, "Inheritance of Holiness."

a brilliant lawyer and "was in a flutter of excitement about the pleasures of the stage."[14] But Anthusa redirected him. "Anthusa saw that all of John's love for God would wither in those circles where vanity and pride ruled. She spoke to her son, she prayed for her son, and with the grace of God, she turned his heart away from the vain career of an orator to the heavenly career of dedication to God."[15] John would go on to become the Patriarch of Constantinople, and his rhetoric training made him one of the best preachers of his day. In fact, people began calling him Chrysostom, which means "golden-tongued" in Greek, because of his great skill in delivering sermons.

John may have learned some of his golden-tongued rhetorical skill from his mother, Anthusa. When John told her that he wanted to leave home, she became very upset. John and his good friend Basil wanted to withdraw from the world and live a kind of monastic life together. John remembered the way in which she entreated him to consider his poor mother before he made this decision. Anthusa sat him down on the bed on which she had borne her children, and as John tells it, "She unleashed streams of tears and added words more pathetic than the tears, making a bitter lament to me in this manner: 'my child,' she said, 'I was not permitted to enjoy your father's virtue for long, since that was the plan that seemed good to God. Your father's death followed on the birth pangs with which I bore you, designating you to be an untimely orphan and me an untimely widow, to learn the dreadful events of widowhood that only those women who have experienced them can rightly understand.'"[16] In between sobs, Anthusa managed to tell John that back when she was a young widow, his toddler self had brought her comfort in the midst of her grief.[17] And his young man self continued to bring her comfort because John looked a lot like his deceased father.[18] Anthusa told John about all the things she suffered, how she had to make financial sacrifices to be able to provide for him and how she had to figure out how to manage household and business affairs. And then she continued her speech: "None of these difficulties convinced me to enter into the union of a second marriage, nor to bring another bridegroom into your father's house. I remained in the midst of

14. John Chrysostom, *On the Priesthood* 1.4.

15. Vasilopoulos, "Inheritance of Holiness."

16. John Chrysostom, *On the Priesthood* 1.5, quoted in Clark, *Women in the Early Church*, 244.

17. "Thus while you were still a child and had not yet learned to talk, when you were at an age when children are an enormous delight to their parents, you furnished me with much comfort. I bore my widowhood nobly." John Chrysostom, *On the Priesthood* 1.5, quoted in Clark, *Women in the Early Church*, 245.

18. "Yet it brought me great comfort amid those horrors to gaze constantly at your face and to cherish for myself a living image of the departed, an image that was almost exactly like him." John Chrysostom, *On the Priesthood* 1.5, quoted in Clark, *Women in the Early Church*, 245.

the stress and the confusion and did not flee the iron furnace of widowhood, aided chiefly by grace from above."[19] Even when financial need arose, Anthusa never dipped into his inheritance. She always paid for everything out of her own funds. In the climax of her speech, she said, "As a return for all these things [which I have done for you], I ask one favor from you, that you do not invest me with widowhood a second time nor again kindle the grief already laid to rest: wait for my death. I shall perhaps depart after a short time."[20]

Those are John's words telling the story as he remembers it, but clearly Anthusa spoke with power and eloquence. John respected and loved his mother, and he ended up staying with her rather than going to live with Basil right away. Anthusa's speech reveals the kind of mother she was: committed, passionate, sacrificial, and determined.

Monica

Monica (331–387), a Christian of Berber descent living in North Africa, was the mother of Augustine. She prayed constantly for Augustine to come to know God. Augustine was a bright young man, and Monica seems to have had an inkling that a good pagan education might eventually lead him to God.[21] She prayed when he started getting interested in philosophy. She prayed when he joined a non-Christian group called the Manichees. She prayed when he left his North African home and moved across the Mediterranean to Milan, Italy. At least once, she was tempted to give up. At that point, God sent her a dream. In the dream, God promised her that one day she would see Augustine a Christian. And indeed, she did. As Augustine wrote, "Lord, you heard her and did not despise her tears which poured forth to wet the ground under her eyes in every place where she prayed. You heard her."[22]

While living in Milan, Augustine received a visit from a fellow African who told him about his own conversion. Augustine was moved. Then sitting outside in a garden, Augustine heard a child say, "Pick up and read," so he picked up the Bible and read a passage that immediately convicted him. He gave his life fully to Christ in that moment.[23]

Augustine then formed a monastic community of celibate men. Interestingly, Monica moved in with them.[24] According to Augustine, the community viewed her as the mother and teacher of them all. She had lived a long, faithful

19. John Chrysostom, *On the Priesthood* 1.5, quoted in Clark, *Women in the Early Church*, 245.
20. John Chrysostom, *On the Priesthood* 1.5, quoted in Clark, *Women in the Early Church*, 245.
21. Cohick and Hughes, *Christian Women*, 177.
22. Augustine, *Confessions* 3.11.19 (Chadwick, 49).
23. Augustine, *Confessions* 8.12.29 (Chadwick, 152).
24. Augustine, *Confessions* 9.4.8 (Chadwick, 160).

life of Christian discipleship, which gave her an authority that the younger men lacked. She was able to share her wisdom with the young men and inspire them in their pursuit of God.[25]

Sisters

Macrina

Macrina (327–379) was the oldest of Emmelia's ten children and had a major influence on her brothers Basil, Gregory, and Peter. Her influence was foretold in a vision that Emmelia had when she was in the midst of her labor pains. In the vision, a figure of superhuman likeness addressed Emmelia's daughter as "Thecla" three times, recalling the influential virgin martyr of *The Acts of Paul and Thecla*. "Thecla" became Macrina's secret name, which her brother Gregory believed foretold Macrina's journey toward Christlikeness through asceticism and a vow of virginity.[26]

When Macrina approached the age of twelve, her father set about arranging her marriage to a young man, who died before the wedding could take place. Claiming that her betrothed was "living in God because of the hope of the resurrection," Macrina vowed to be true to him and not consider another marriage.[27] Instead, she devoted herself to Christ and serving her mother, Emmelia. Although her family initially did not approve of this decision, they soon recognized that they could not function without her leadership.

When her father died in 340, Macrina became a leader in the household, filling the roles of father, teacher, adviser, and spiritual mentor. When Macrina's youngest sibling, Peter, was born in 341, Macrina took it upon herself to direct his education; she taught him to love philosophy and theology.[28]

Although Macrina did not have the option of a formal education like her brothers, she read extensively and developed a deep understanding of philosophy. Kevin Corrigan writes that Macrina was "evidently a genius."[29] Corrigan argues that she must have had one of the most extensive informal educations of the fourth century, as she was not only the head of an intellectual family but also the mentor of two Cappadocian fathers, her brothers Gregory of Nyssa and Basil of Caesarea.

25. Cohick and Hughes, *Christian Women*, 181–83.
26. Cohick and Hughes, *Christian Women*, 163.
27. Gregory of Nyssa, *Life of St. Macrina*, 25.
28. Gregory of Nyssa, *Life of St. Macrina*, 31.
29. Corrigan, introduction, 15.

Gregory admitted that Macrina, like a true teacher, often called him out on his errors. When Gregory complained about his responsibilities as bishop, Macrina rebuked him and admonished him to see his role as a blessing from God.[30] Similarly, she both rebuked and encouraged her brother Basil. When brilliant Basil came home all puffed up with his high-level education, Macrina took him to task for caring more about worldly things than about the things of God. Her arguments and attitude must have been both fierce and compelling because Basil ended up giving up his worldly life and adopting a life of asceticism.[31]

While influencing her family, Macrina also had an influence on her wider community through her devotion to embodying and performing acts of Christian love. In Cappadocia, people of high social status like Macrina's family often stored up a surplus of goods so as to avoid suffering during times of drought or famine. Macrina, however, encouraged her mother, Emmelia, to share their clothing and food, a practice that was completely countercultural. Macrina also emancipated her slaves and encouraged her family's servants to consider themselves their equals, transforming them all into sisters in a quasi-monastic community in her home.[32]

Gregory concluded *Life of Macrina* with his witness of her death, which he portrayed as her final sacrifice of love to her Lord. Gregory realized the depths of her faith when he saw her face death unafraid, longing to be united with her bridegroom, Christ. For Gregory, Macrina served as a model for a Christian life worthy of the name.

Gregory also honored his sister in *On the Soul and the Resurrection*, a treatise about the afterlife in which he portrayed Macrina as a wise philosopher, akin to Socrates, and himself, in humble deference, as her student. The treatise perhaps arose out of Gregory's final conversations with his sister on her deathbed, where she consoled him with wisdom on suffering and resurrection "as if she were inspired by the Holy Spirit," leading Gregory to sense the presence of God.[33]

Marcellina

Like Macrina, Marcellina (ca. 330–398) was the oldest child in her family, and when her parents died, she played a major role in raising her two younger

---

30. Gregory of Nyssa, *Life of St. Macrina*, 39.
31. Gregory of Nyssa, *Life of St. Macrina*, 26.
32. Cohick and Hughes, *Christian Women*, 166–67.
33. Gregory of Nyssa, *Life of St. Macrina*, 35. See also Gregory of Nyssa, *On the Soul and the Resurrection*.

brothers and inspiring them in the pursuit of holiness. Also like Macrina, Marcellina never married. She and her brother Ambrose, who eventually became bishop of Milan, felt very strongly about the importance of celibacy and the ascetic life. They encouraged each other in this pursuit and tried to inspire others in Milan to take up the ascetic challenge.[34]

As mentioned in chapter 2, liturgical services developed in response to women's desire to become consecrated virgins. Gradually, these women also began to wear a distinctive veil as a sign of their religious commitment. Marcellina "took the veil" and became a consecrated virgin on Christmas Day 353. When Ambrose wrote the church's first major treatise on virginity, he dedicated it to Marcellina.[35]

All throughout their lives, the brother and sister corresponded by letter. Ambrose gave Marcellina information on how some of his interactions with the emperor were going. Marcellina presumably offered him her thoughts and encouragement in response, though unfortunately none of her letters have been preserved.

Summary of Mothers and Sisters

Women like Marcellina, Macrina, Monica, Anthusa, Emmelia, and Nonna played a role in the mission of the church through their own holiness and through the example they set for others. They also played a role in the development of theology and church practices through their relationships with their sons and brothers, who became influential bishops and theologians. As W. H. C. Frend has noted, "Christian womenfolk in the family played a great part in forming the outlook of Basil of Caesarea, John Chrysostom, and Ambrose of Milan. Each owed his later, strongly held views to the influence of a mother or sister in the decade 350–360."[36] The same could be said of Gregory of Nazianzus, Gregory of Nyssa, and Augustine.

Nonna's son Gregory, Emmelia's son Basil, and Anthusa's son John Chrysostom became three of the most important bishop theologians (or "hierarchs") in the early church. Together, Nonna, Emmelia, and Anthusa are known as the "three holy mothers of the three hierarchs." Their feast day, celebrated each year in the Eastern Orthodox Church on the Sunday following the Feast of the Presentation of Christ in the Temple, is an opportunity for the church to hear their stories and to meditate on how

34. "Marcellina"; "St. Marcellina."
35. Mara, "Marcellina," 670. See also "St. Ambrose."
36. Frend, *Rise of Christianity*, 562.

these saints honored God with their lives, particularly through their role as mothers.

These are just a few of the women who had an impact on the faith of their sons and brothers; they were not isolated cases. On the contrary, according to Frend, "The influence of the women, especially educated women, on the religious life of the time was very considerable."[37]

Empresses

Some women influenced the mission of the church not only as mothers and sisters but also as empresses. These women cultivated the faith of their male relatives, but they also used their imperial power to fund church-building projects, shape ecclesiastical and political policy, and bestow charity. Their influence on the Christianization of the Roman Empire was substantial.

Helena

Helena (248?–328?) created a new role for women in the church, the role of the Christian empress. When her son Constantine committed himself to the Christian faith, he and his advisers had to reimagine what his role as emperor of the Roman Empire meant in light of his adherence to the Christian God. They decided that "pagan sacrifices [should be] forbidden, temple treasures seized, gladiatorial contests ended . . . and laws . . . enacted against sexual immorality and ritual prostitution."[38] Constantine returned confiscated property to Christians, started church building projects, and abolished crucifixion. Constantine and his mother, Helena, also reimagined the role of empress. Ultimately, what they landed on was a vision of empress that enabled women to have more power in the imperial realm of the Roman Empire than they had ever had before. According to Diliana Angelova, "Christian imperial women came to assume the trappings of power and to wield concrete authority in unprecedented ways."[39]

In 324, Constantine defeated the Eastern emperor Licinius and became the sole emperor of the Roman Empire. Licinius had been executing Christians and destroying churches in the East, whereas Constantine had been favoring Christians with his policies in the West.[40] Therefore, when Constantine's rule expanded to the East, the Christians there rejoiced, but the pagans feared

37. Frend, *Rise of Christianity*, 561.
38. Wasson, "Constantine I."
39. Angelova, *Sacred Founders*, 6.
40. Wasson, "Constantine I."

the effects of his pro-Christian policies. Constantine had barely started the process of solidifying his rule and Christianizing the Eastern part of the empire when he was called to Rome for a celebration of his twenty years as emperor. At this crucial time in Constantine's rule, he sent his mother, Helena, as a diplomat to the Eastern part of the empire. She went "to propagate Christianity and to appease dissatisfaction concerning Constantine's policy of Christianization."[41] By this point, Constantine had given her the title "Augusta" (meaning "honored" or "venerable") to signify the power and authority he had invested in her. And so, according to Lynn Cohick and Amy Hughes, "Helena Augusta was the face of Constantine's Christianization campaign in Palestine and the eastern provinces."[42]

While she was in Palestine, Helena oversaw the building of three churches: the Church of the Holy Sepulchre to commemorate the place where Christ was said to have been entombed, the Church of the Ascension on the Mount of Olives, and the Church of the Nativity. Helena visited and worshiped in numerous other churches, demonstrating her Christian piety. She also made use of the power Constantine had invested in her to release Christians who had been imprisoned or enslaved during the years of persecution and to return property that had been confiscated from them. She also distributed money to both poor people and military units.

Helena was eighty years old when she went on her diplomatic mission. "Whether she succeeded in Christianizing the still largely pagan population of the eastern provinces, we do not know, but [after her visit] many of Constantine's subjects definitely began to feel sympathy for their emperor's religion."[43] It was normal for emperors or their representatives to visit cities in order to enforce policies and garner goodwill, but what was unique in Helena's case was that she helped to enforce a new religion, Christianity. Through her presence, pagans were exposed to a vision of what Christian royalty looked like. They observed her piety in Christian churches, her charity in giving to poor people, her opposition to other faiths, and her favor toward Christian subjects. She gave gifts to every church in the region, which must have impressed upon "many pagans that they could not expect much good from this Christian ruler. Many may have wanted to be on the safe side and adopted the religion of their emperor and his mother."[44]

Helena and Constantine did much to Christianize the Roman Empire. Some of this Christianization took the form of "changing the literal architecture of

41. Drijvers, *Helena Augusta*, 55.
42. Cohick and Hughes, *Christian Women*, 116.
43. Drijvers, *Helena Augusta*, 70.
44. Drijvers, *Helena Augusta*, 70.

the land" through using imperial funds to erect churches and tear down pagan temples.[45] Constantine also called the Council of Nicea to clarify Christian doctrine. And Helena modeled Christian piety through her church attendance and charity. Her very person became a symbol of the Christian empire when Constantine placed her image on a coin that circulated throughout the Roman Empire. When people saw her image on the coin, they may have thought of the way in which she—a regal, Christian woman—was a pillar of their empire.[46]

Empresses after Helena looked to her as a model of how to combine Christian faith with imperial power. After Helena, the expectation for future empresses was that they had the power to fund church-building projects, shape ecclesiastical and political policy, and bestow charity. Helena became the model not only for subsequent Roman and Byzantine empresses but also for queens in medieval Europe.[47]

Pulcheria

Pulcheria (399–453) was a particularly influential Christian empress who inhabited and expanded the role of the Christian empress. Like Helena, she was able to fuse imperial power and wealth with Christian virtue and charity. Notably, she was proclaimed a "protectress of the faith" for throwing her imperial weight behind the orthodox position at the Council of Chalcedon in 451.[48]

Pulcheria's leadership in the Roman Empire began when she was only ten years old. It was at that point that her father died. Her younger brother, Theodosius II, was only eight. Just like Macrina and Marcellina, Pulcheria took on the role of teacher-mentor for her brother. She fired her brother's tutor and began directing her brother's education herself. Since her brother was legally the emperor and she was the main influence on him, she was essentially running the empire at age fifteen.

Part of the task of running the empire well, in Pulcheria's mind, was making sure that both she and her brother were faithful to God. Toward that end, she took her brother to church regularly, prayed throughout the day, gave gifts to the church, honored the priests, and took a vow of celibacy. She even retained this vow of celibacy when she later married.[49]

---

45. Cohick and Hughes, *Christian Women*, 116.
46. Drijvers, *Helena Augusta*, 41–42.
47. "Byzantine" is the name given by contemporary scholars to the eastern part of the Roman Empire after the western part of the empire fell to the barbarians in the fifth century. The Byzantine Empire lasted until 1453, when it fell to the Muslim Turks.
48. Cohick and Hughes, *Christian Women*, 238.
49. Cohick and Hughes, *Christian Women*, 228.

Pulcheria's vow of celibacy earned her a great deal of respect from her surrounding culture. When Atticus, the Patriarch of Constantinople, wrote a treatise on celibacy, he dedicated it to Pulcheria. Either Atticus or his successor, Sisinnius, also brought one of Pulcheria's robes to the church and laid it on the altar where he prepared the Eucharist.[50] This act was a way of honoring Pulcheria for her commitment to Christ and also incorporating some of her presumed holiness into the eucharistic service. The Patriarch also welcomed Pulcheria to take Communion along with her brother, Emperor Theodosius II, and the other priests. It was an unusual move. The emperor was believed to have a special anointing and authority that were on par with the anointing and authority of a priest, but Pulcheria was neither a priest nor an emperor. She was a laywoman. Nevertheless, because of her special relationship to the emperor, her clear role in advising him and helping to run the empire, and her status as a virgin, the Patriarch stretched the rules and admitted her to the special Communion time for the emperor and the priests.

But then Nestorius became the Patriarch of Constantinople. Pulcheria was at this point about twenty-eight years old, and she had grown used to being included in the special Communion for the emperor and the priests. As she prepared to enter the sanctuary on Easter Sunday, Nestorius stopped her. He accused her of grasping at power that was inappropriate for her, a layperson and a woman. She responded by comparing herself to the Virgin Mary and pointed out that it was a woman, after all, who had given birth to the Messiah. In her vow of celibacy, Pulcheria, like other virgins, was modeling her life after that of the Virgin Mary, but she was also modeling her life after Christ. Her sacrifice gave her an authority in society, and she was displeased when Nestorius refused to recognize that authority. Pulcheria's problems with Nestorius didn't end there. Nestorius later accused her of sexual immorality.[51] Three years later, however, Nestorius himself was excommunicated by the church at the Council of Ephesus for his Christology.[52]

In 450, Emperor Theodosius II died. Pulcheria sensed there would be competition over the throne, so for the stability of the empire, she decided to marry, under the condition that her husband, Marcian, would respect her vow of celibacy. With Marcian as emperor, Pulcheria preserved authority as a leader of the empire.

50. Cohick and Hughes, *Christian Women*, 229.
51. Cohick and Hughes, *Christian Women*, 230.
52. Nestorius claimed that Christ had two persons, one divine and one human, but Cyril of Alexandria and others argued that Christ's divine and human natures were united in one person. Cyril wrote to Pulcheria to make sure she was on his side of the debate, even though her brother, the emperor, was on Nestorius's side.

Pulcheria's imperial status coupled with her religious devotion helped her become a major influence in the church. Like Helena, she was a philanthropist, built churches, and shaped ecclesiastical and political policy. She was "the only empress recorded to have played a direct part in imperial councils while the emperor was alive."[53] She helped to advance orthodoxy through her involvement with the Council of Chalcedon in 451, and for this, the bishops proclaimed her the "new Helena" and her husband the "new Constantine."[54]

Queens

Now we shift from the world of the Roman Empire to that of medieval Europe, where several queens played a notable role in the mission of the Western church. Significantly, three queens—Clotilda, Bertha, and Ethelberga—married pagan kings and facilitated the conversion of these kings and their kingdoms to Christianity. Queen Radegund founded two monasteries and inspired others through her piety and charity. Queen Margaret reformed the church of Scotland.

These queens had an influence in their own day, but their influence was augmented in later years through the rise of the cult of the saints. As the pagan tribes of Gaul and Britain converted to Christianity, both the clergy and the common people began to show great interest in the lives of holy people, particularly martyrs but also others who were deemed by their contemporaries to have had a strong connection with God. At this time, the canonization of a saint "remained a very informal process. It entailed the inscription of the name of the candidate for sainthood in the local catalogue of saints along with the subsequent issuance of an order by the Church that the faithful publicly recognize or venerate the new saint."[55] The stories of saints were recounted on the anniversaries of their deaths, and the clergy began to realize that they could hold up the stories of saints in order to inspire ordinary people to more fervent faith. Clotilda, Bertha, Ethelberga, Radegund, and Margaret came to be regarded as saints in medieval Europe.

People who came to saints' day festivals didn't come just to hear the stories of saints. They came because they also wanted to feel the power of the saints. As Peter Brown notes, people came "to participate. They wished to be touched, if only for a blessed moment, by the burst of glory associated with

53. Cohick and Hughes, *Christian Women*, 230.
54. Drijvers, *Helena Augusta*, 183.
55. Schulenburg, *Forgetful of Their Sex*, 4.

heroes and heroines."[56] They believed that saints had real power. When they assembled for festivals or visited the tombs of saints, they believed that the power of the saints would be able to work miracles, heal illness, and expel demons. Thus, saints like Radegund and Margaret continued to exert influence long after their bodies had passed from life to death.

Clotilda

Clotilda (474–544) was the mother of Christian Europe. Not only did she play a role in converting her husband and kingdom to Christianity, but her great-granddaughter and great-great-granddaughter also played a role in converting their husbands and kingdoms to Christianity. Clotilda was born in Gaul (modern-day France). She was raised Catholic by her mother, Caretena, but then her parents were killed and her sister exiled by her Arian uncle, King Gundobad.[57] She remained in Gundobad's court. When Clotilda was old enough to marry, she was noticed by a delegation from Clovis, king of the Franks. As the story goes, a series of betrothal gifts followed, but Clotilda kept the entire process a secret because she suspected that Gundobad would not approve of the marriage. "Considering that Gundobad had killed her parents and exiled her sister, and continued to espouse Arianism, Clotilda was no doubt anxious to escape from his court and to start a new life."[58] Although King Clovis was a pagan, some scholars think that Clotilda's Catholic faith may have been attractive to him as a way of connecting to the growing power of the Catholic Church.[59] Clovis and Clotilda were married in 493.

In telling Clotilda's story a century later, Bishop Gregory of Tours wrote that throughout her marriage to Clovis, Clotilda "unceasingly urged the king to acknowledge the true God, and forsake idols."[60] Historian Jane Schulenburg argues that Clotilda played the role of a "trusted religious adviser" in Clovis's life. She modeled what Christian ideas looked like in practice, and she gave Clovis incentive to convert. No one knows for sure the extent of Clotilda's influence on Clovis, but certainly she was "able to provide the crucial groundwork for Clovis' official conversion."[61]

56. P. Brown, *Cult of the Saints*, xxvi.
57. Schulenburg, *Forgetful of Their Sex*, 470. Arians believed that God the Father created God the Son at a particular moment in time.
58. Schulenburg, *Forgetful of Their Sex*, 182.
59. Schulenburg, *Forgetful of Their Sex*, 182.
60. Gregory of Tours, "History of the Franks." The story of Clotilda in *The History of the Franks* by Gregory of Tours is the earliest account that exists. Although Gregory wrote the *History* about a century after Clotilda, he did have some written sources at his disposal that are now lost. Wood, "Gregory of Tours and Clovis."
61. Schulenburg, *Forgetful of Their Sex*, 185.

When Clotilda gave birth to her first child, Ingomir, she longed to baptize the baby. Baptism would ensure that even if Clovis didn't convert to Christianity, the future sovereign of the kingdom would be Christian. Unfortunately, Ingomir "died in his white baptismal robe," giving Clovis good reason to continue to reject his wife's religion.[62] When a second son was born, it seemed that he would die like the first, but Clotilda poured out her heart in prayer "and by God's will the child recovered."[63]

At this point, Clovis was in the process of fighting every other king in the region to become the sole king of the Franks. It so happened that when he was in the midst of a great battle against the Alamanni, he decided to ask Clotilda's God to help him win the battle. He had already called on his pagan gods, but to no avail. He told Clotilda's God that in exchange for giving him victory, he would become a Christian. As soon as he did so, the tides turned and his army won the battle. Clovis returned and told the exuberant Clotilda "how he had won the victory by calling on the name of Christ."[64] Clotilda summoned Bishop Remigius, and Remigius instructed Clovis in Christian doctrine. Clovis was then baptized, a "new Constantine," along with three thousand of his soldiers and many of the common people in his kingdom.[65] The region would have to be reevangelized by missionaries like Columbanus in the seventh century, but Clotilda was still remembered as a saint for her role in converting Clovis and the Franks to Christianity.

Clotilda's story became part of the way the Franks made sense of who they were. "Hagiographers shaped the historic destiny of the Franks as a divine mission in which women played a leading role."[66] In the ninth century, a Carolingian author drew on Gregory's *History of the Franks*, along with other sources, to write Clotilda's *Vita* (life story). This author heightened Clotilda's significance by comparing her to a martyr: "None would have thought that this holy woman . . . suffered pain and torment in this life since she did not share the fire and sword of the martyr. But the sword pierced her soul in the killing of her father and her mother's drowning, the exile of her sister and her own marriage to a pagan king. Her sweetness softened the hearts of a pagan

62. Gregory of Tours, "History of the Franks."
63. Gregory of Tours, "History of the Franks."
64. Gregory of Tours, "History of the Franks."
65. It is important to note that Clovis's conversion (and that of Ethelbert and Edwin in the stories that follow) was an "ecclesiastical conversion," not an "inner conversion." These conversions were "the result of a gradual, deliberate process. Also the new converts do not necessarily undergo the heightened emotional or spiritual experiences which are essential to inner conversions." Schulenburg, *Forgetful of Their Sex*, 178.
66. McNamara and Halborg, *Sainted Women*, 3.

and ferocious people, namely the Franks, and she converted them through blessed Remigius with her holy exhortations and unremitting prayers."[67]

Clotilda's story continued to be told and retold. She was seen as a "second Helena," and she became a model for future queens of Europe.[68] Her granddaughter Clotsinda received a letter from Bishop Nicetius that urged her to lead her Arian husband, king of the Lombards, to Catholic faith, just as Clotilda had led Clovis.[69] Clotilda's great-granddaughter Bertha and great-great-granddaughter Ethelberga were also encouraged by bishops to convert their husbands to Christianity. Schulenberg, who has traced the history of "domestic proselytization," says that popes and bishops viewed Christian queens as "emissaries for the Church," as people who had real power to influence the future of the church.[70]

Radegund

Clotilda's son Clothar conquered a kingdom to the east (Thuringia) and chose a twelve-year-old princess to be his future wife.[71] Her name was Radegund (525–587), and she became a respected and influential Christian leader. "Even during her lifetime, she was recognized as a saint."[72] She knew she would be married to King Clothar when she turned eighteen, so she fled, hoping to escape the marriage. But King Clothar pursued her and made her one of his six wives. When she was a child, she had dreamed of martyrdom; instead, marriage became her cross to bear. King Clothar was "rough, brutal, unfaithful, and often drunk."[73] Radegund, by contrast, was pious, generous, and dedicated to ascetic practices. "Around the year 550, Clothar had Radegund's brother, of whom she was very fond, killed. Shortly thereafter the queen, probably in her late twenties and no longer able to tolerate the marriage, left her husband."[74] She persuaded Bishop Medard to ordain her

---

67. McNamara and Halborg, *Sainted Women*, 47.

68. Schulenburg, *Forgetful of Their Sex*, 179–80.

69. Schulenburg, *Forgetful of Their Sex*, 188. Although Clotsinda did not ultimately succeed, another Lombard queen, Theodelinde, did.

70. Schulenburg, *Forgetful of Their Sex*, 191.

71. "The trauma of that experience is vividly preserved in the poem 'The Thuringian War,' written more than thirty years later either by Radegund herself or by her friend Vanantius Fortunatus (d. 609) with her verbal collaboration." McNamara and Halborg, *Sainted Women*, 61.

72. Schulenburg, *Forgetful of Their Sex*, 20. Radegund's life "is one of the best documented of this early period. Two contemporary saints' Lives, as well as Gregory of Tours' *History of the Franks* and the *Glory of the Confessors*, describe the events of Radegund's life as royal ascetic and model nun." Schulenburg, *Forgetful of Their Sex*, 18–19.

73. "St. Radegund."

74. Schulenburg, *Forgetful of Their Sex*, 19.

a deaconess and went on to found two monasteries, one in the city of Tours for men and another in Poitiers for women, which she may have also joined.[75] "The community [in Poitiers] grew rapidly, numbering as many as two hundred nuns living together at one point."[76]

Monasteries help explain how Frenchmen like Radegund's husband, Clothar, ever reformed and how France ever became a beacon of Christian civilization. Such reform flowed out of monasteries like the ones Radegund founded. In monasteries, people spent time reading the Scriptures and praying. They didn't automatically become more Christian than their peers outside the monastery, but as Mark Noll says, much that "approached the highest, noblest, and truest ideals of the gospel was done either by those who had chosen the monastic way or by those who had been inspired in their Christian life by the monks [and nuns]."[77] Thus, through her own holy life and through the monasteries she founded, Radegund influenced the Christianization of the Franks.

Radegund was particularly known for her ascetic disciplines and for her charity. When still at court, she could be found handing out gifts to poor people who gathered outside as the king feasted.[78] And even after she left her husband, she still had control of substantial wealth, which she distributed to poor people and churches. She also maintained a role in political affairs and worked to broker political peace in the Frankish realm.[79]

In establishing monasteries, dispensing charity, and influencing political affairs, she carried forward the mantle of the Christian queen, which had been inaugurated by Helena and developed by Pulcheria and Clotilda. Even after her death, as Radegund's *Vita* was read in monasteries and churches, she continued to exert influence.[80]

Bertha

Bertha (539–612), the great-granddaughter of Clotilda, became another important link in the chain of influential Christian queens spread out across Europe.[81] In 596, Pope Gregory sent missionary monks to Britain.[82] They landed in Kent, the kingdom of Ethelbert and Bertha, and were given permission to

---

75. McNamara and Halborg, *Sainted Women*, 75, 88–89; Schulenburg, *Forgetful of Their Sex*, 19.

76. Irvin and Sunquist, *History of the World Christian Movement*, 238.

77. Noll, *Turning Points*, 84.

78. McNamara and Halborg, *Sainted Women*, 7.

79. Schulenburg, *Forgetful of Their Sex*, 19–20.

80. Schulenburg, *Forgetful of Their Sex*, 20.

81. McNamara, "Living Sermons," 24.

82. Christianity had already reached Britain during the days of the Roman Empire, but Christians had fallen on hard times after the fall of the Roman Empire. The Anglo-Saxons

settle and evangelize in Canterbury. Bede tells the story in his *Ecclesiastical History of the English People*, which he wrote in 731.[83] Bede explains that Bertha was already a Christian when the missionaries arrived. She had brought a priest with her when she married Ethelbert. Once in Kent, Bertha and the priest found an old church to worship in, left over from the days of Roman occupation.[84] After Pope Gregory's missionary monks arrived and people from the countryside were baptized, they joined Bertha in worship.

Some scholars think it was actually Queen Bertha who wrote to the pope in the first place, asking him to send missionaries to help convert her husband.[85] But whether she did or not, "it was partly, no doubt, by her influence that Ethelbert was induced to receive the Roman mission."[86] It is also clear that Pope Gregory recognized Bertha as a strategic emissary for the church. In 601, Pope Gregory wrote her a letter. He started off with praise for her faith and her work in aiding the missionaries he had sent. Then he compared her to "Helena of illustrious memory" and urged her to work even harder for the conversion of her husband and the entire kingdom.[87]

Interestingly, Bede makes no mention of Pope Gregory's letter in his description of Ethelbert's conversion. It may be that Bede simply had no access to it, but it also may be that the letter detracted from the vision of history Bede hoped to communicate. For one thing, Bede wanted to portray Ethelbert as a zealous leader. He may have felt that giving too much credit to Bertha would detract from this vision of Ethelbert as a leader. He also may have minimized Bertha's role because she was a Frank and he wanted to portray Rome, not the Franks, as having the most substantial impact on England's conversion.[88]

Even though Bede may have deliberately downplayed Bertha's significance in the conversion of England, others did not. According to Schulenburg, "For her role in the conversion of the king and of the area of Kent, Bertha was recognized as a popular saint with a local cult centered around Canterbury."[89]

who had taken over rule of Britain were pagan, so Pope Gregory decided to send monks to introduce them to Christianity.

83. Bede's sources were many: official documents housed at various monasteries and episcopal sees, saints' lives, and oral testimonies. He wrote in part to give clergy and kings in his day examples of people to emulate.

84. Walls of Bertha's church still exist today and are part of a new church that has been built on the same site. This church is "England's oldest parish church in continuous use." "Canterbury."

85. Beeson, *Church's Other Half*, 9; Schulenburg, *Forgetful of Their Sex*, 194.

86. Stubbs, "Bertha."

87. Gregory the Great, *Epistle 29*.

88. Schulenburg, *Forgetful of Their Sex*, 192–93.

89. Schulenburg, *Forgetful of Their Sex*, 195.

Ethelberga

Ethelberga (605–647), daughter of Bertha and Ethelbert, great-great-granddaughter of Clotilda, became another emissary of the church in the domestic and political realms. After her parents died, her brother arranged for her marriage to Edwin, a polygamous pagan king in northern England. According to Bede, Edwin "gave an assurance that he would place no obstacles in the way of [Ethelberga's] Christian Faith." Edwin also said that he would convert to Christianity if his advisers found Christianity "more holy and acceptable to God than their own [religion]."[90] So Ethelberga moved to Northumbria, taking her chaplain, Paulinus, and a few Christian companions with her.

The next year Ethelberga gave birth to a daughter, Eanfled. According to Bede, the very night that Eanfled was born, an assassin tried to kill King Edwin. Chaplain Paulinus tried to use the intensity of the evening to get Edwin to convert to Christianity, but Edwin said he would do so only "if God would grant him life and victory over the king his enemy who had sent the assassin." Edwin did, however, give permission for Paulinus to baptize Eanfled, who became "together with twelve others of her family . . . the first of the Northumbrians to receive Baptism."[91]

As Bede tells the story of Edwin's long, drawn-out conversion, he makes the climax of the story a vision Edwin received. Just as Bede downplayed Bertha's role in Ethelbert's conversion, he also may have downplayed Ethelberga's role in Edwin's conversion. As Stephanie Hollis says, "Bede offers no portrait of a queen converter."[92] However, Ethelberga's power didn't escape the notice of Pope Boniface, who sent both her and Edwin a letter. In Boniface's letter to Ethelberga, the pope affirmed her for her faith and said that God was giving her "an opportunity to kindle a spark of the true religion" in Edwin. "My illustrious daughter, persevere in using every effort to soften the hardness of his [King Edwin's] heart by teaching him the laws of God. Help him to understand the excellence of the mystery which you have accepted and believe. . . . Melt the coldness of his heart by teaching him about the Holy Spirit, so that the warmth of divine faith may enlighten his mind through your constant encouragement."[93] Thus, even if Bede later minimized Ethelberga's role, Pope Boniface saw her as an active agent, as a teacher and encourager, someone who could bring about Edwin's conversion. Edwin did end up converting to

90. Bede, *History of the English Church and People* 2.9.
91. Bede, *History of the English Church and People* 2.9.
92. Hollis, *Anglo-Saxon Women*, 218.
93. Bede, *History of the English Church and People* 2.11.

Christianity, and together with "all the nobility and a large number of humbler folk," he was baptized in 627.[94]

Margaret

Many other Christian queens facilitated the conversion of their husbands and/or kingdoms to Christianity; the last queen presented here is Margaret, Queen of Scotland (1045–1093).[95] Margaret was born in Hungary. She was English, but her father had been exiled after the Danes conquered England in 1016. When she was a little girl, her family moved back to England because her father was an heir to the throne. However, when her father died and William the Conqueror took over England, Margaret's family found their way to Scotland. There King Malcolm III became their protector. Eventually, Margaret married King Malcolm. Here her *Vita* resembles that of Radegund, as both women were forced to marry men they didn't want to marry. In both cases, the men were rough and violent and the women were spiritually devout. While Margaret prayed, Malcolm was off "raiding Northumberland, burning churches, and pitilessly disposing of the conquered. Men of working age were taken captive; women, children, and the aged were killed."[96] As Kathleen Jones notes, "The procedure was standard for the time, but Malcolm was a very enthusiastic raider."[97]

But here the *Vita* of Margaret departs from that of Radegund, for whereas Radegund fled King Clothar's court and lived out the rest of her days in a monastery, Margaret remained at court and had a reforming influence on her husband. She "assumed a prominent, truly collaborative position as partner and indispensable counselor of the king."[98] According to Margaret's *Vita*, Malcolm adored his wife and allowed her to bring her desired reforms to his court. Where there was once drunkenness, she introduced restraint. Where there was rudeness, she brought politeness and beauty. She used her new resources to serve poor people and brought prayer to the court. In order to encourage knights to stay for prayers after eating their meal, "Margaret

---

94. Bede, *History of the English Church and People* 2.14. Of course, the road to deeper Christianization would take centuries. And often future kings would convert back to paganism. But this does not obscure the importance of these initial conversion stories and the women behind them.

95. "Her remarkable biography was written by her contemporary and confidant, Turgot, prior of Durham and bishop of St. Andrews" (Schulenburg, *Forgetful of Their Sex*, 20). For other influential queens, like Eormenhild, Eadgyth, Ludmilla, Dubrawa, Olga, and Anna, see Schulenberg, *Forgetful of Their Sex*, chap. 4.

96. Jones, *Women Saints*, 122.

97. Jones, *Women Saints*, 122.

98. Schulenburg, *Forgetful of Their Sex*, 20.

introduced the practice of the Grace Cup, a cup of wine from the queen's own table sent down for those who stayed for the grace. This practice became known as St. Margaret's Blessing and for centuries remained a custom followed at Scottish feasts."[99] King Malcolm never learned to read and he never stopped raiding other territories, but Margaret did get him to start praying.

Margaret founded a monastery, built a church, and led a group of women in embroidering linens for use in worship, all of which helped to deepen Christian devotion in Scotland. Christianity had been in Scotland for five hundred years, but it was in need of reform. Malcolm basically gave Margaret free rein to reform the entire church of Scotland, to hire new priests, and to bring worship into line with what was being done in other parts of Europe. Ultimately, this meant lengthening the period of Lent, celebrating Easter consistently, kneeling in church, and taking Communion every Sunday. For her skilled diplomacy, piety, charity, and missional influence, Margaret's biographer said she was a "second Helena."[100]

Conclusion

Women in late antiquity and the Middle Ages were influential in bringing others into a knowledge of Christ through their roles as mothers, sisters, empresses, and queens. These women influenced the development of theology and church practices, sometimes through their own imperial authority and sometimes through their relationships with male relatives who were church and political leaders. In some cases, these men might not have even become church leaders if not for a woman's influence in their lives. Such was the case with Macrina's influence on her brothers, Anthusa's influence on her son John Chrysostom, and Marcellina's influence on her brother Ambrose. Highlighting their stories draws attention to the importance of the kingdom work that takes place in the home.

Far too often in the contemporary telling of church history, the influence of women is overlooked. That has not always been the case. The authority, influence, and piety of Empresses Helena and Pulcheria were recognized by their contemporaries. Helena stood as a beacon of Christian piety for the Roman Empire and gave successive generations of Christian empresses and queens a vision of what it looked like to merge piety with royal identity and power. Pulcheria was declared a "protectress of the faith" at the Council of Chalcedon. Western queens Clotilda, Bertha, and Ethelberga were celebrated as

99. Jones, *Women Saints*, 123.
100. Jones, *Women Saints*, 125.

saints for converting their husbands and kingdoms to Christianity. Radegund's piety was well known, and her influence grew when she founded a monastery. Margaret was celebrated for reforming the court and church of Scotland.

Chapter 1 described how women in church history have passed the baton of religious leadership throughout the centuries. These baton passes have not been the formal passes of apostolic succession. Nevertheless, the succession of Christian mothers, sisters, empresses, and queens was a kind of passing down of women's religious authority. Popes invoked the names of Helena and Clotilda in order to motivate queens who came after them. Hagiographers compared their subjects to notable women from history. Radegund's friend Fortunatus linked her leadership with that of previous women, including Eustochium, Paula, Melania, Marcella, and Thecla.[101]

Fortunatus and many other Christians in history have done a far better job than many contemporary Christians of bringing to mind women's religious leadership. In late antiquity and the early Middle Ages, clergy and common people alike celebrated the achievements of Christian queens. They looked to them as role models and intercessors. They told their stories on the anniversaries of their deaths and read them aloud in monasteries. Only later did these women's accomplishments become forgotten.[102]

101. Smith, "Radegundis peccatrix," 312.
102. Schulenburg, Forgetful of Their Sex, 208.

4

Medieval Nuns

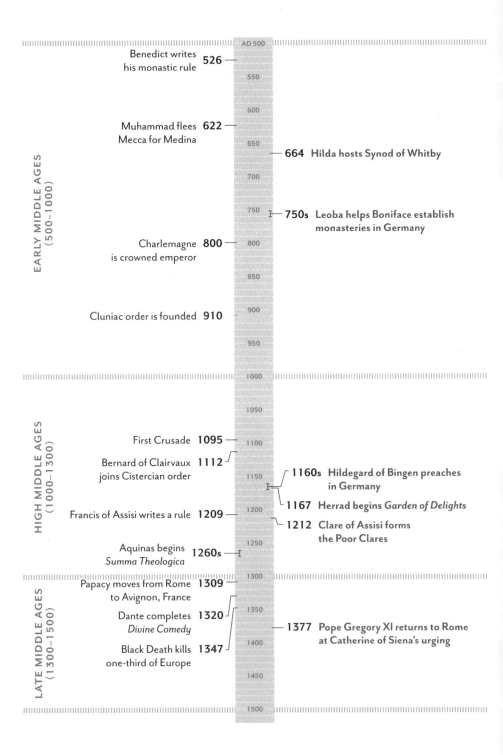

EARLY MIDDLE AGES (500–1000)

Benedict writes his monastic rule **526**

AD 500

550

600

Muhammad flees Mecca for Medina **622**

650

— **664** Hilda hosts Synod of Whitby

700

750 ⊢ **750s** Leoba helps Boniface establish monasteries in Germany

Charlemagne is crowned emperor **800**

800

850

Cluniac order is founded **910**

900

950

1000

HIGH MIDDLE AGES (1000–1300)

1050

First Crusade **1095**

1100

Bernard of Clairvaux joins Cistercian order **1112**

1150 ⊢ **1160s** Hildegard of Bingen preaches in Germany

1167 Herrad begins *Garden of Delights*

Francis of Assisi writes a rule **1209**

1200

1212 Clare of Assisi forms the Poor Clares

1250

Aquinas begins *Summa Theologica* **1260s** ⊢

LATE MIDDLE AGES (1300–1500)

1300

Papacy moves from Rome to Avignon, France **1309**

1350

Dante completes *Divine Comedy* **1320**

— **1377** Pope Gregory XI returns to Rome at Catherine of Siena's urging

Black Death kills one-third of Europe **1347**

1400

1450

1500

Chapter 2 showed how women shaped the development of early Christian monasticism by founding and joining monasteries and by living holy lives in the deserts of Egypt and Syria. Chapter 3 argued that monasteries like the one Radegund founded in sixth-century Poitiers were essential to the Christianization of Europe. This chapter more fully unpacks how monasteries impacted Christianization. According to JoAnn McNamara, nuns served as "living sermons," showing others what it looked like to live lives of "humility, self-abnegation, service, and above all charity."[1] Medieval nuns also contributed to the mission of the church through their prayers, book production, counseling, preaching, and teaching.

Nuns in the Middle Ages lived in convents away from the hustle and bustle of cities.[2] They dressed in simple habits, either white, brown, or black, depending on the religious order to which they belonged. They wore veils to signify their virginal state and their connection to the Virgin Mary.[3] They ate simple foods, often in silence, while a member of their community read to them from the Bible or the writings of the church fathers. They gathered eight times each day to pray, even rising in the middle of the night for one of these services.

Convent life gave women an unprecedented opportunity for education. Most women in the Middle Ages were illiterate, but nuns learned Latin in order to chant the Psalms and had the opportunity to read centuries-old books by the church fathers.[4] Some served in convent schools, teaching girls to read. Others served as nurses in nearby hospitals. Wherever they were, nuns always listened for the bell that called them to prayer.

On important church holidays, nuns walked in procession down the streets of the town with monks and priests, all the while chanting the liturgy. They

---

1. McNamara, "Living Sermons," 28.

2. Throughout this chapter, we will use both terms, "convent" and "monastery." The former refers only to houses of women, while the latter can refer to houses of men and/or women.

3. This veil was the only piece of a nun's clothing that was "distinctly female." It was also one of the oldest traditions in the Christian faith, dating back to the consecrated virgins of the early church. Johnson, *Equal in Monastic Profession*, 236.

4. Although being a nun in the Middle Ages meant a woman was more likely than other women to be literate, not all nuns were literate or knew Latin. For example, while most nuns in twelfth-century France were literate, that was not the case for many nuns in twelfth-century England (Thompson, *Women Religious*, 72). By contrast, literacy was the norm in many convents in sixth-century Gaul (Beach, *Women as Scribes*, 9). It seems that the decreased literacy in twelfth-century England was in part related to the decrease in "double houses." Beach, *Women as Scribes*, 11.

had the honor of walking at the front of the procession, and their vocation garnered respect from the townspeople gathered for the event. Medieval
people considered nuns to be holier than married women, and that holiness
gave nuns prestige and authority in society. Their prayers were thought to be
particularly effective. For these reasons and others, "throngs of adult women
in this period sought the monastic life."[5] There were so many nuns in England and France that no one lived "more than a day's journey from a female
monastic community, and most were closer than that."[6]

Becoming a Nun

The choice to become a nun was often a communal rather than an individual
decision. Say a family had six children, three of them girls. Knowing that a
hefty sum of money (a dowry) was necessary for the marriage of a daughter,
a family might decide to marry only two of its daughters and send the third
to the nearby convent. Some families sent a daughter to a convent when she
was as young as seven years old. Often families nurtured relationships with
particular monasteries. Sometimes the seven-year-old would have an older
sister or aunt who was already at the convent where her parents were sending
her. Parents couldn't force a daughter to become a nun—she had to make her
own decision to "take the veil" when she turned twelve years old. However,
because family played such a major role in the lives of medieval people, because the convent came to feel like home, and because nuns were privileged
members of society, most girls did take the veil when they came of age.

When women entered a convent, either as child oblates or adults, they did
not fully sever ties with their family. They constantly prayed for their family
(indeed, this was one of the reasons it was good to have a family member in
a monastery), their family could visit, and their family could even call them
home for a time to help care for a sick relative. Families would often donate
money and land to the monasteries where their relatives lived. Occasionally,
a family would even earmark a donation specifically for a relative to cover the
cost of that person's food or clothing. And even though nuns took a vow of
poverty and weren't supposed to own anything once they joined a monastic
house, abbesses tended to stretch the poverty vow a bit, especially if it meant
that their house could remain solvent and their nuns could stay sufficiently
fed and clothed.

5. Johnson, *Equal in Monastic Profession*, 247.
6. Venarde, *Women's Monasticism*, 16. A day's journey was likely about fifteen miles. See
Labarge, *Mistress, Maids, and Men.*

Some communities didn't even require women to take a vow of poverty, making them attractive for nobility who did not want to surrender their wealth and autonomy. A noblewoman could become a canoness by taking a temporary vow instead of a lifelong vow and could decide a few years later to leave the community in order to get married.[7] It was not uncommon for medieval women to spend part of their lives as a canoness or nun and another part as a married woman. Hedwig of Silesia is an interesting example. She was raised in a monastery. When she came of age, she married a duke. After having seven children, "she took a vow of chastity and devoted herself to acts of charity."[8] Other women chose to join monasteries after the deaths of their husbands.

Double Houses

Many of the earliest convents in Europe were established by kings, queens, nobles, and aristocrats. Because their founders endowed them with land and resources, these convents were able to sustain large communities of women, sometimes more than several hundred nuns. The nuns themselves were often members of the royal and aristocratic classes. Many of these nuns lived together with monks in "double houses."

During the early Middle Ages, more double houses were headed by an abbess than by an abbot.[9] Hilda was one such abbess. She headed a double house in Whitby that became "the most celebrated religious house in the northeast of England in the seventh century."[10] Hilda had been a member of King Edwin's court and had been baptized with him in 627 (see chap. 3). She was Edwin's great-niece and had come to live with Edwin and Ethelberga after her father died. When she became the abbess at Whitby, Hilda taught the monks and nuns "the strict observation of justice, piety, chastity, and other virtues."[11] She was considered such a wise person that kings sought her counsel. A sure sign of her wisdom and influence is seen in the fact that five of the monks from her monastery became bishops.

Scholars don't know exactly how the men and women in double houses lived, and their interactions with members of the opposite sex likely varied by

7. Griffiths, *Garden of Delights*, 30. However, by the twelfth century, after efforts to regulate monasticism, the majority of communities were organized around a formal rule, like the Benedictine Rule, and women who joined these communities committed themselves to these rules.

8. Mulder-Bakker, "Holy Women," 326.

9. Thompson, *Women Religious*, 54–55. By the twelfth century, the double houses that existed were led by men.

10. Deen, *Great Women*, 34.

11. Bede, *History of the English Church and People* 4.23.

location. Certainly they slept in separate buildings, but they may have eaten and worked together. It's clear that at some double houses they chanted their daily prayers together, because this practice was explicitly forbidden later. The vision for double houses came from practices in the early church. Just as some men and women had shared their resources in the early church, so medieval monks and nuns sought to follow their example. The story of Jesus looking down from the cross to tell the apostle John to care for his mother, Mary, also became an important motivation for monks to care for nuns.[12] Since only men could be ordained and administer the Eucharist, some male priests were charged with administering the Eucharist for nuns. This responsibility, along with hearing confession and advising nuns in other capacities (i.e., financial, legal, etc.), was called the *cura monialium*, the "care of the nuns."

Before the tenth century, most monastic communities were Benedictine (meaning they followed the sixth-century rule written by Benedict), but during the High Middle Ages (1000–1300), new orders developed, some of which founded more double houses. The Premonstratensians, the Arrouaisians, the Gilbertines, and the order of Fontevrault all developed double houses. The order of Fontevrault, founded by Robert of Arbrissel, actually placed the male members of the community in a subservient position to the female members. Because women in the medieval world were less privileged than men, Robert believed that serving them would aid his own quest to become more Christlike and would also aid in the sanctification of his male followers.[13]

Interestingly, husbands and wives would sometimes join double houses together. After raising their children, these married couples would decide to intensify their Christian devotion by living as brother and sister in a monastery. Sometimes one or two sons or daughters would join their parents in the decision to renounce the world and take up a life of prayer.[14] However, by the end of the twelfth century, the suspicion that men and women couldn't really control their sexual urges and the fear of scandal became too much of a strain on these communities. Double houses began to dissolve, and houses for women were built at new locations several miles away.

Poverty, Celibacy, and Christian Witness

The earliest nuns and monks were inspired by Jesus's words to the rich young ruler: "If you want to be perfect, go, sell your possessions and give to the poor,

12. Griffiths, *Garden of Delights*, 38–39.
13. Thompson, *Women Religious*, 115.
14. Thompson, *Women Religious*, 84–85, 117.

and you will have treasure in heaven. Then come, follow me" (Matt. 19:21). They were also inspired by the passage in which Jesus talks about people living celibate lives "like eunuchs for the sake of the kingdom of heaven. The one who can accept this should accept it" (19:12). Poverty, lifelong celibacy, and obedience to one's superior became central to the monastic ideal.

Nuns and monks in the early and medieval church were honored for overcoming natural human desire for wealth, sex, and autonomy. People in the ancient and medieval world believed that compared to men, women had stronger sex drives, greater need for physical comfort, less moral fortitude, and less rational power to overcome their bodily desires. So when a woman became a nun and demonstrated her ability to live without a husband, children, sex, and material possessions, it was particularly impressive.

In the early Middle Ages, nuns and monks often accompanied missionaries when they went out to evangelize new areas. For example, when the Anglo-Saxon missionary Boniface evangelized in eighth-century Germany, a number of nuns from double houses in England, including his cousin Leoba, went with him.[15] Just as their lives inspired people in Christian lands, so they served as "living sermons" in non-Christian lands, arousing interest in the faith through their impressive commitment to poverty and chastity. By establishing monasteries, Leoba and other missionary nuns also "provided an essential center for servicing, sheltering, and training female converts."[16]

Anchoresses

Anchoresses lived out their devotion to God in a small room attached to a church or monastery called an anchor-hold. An anchoress never left her anchor-hold. The only light she received came in through a small window, through which people also passed her food and water. In order to provide resources necessary for her own care, an anchoress would spend some of her time making baskets, spinning wool, weaving, embroidering, or even copying books. These goods would then be given to the community.

Some women became anchoresses after first being wives and mothers. Ava Inclusa (d. 1127) had two sons before she became an anchoress. She also knew Latin and, from her anchor-hold, became the "earliest known German poetess," writing poems about salvation history and the Holy Spirit.[17] Julian of Norwich was a fourteenth-century English anchoress, mystic, and theologian.

15. Rudolf of Fulda, "Life of Leoba."
16. McNamara, "Living Sermons," 32.
17. Mulder-Bakker, "Holy Women," 323.

She recorded her visions in *Revelations of Divine Love*, now judged to be a spiritual classic.

Towns prided themselves on having an anchoress in their midst. Most anchoresses were educated and knew the content of Scripture well.[18] People visited them for prayer and advice. Sometimes young girls went to live with an anchoress for a period of time in order to be educated. The mystic Margery Kempe visited Julian of Norwich in 1413 and shared her own mystical visions with Julian in order to gain Julian's perspective, for, wrote Margery, "the anchoress was an expert in such things and could give good advice."[19]

In the early Middle Ages, there were some anchoresses, but the vocation really exploded between the twelfth and thirteenth centuries, particularly in Germany.[20] There were far more women living as anchoresses than men living as anchorites (as male anchor-hold dwellers were called).[21] In England, "there were around twice as many female recluses [anchoresses] in the 14th and 15th centuries and around three times as many in the 13th century."[22]

Some anchoresses attracted quite a following. Communities that gathered around an anchoress often became monastic communities after the death of the anchoress. Hildegard of Bingen's community was established this way. She herself had gone to live with the anchoress Jutta at a monastery in Germany when she was a little girl. Gradually, others came to live in Jutta's presence at the monastery. Jutta became their magistra, and at her death, she appointed Hildegard to take over as magistra.[23]

Hildegard of Bingen

Hildegard of Bingen (1098–1179) is one of the most gifted humans to have ever lived. She was a theologian, scientist, composer, playwright, preacher, philosopher, counselor to popes and emperors, abbess, natural healer, and Christian mystic who was named a Doctor of the Church for her astounding volumes of theology.

Hildegard's visions came to her when she was "fully awake in mind and body," not asleep, and the visions often corresponded with bodily illnesses,

18. Beach, *Women as Scribes*, 36.
19. Kempe, *Book of Margery Kempe*, 77. Margery Kempe herself is a fascinating figure, as she wrote "the earliest autobiography in English." See "Book of Margery Kemp."
20. Beach, *Women as Scribes*, 35–36.
21. Simons, *Cities of Ladies*, 74.
22. Wellesley, "Life of the Anchoress."
23. "Magistra" was the term given to a female leader who submitted to a male abbot instead of having sole authority over the monastic community, as an abbess would.

like migraines.[24] When she was forty-three years old, she had a vision in which a heavenly voice told her to write down all that she saw. Hildegard recruited the monk Volmar to be her amanuensis.[25] With the help of Volmar and her mentee, the young nun Richardis von Stade, Hildegard produced a body of theological work that is as stunning in depth as it is in breadth. Her first work, the *Scivias* (*Know the Ways of God*), contains twenty-six visions and her related theological observations; the *Scivias* uses images of the natural world to explore the history of creation and salvation.

After reading the *Scivias*, Pope Eugenus III recognized the value of Hildegard's work and encouraged her to keep writing.[26] She went on to write *Liber Vitae Meritorum* (*The Book of Life's Merits*), which examines humanity's responsibility for its moral choices through a series of dialogues between vice and virtue, and *Liber Divinorum Operum* (*The Book of Divine Works*), which unpacks God's relationship to all creation and his role in human salvation.

Hildegard also wrote two medical books that detailed the common illnesses she had treated in the infirmary at her convent, natural remedies, and strategies for prevention. In one of these books, *Causes and Cures*, Hildegard incorporated her theological assessment of how sin affects human health. According to Hildegard, sin blocks the flow of *viriditas*—the "greening power of God," or the divine source of life and vitality that flows through all things.[27] Thus, Hildegard promoted the practice of virtue in order to promote health.

Hildegard once wrote, "There is the music of heaven in all things, but we have forgotten to hear it until we sing." Toward that end, she composed seventy songs and taught them to her nuns. She also wrote "the first known morality play," which she called *Ordo Virtutum* (*Play of Virtues*).[28] Her nuns performed this play, in costume, for a visiting dignitary. She even made up a new language, which her nuns could use to converse with one another.

Hildegard was also "the first Western philosopher to articulate the complete concept of sex complementarity."[29] She believed that men were more

24. Newman, introduction, 11–12.

25. An amanuensis was a scribe who took down an author's dictation.

26. Newman, introduction, 13–17.

27. "What Is Hildegard's Viriditas?" Hildegard "often concluded her letters with the words, 'stay green and moist,' which for her meant openness to the Spirit of God." Malone, *Four Women Doctors*, 28.

28. Newman, introduction, 9, 13. There is a wonderful rendition of this in the 2009 film *Vision: From the Life of Hildegard von Bingen* (directed by Margarethe von Trotta [Zeitgeist Films, 2011]).

29. Allen, *Concept of Woman*, 408. Before her, some philosophers had developed a "sex unity" position, which held that women were equal to men, but in order to hold that position, these philosophers had minimized the differences between men and women.

courageous and women more merciful, but neither courage nor mercy was inherently more valuable.[30] Moreover, "Hildegard frequently argued that men ought to develop the feminine qualities of mercy and grace, while women ought to develop the corresponding masculine qualities of courage and strength."[31] Whereas previous philosophers like Aristotle had argued that men were superior to women because of their ability to concoct seed, Hildegard argued that women had more than a passive role to play in the making of a child.[32] In order to develop her theory of sex complementarity, Hildegard drew from biblical and philosophical sources as well as her knowledge of human bodies and personalities, which she gained through treating people in her infirmary. Her work on gender failed to influence the wider culture, as it was overshadowed by the rediscovery of Aristotle's works and the incorporation of his theories into the curriculum of the Western universities.[33] More recently, however, scholars have reclaimed Hildegard's theology, particularly her attention to the feminine attributes of God and her use of titles like "Sapientia" and "Lady Wisdom" for God.

Hildegard was an inspiring leader in her time, and many joined the Benedictine convent under her leadership. In 1148 she moved her community to Bingen, and in 1165 she founded another community in Eibingen. Pope Benedict XVI made Hildegard a Doctor of the Church in 2012.[34]

Prayer, Charitable Work, and the *Vita Apostolica*

If a medieval anchoress or nun were asked how she was involved with the mission of the church, the first thing she would say is that she was "one who prayed." The primary work of nuns and monks was prayer. Prayer was, for them, not only about growing in a personal relationship with God but also about interceding on behalf of the entire community. Medieval society was communal. Everyone had a part to play, and the part played by monks and nuns was necessary, just as the parts played by merchants, farmers, soldiers, and kings were necessary. Merchants, farmers, soldiers, and kings didn't have much time to spend in prayer, so medieval people relied on the prayers of monastics and their acts of piety to improve the moral standing of the community before God. The prayers and piety of the nuns and monks helped to counteract the sins of the wider community. As trade and towns continued

30. Allen, *Concept of Woman*, 297.
31. Allen, *Concept of Woman*, 298.
32. Allen, *Concept of Woman*, 299.
33. Allen, *Concept of Woman*, 413.
34. "St. Hildegard of Bingen."

to grow, and with them the sins people associated with a market economy, such as greed, envy, and laziness, the role of "those who prayed" became all the more necessary.

Nuns were also involved in the mission of the church through their charitable work. Nuns looked out for widowed women and orphaned children, caring for them and raising the children when there was no one else to do so. Many convents had a guesthouse where travelers could stay for a night. Convents were places where people could flee when in danger. They were places where poor people could get a hot meal or where peasants could go for a loan or for help in resolving a dispute.

Nuns also cared for sick and abandoned people, both at the convent infirmary and out in the community. Gradually, they began to found hospitals. Their convent libraries usually contained whatever information about healing and medicine was available at the time. "It may be that some basic nursing was part of the education of nuns in monasteries that ran hospitals, or perhaps the common expectation that women would care for the health of family members predisposed nuns to be sensitive nurses."[35] Monks also had medicinal knowledge and founded hospitals, but usually nuns did the actual nursing work.

In the early thirteenth century, Francis and Clare of Assisi developed a new form of monastic life by committing themselves to radical poverty. Rather than living in a monastery and deriving support from land and endowments, Francis and his followers were mendicant. They wandered around in the growing urban centers of Europe, caring for sick people and begging for their food. They also preached. Through their preaching and poverty, they saw themselves as imitating the lives of the apostles in the early church. Compelled by this *vita apostolica*, Clare established a community of women that became known as the Poor Clares. Although medieval social convention kept the Poor Clares from being able to beg in the streets, as Clare had wanted to do, Clare did get her monastic rule approved by the pope, which allowed her to pursue the same poverty as did Francis.[36]

Art, Contemplation, and Devotion

One of the ways nuns sought to deepen their devotion was through the use of art, and their use of devotional art eventually spilled out into wider medieval society. Nuns did not have access to formal training in art, and their art hasn't been valued by later art critics. However, Jeffrey Hamburger has highlighted

35. Johnson, *Equal in Monastic Profession*, 51–52.
36. Lawrence, *Medieval Monasticism*, 238–68.

the theological insights of a collection of simple drawings made by nuns in fourteenth-century Germany. One drawing is of the crucifixion. Christ's whole body is the deep, red color of blood, and the blood pours off his outstretched arms, slumped head, and body. At the foot of the cross, a monk on the left and a nun on the right grasp the cross with their arms. The blood, however, does not stain them. They are spotless.[37] They have been washed clean in the blood of the lamb (Rev. 7:13–14). Their faces are sad, serious, deeply reverent. The image is simple, but it captures the complex emotion and the fitting response to the theological reality of being washed clean by Jesus.

No one knows the name of the nun who drew this piece, but it and other pieces like it were used by nuns to deepen their spiritual lives. Nuns would sit and meditate on an image either they or someone else had drawn. Looking at the image was a way of bringing themselves into closer connection with Christ. Their meditation on the image was informed by their experience of communal prayer, chanting the Psalms, and viewing the tapestries hanging in the church. These nuns developed their own visual culture within their convent, and that visual culture, in turn, shaped their devotion to Christ.

According to Hamburger, nuns were far more dedicated to the use of images in their devotional lives than were male monks, priests, and theologians. Sometimes nuns expressed apprehension over the use of images in devotion, wondering if art detracted from the worship of the nonphysical God. But ultimately they realized that if Jesus was the nonphysical God in human flesh, then the use of physical objects, images, and bodily experiences in devotion was a way of honoring the reality of the incarnation.[38] "Whereas male theologians rarely mentioned works of art except to criticize them or, on occasion, to concede their utility for pastoral purposes, nuns made them an integral, even indispensable, part of their piety."[39] As certain nuns became renowned for their spiritual fervor, their use of images in the spiritual life was lifted up as exemplary, or at least as permissible. And their practice began to transform devotional practices outside the convent. Looking at the heightened use of images in devotional practices throughout Europe in the thirteenth and fourteenth centuries, Hamburger suggests that this increase was due to Flemish and Rhenish[40] nuns increasingly connecting images with their own devotion. "By the end of the western middle ages," he says, "images

---

37. Hamburger, *Nuns as Artists*, 1–2.

38. This was the same argument that the church had upheld at the seventh ecumenical council back in 787 allowing the use of icons in worship.

39. Hamburger, *Nuns as Artists*, 4.

40. Flemish nuns lived in Flanders, in present-day Belgium; Rhenish nuns lived near the Rhine River in France.

had joined texts as recognized sources of religious authority and devotional authenticity."[41] Nuns, though cloistered, contributed to the growing use of art in worship and devotion.

Intellectual Mission and Reform: Herrad's *Garden of Delights*

Some nuns were also active in the intellectual mission of the church and in the efforts to reform the church of its abuses, such as simony and clerical concubinage.[42] They, like other reformers, wanted to curb the vices of pride and greed that continued to plague church leaders. Herrad, an abbess in twelfth-century Germany, was one of these reformers. She produced a beautifully illustrated book called *Garden of Delights* to cultivate the intellect and virtue of her nuns.[43] In it were excerpts from the church fathers, passages of Scripture, and some texts she herself wrote. Herrad arranged the texts in order to tell the story of salvation history.

The illustrations in *Garden of Delights* offer vivid evidence of Herrad's interest in reforming the church and cultivating virtue in her nuns. At one point, she depicts sanctification "as a grand conflict between the Virtues and Vices, who are depicted as female knights dressed for battle, heavily armed with chain mail, helmets, and weapons. . . . The Virtues carry swords, and the Vices spears. They confront each other across the facing page."[44] The first female knight to appear on the page is Pride, carrying a spear. The female knight Humility is able to defeat her. In the ensuing pages, the knights named Faith, Love, and Prudence defeat Idolatry, Envy, and Vainglory.

In the past, scholars tended to assume that nuns did not participate in the intellectual currents of the day because they were not able to attend medieval universities. Herrad's *Garden of Delights*, among other discoveries, reveals that nuns did participate in intellectual debate, which was a key element of the church's mission in twelfth-century Europe.[45] While Herrad was preparing her book, debates were raging about whether the pope or the king should have more power. By choosing to put texts in support of papal power in her book, Herrad showed which side of the debate she was on. She wanted the

41. Hamburger, *Nuns as Artists*, xxi.

42. "Simony" is the buying and selling of spiritual benefits.

43. Fiona Griffiths argues that "Herrad's garden title stands as a reminder to her audience that knowledge, when used inappropriately, was the source of humanity's exile from God; however, when used properly, as Herrad teaches it can be, knowledge could become the means for reconciliation." Griffiths, *Garden of Delights*, 19.

44. Griffiths, *Garden of Delights*, 197.

45. Griffiths, *Garden of Delights*, 4.

nuns who read *Garden of Delights* to be well informed and to know the best arguments in favor of papal power.

Herrad was also concerned about corrupt priests. Her nuns depended on priests to provide the sacraments necessary for medieval church life: confession and Communion. A nun might confess pride, but if she confessed to a corrupt priest, who didn't make any effort to overcome pride in his own life, she likely wouldn't get very good advice from him. This problem was one of the primary reasons Herrad compiled *Garden of Delights*. Even if her nuns received bad advice from the priests who served them, they wouldn't have to depend on those priests for their spiritual nourishment. They could get theological training and spiritual advice from *Garden of Delights*. The book would not only educate them but also help them discern whether the priests serving their community were spiritually mature or not. Herrad took further action to ensure that her flock received consistent spiritual nourishment from priests by founding two monasteries for monks who could then take over the *cura monialium* for her community.

Book Production and Preaching

Another way in which nuns were active in the intellectual mission of the church was through their role in book production. The only way to replicate books during this period was by hand. Scribes spent hour after hour painstakingly copying texts. One such woman was Bertila, "the first abbess of Chelles, who sent manuscripts to missionaries and newly established abbeys in England" in the seventh century.[46] Bertila's proficiency in Latin enabled her to prepare new copies of the Bible and spiritual classics for use in England. The eighth-century English nuns who went with missionary Boniface to Germany also produced books. The intellectual skill of these nuns was admired not only for its own sake but also as "evidence of female sanctity."[47] Moreover, their work preparing copies of the Bible and other books for use in missionary lands was indispensable to the spread of the gospel.

Some nuns in England, Ireland, Italy, and Germany were active in book production between the sixth and the eleventh century, but book production really took off in twelfth-century Germany because of a reform movement. As reformers penned texts on topics like clerical celibacy and papal power, scribes hurried to reproduce these texts. They also copied Scripture and texts by the church fathers for monastery libraries. Many women were as excited about

46. Beach, *Women as Scribes*, 14.
47. Beach, *Women as Scribes*, 9.

church reform as men, and growing numbers of women chose the monastic profession during this period. "Between 1100 and 1250, 350 new [convents] were founded" to accommodate these women who wanted to become nuns.[48] Some women in these convents became scribes. One such woman, Diemut, was an anchoress at a renowned German monastery. The epitaph on her tomb reads, "Diemut, a recluse of pious memory who with her own hands created a library for St. Peter's."[49] During her lifetime, Diemut copied forty books, which was quite a feat, given the strenuous nature of scribal work. Diemut and the nuns who copied books for use in twelfth-century Germany were doing important missional work. Their books "made possible the biblical study and devotional reading so central to the intellectual and spiritual life prescribed by monastic reformers in the eleventh and twelfth centuries."[50]

In addition to copying existing texts, a few scribes even wrote their own sermons, biblical commentaries, and biographies. The nuns of a double house in Germany called Admont were particularly adept at writing. One of the nuns, Gertrude, was so impressed with the sanctity and intellectual prowess of her abbess that she wrote the woman's biography, which then continued to inspire the spiritual and intellectual growth of the monastery's inhabitants. Several of the nuns at Admont were quite educated and skilled in biblical interpretation. When a monk was not able to give the customary daily sermon to the nuns, one of the nuns preached in his place. And instead of chastising the nuns, the abbot in charge of the *cura monialium* praised them. "They are exceedingly lettered," he wrote, "and wonderfully trained in the knowledge of sacred Scripture." This abbot was himself an author, and he enlisted the help of several nuns in preparing his biblical commentaries.[51] Medieval historian John Van Engen thinks that in all likelihood the nuns did more work on these biblical commentaries than the abbot. It was the nuns who "did the real work, drove the exegetical conversation forward, [and] composed the Latin text."[52]

The nuns at Admont preached to one another when their priest was unable to do so, but a few medieval women preached to mixed audiences. Hildegard went on four preaching tours of Germany and preached to monks, clergy, and townspeople alike. In thirteenth-century Italy, Rose of Viterbo also preached to mixed audiences, and the anchoress Umiltà of Faenza wrote and delivered

48. This is compared to "only approximately 70 convents for women in Germany in 900" and 150 convents in 1100. Beach, *Women as Scribes*, 29.
49. Beach, *Women as Scribes*, 32.
50. Beach, *Women as Scribes*, 60.
51. Beach, *Women as Scribes*, 72–73.
52. Van Engen, "Voices of Women," 208.

sermons from within her anchor-hold.[53] Umiltà achieved renown, and people set up little cells near her anchor-hold so they could benefit from her teaching. A century later, Catherine of Siena preached to mixed audiences. Preaching to mixed audiences was not an activity that many medieval women engaged in, and some of those who did were declared heretics, but Hildegard, Rose, Umiltà, and Catherine were not condemned for their public preaching. Some people criticized them, but the Roman Catholic Church ultimately canonized these women as saints. Later, the Church even declared Hildegard of Bingen and Catherine of Siena Doctors of the Church, meaning they were trustworthy teachers of doctrine alongside the likes of Augustine and Aquinas.

Catherine of Siena

Catherine of Siena (1347–1380) spent her life bringing healing and reconciliation to the church. From a young age, Catherine felt a mystical connection to God and was attracted to the religious life, prompting her to take a vow of virginity. Her family really wanted her to marry and pressured her to change her mind by reducing her to a servant in her own home. Catherine transformed this burden into an extension of grace by "visualizing family members as the holy apostles and her parents as the divine family."[54] When they suggested that she focus on her beauty to attract suitors, Catherine cut off her hair. At age seventeen, while she was stricken with smallpox, Catherine finally convinced her family to allow her to take holy orders. She was accepted as a Dominican tertiary, meaning she could pursue a religious life within the walls of her own home. She continued to live with her parents but took a vow of silence, which she kept for three years. During this time, she learned to "build an internal cell [in her mind] to which she could go to meditate," a discipline she would later pass on to her followers.[55]

Catherine stepped out of this purely contemplative life after she received a vision of being united in marriage to Christ.[56] Like Christ, she felt tremendous compassion and wanted to serve poor and sick people. When a wave of the Great Plague (Black Death) swept through Italy in 1374, Catherine and her

53. Kienzle and Walker, *Women Preachers*, 148, 159. Looking especially at the art of the Middle Ages, one can see that medieval Christians understood Mary of Magdalene and Martha of Bethany to be preachers. There were also many paintings of the fourth-century Catherine of Alexandria preaching to pagan philosophers before being martyred. Kienzle and Walker, *Women Preachers*, 181–86.

54. Petroff, *Medieval Women's Visionary Literature*, 239.

55. Petroff, *Medieval Women's Visionary Literature*, 239.

56. Petroff, *Medieval Women's Visionary Literature*, 240.

followers—most of whom had already lost members of their own families to the plague—nursed those who fell ill. In all, the Black Death killed about one-third of Europe's population during this time. "As far as most people were concerned, the devil was stalking the land, wreaking the vengeance of God on a sinful people."[57] Catherine and her followers tended those whom others had abandoned.

People criticized Catherine for being out in society as a single woman in a mixed company of men and women. She wrote, "My very sex . . . puts many obstacles in the way. The world has no way for a woman to mix so freely in the company of men." She heard the Lord respond, "With me there is no male or female."[58] She also learned to protect herself from criticism by "dwelling in the cell of self-knowledge" and by remembering what God had told her: "I make you free so that you are subject to no other except me."[59] People also criticized her for refusing to eat and sleep. It is said that for many years she "survived on the Eucharist alone."[60] Catherine fasted to such an extent that she ceased to menstruate. Her exact reasons for doing so are unclear, but one scholar has argued that her ascetically trained body gave her an ability to command respect and authority, which other medieval women lacked.[61]

In 1374, Catherine was twenty-seven years old and a greatly admired religious leader. People flocked to her, and "a team of three priests had to accompany her everywhere in order to hear the confessions of those whose lives had been transformed by Catherine's life and teaching."[62] Catherine also wrote letters to political figures, including the pope. During the reign of Pope Clement V (1305–1314), the papacy had moved from Rome to Avignon, France. Many considered this move scandalous because it devalued the consecration of Rome and led to popes engaging in corrupt political dealings in France. Thus, in 1376, Catherine worked tirelessly to bring Pope Gregory XI back to Rome. Catherine wasn't working from Italian nationalistic pride; rather, she desired to heal divisions within the church, restoring it to order and its proper function. Her persistence and growing spiritual clout convinced Pope Gregory XI to return the papacy to Rome. But then he died. Pope Urban VI was elected in Rome, and a faction of the church responded by electing a rival pope in Avignon.

57. Malone, *Four Women Doctors*, 40.
58. Luongo, *Saintly Politics*, 62–63.
59. Malone, *Four Women Doctors*, 62.
60. Malone, *Four Women Doctors*, 48.
61. White, "Hungering for Maleness," 157.
62. White, "Hungering for Maleness," 46.

By this time, Catherine was seriously ill. She did not, however, stop writing. Over the span of just three days, she dictated a book called *The Dialogue*, which described Jesus as the bridge of salvation. When she died in 1380 at age thirty-three, her last words were "Father, into your hands I commit my spirit."[63] She was declared a saint in 1461 and a Doctor of the Church in 1970.

Obstacles Faced by Nuns

Catherine's story reveals some of the obstacles medieval nuns faced—for example, the expectation that they should not mix with men in the public square. Herrad's story reveals another obstacle: nuns were dependent on male priests for the sacraments of confession and Eucharist. This dependence meant that their communities were often poorer than male monastic communities because nuns had to pay priests for sacramental services, whereas male communities did not. Moreover, sometimes the priest who administered the *cura monialium* was corrupt. Herrad wrote *Garden of Delights* and founded a monastery to deal with this problem, but sometimes there was nothing an abbess could do if her community was assigned a corrupt priest.

Another obstacle for nuns was that medieval society thought of women as being more carnal, more sinful, and more susceptible to temptation than men. Part of the problem was that a number of important writings in the Christian tradition contained this negative perspective on women. During the eleventh-century Gregorian Reform, as the church began to insist on a celibate priesthood (celibacy had long been the ideal but not the norm for priests), there was "a deluge of propaganda against marriage, and women in particular."[64] When reformers looked to the church fathers for help reforming the church, they found aspects of this antiwoman sentiment in some of their writings.[65] It seems that many medieval monks and priests were afraid that women would cause them to break their vow of celibacy. Thus, women in general—and nuns in particular—became scapegoats. They were blamed for being temptresses.

But although many male monks and priests saw medieval nuns as particularly "ripe to fall into sexual sin," the data from medieval monasteries reveals that there was no statistical difference between monks and nuns in terms of

63. "Catherine of Siena."
64. Malone, *Four Women Doctors*, 25. Another tragedy is that married priests were forced to send their wives away. This requirement caused "huge social disruption as thousands of families were left destitute. Many were sold into slavery." Malone, *Four Women Doctors*, 25.
65. See the discussion in chap. 1 under the heading "Women's Leadership Curtailed."

their ability to keep their vow of chastity.[66] In both male and female houses, only three or four out of a hundred fell into sexual sin.[67] Penelope Johnson says that "female lapses usually occurred when the monastic environment was a small, isolated, and financially strapped institution in which morale must have been low and life particularly hard."[68]

In fact, women were not a threat to male virtue as much as men were a threat to women's virtue. While the circumstances of every story that has come down to us are not known, there is evidence that some medieval nuns were raped. "The story of Christina of Markyate tells of her terrifying experience with Bishop Ralph Flambard, who tried to seduce her by getting her alone in his apartments and would have raped her had she not outwitted him. Equally, men could and sometimes did enter nunneries in search of a woman."[69] When women did fall into sexual sin, their sexual partner was most often a priest who was responsible for the *cura monialium*. Perhaps in some cases both partners were willing participants in the sexual liaison, but at other times a nun may have felt coerced into committing sexual sin for fear of retaliation if she refused.

Sometimes the negative perspective on women faded into the background, especially when preachers took to the streets to arouse more interest in the monastic life and when new monasteries were formed and old ones became interested in renewal. During such times, women were welcomed as sisters in the faith, capable of making the sacrifices being demanded of them. Houses for women were founded alongside houses for men during these times of monastic reform. Women took part "alongside men as scribes, readers, preachers, authors, and editors."[70] Male houses willingly took on the responsibilities of the *cura monialium*.

At other times, however, monks and priests found the *cura monialium* to be a burden on their time and energy and complained about nuns being in public instead of staying cloistered. And as church leaders heard these complaints and struggled to accommodate the large number of women wanting to join the monastic life, they favored solutions that seemed to help men, but at women's expense. Fewer houses for women were formed.[71] The houses that

66. Johnson, *Equal in Monastic Profession*, 112.
67. Johnson, *Equal in Monastic Profession*, 123.
68. Johnson, *Equal in Monastic Profession*, 121.
69. Johnson, *Equal in Monastic Profession*, 124.
70. Beach, *Women as Scribes*, 130.
71. In 1198, for example, an order came from the pope himself "forbidding the further admission of women to any Premonstratensian house." However, the situation was complicated. Even though these kinds of orders were made about both Premonstratensian and Cistercian houses, it seems that in some places the orders were not followed. Some monasteries continued to accept

did exist for women were capped at a certain number and were brought more closely into the structures of established orders. Abbesses saw their authority decrease. The position of magistra became more common than that of abbess (magistras had less authority because they submitted to an abbot rather than to a bishop). Johnson describes the cycle this way: "Women tended to share in the enthusiasm in . . . cycles of renewal, but as the impulse became institutionalized, they were usually marginalized or squeezed out entirely."[72]

Another obstacle medieval nuns faced was having their property confiscated. Sometimes monks took their land, and sometimes laypersons did. For example, a group of nuns in tenth-century France were kicked out of their convent when a wealthy duke decided that he wanted to house a group of monks there. In a kind of "musical monastics," the duke uprooted the women, moved them to a new location, and installed his community of monks in their place. As Johnson notes, "There must have been some very hard feelings among the women, but no evidence survives since it certainly behooved them to be discreet and act grateful that they were not being disbanded out of hand."[73]

Conclusion

Medieval nuns were essential to the flourishing of both church and society. Through their prayers, they interceded on behalf of those in the wider community. They cared for sick people and created libraries for the intellectual and spiritual nourishment of the faithful. They raised orphans, taught oblates, housed travelers, offered counsel, and protected those in danger. They served as missionaries, establishing monasteries in foreign lands. Even in their own lands, they served as "living sermons," demonstrating what it looked like to live a life committed to serving God and neighbor.

Some scholars have wrongly assumed that because women couldn't attend medieval universities, they did not participate in the intellectual, artistic, and exegetical interests of the period. Despite their lack of opportunity, however, medieval women found ways to contribute to the artistic and intellectual life of the church. Nuns in Belgium and France created drawings of Christ's incarnation and crucifixion. Their use of art in devotion augmented the use of art in devotional practices outside the monastery as well. Nuns at Admont preached and created biblical commentaries, and Herrad wrote *Garden of Delights*.

---

women as members. Nevertheless, the fact that such orders came from the pope still constitutes a major obstacle that women—but not men—faced. Beach, *Women as Scribes*, 109–10.

72. Johnson, *Equal in Monastic Profession*, 4.

73. Johnson, *Equal in Monastic Profession*, 36.

Herrad, Hildegard of Bingen, and Catherine of Siena critiqued the abuses that were plaguing the church of their day. By speaking out on these topics, these women showed that they were active in reforming the medieval church.

Medieval nuns faced many obstacles. Fewer monasteries were founded for them, in part because women controlled fewer resources. Many times women were told they couldn't join monastic communities because priests didn't want to take on the *cura monialium*. Women were accused of being temptresses, and some faced the threat of unwanted sexual advances from corrupt priests. But nuns persevered through these obstacles. They contributed to the mission of the church in myriad ways, and many of them challenged negative views of women by being virtuous, hardworking, theologically literate people.

5

Beguines and Mystics

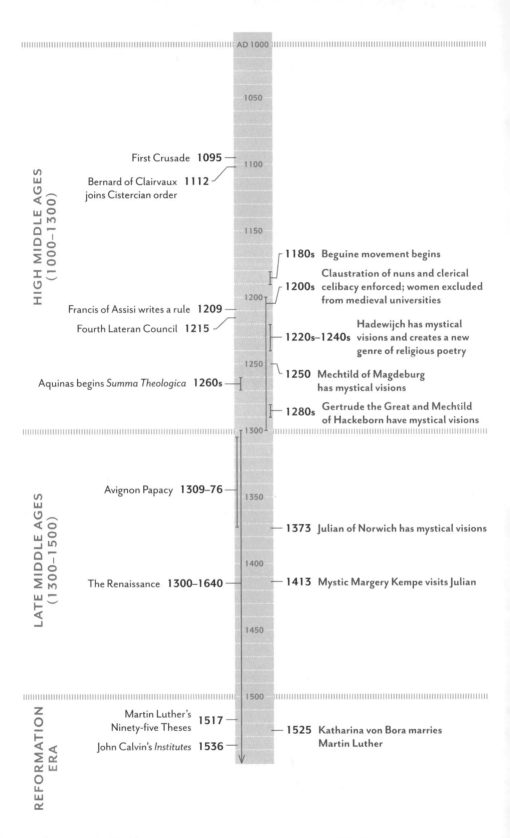

AD 1000

1050

HIGH MIDDLE AGES (1000–1300)

First Crusade **1095**

1100

Bernard of Clairvaux **1112** joins Cistercian order

1150

1180s Beguine movement begins

1200s Claustration of nuns and clerical celibacy enforced; women excluded from medieval universities

1200

Francis of Assisi writes a rule **1209**

Fourth Lateran Council **1215**

1220s–1240s Hadewijch has mystical visions and creates a new genre of religious poetry

1250

1250 Mechtild of Magdeburg has mystical visions

Aquinas begins *Summa Theologica* **1260s**

1280s Gertrude the Great and Mechtild of Hackeborn have mystical visions

1300

LATE MIDDLE AGES (1300–1500)

Avignon Papacy **1309–76**

1350

1373 Julian of Norwich has mystical visions

1400

The Renaissance **1300–1640**

1413 Mystic Margery Kempe visits Julian

1450

1500

REFORMATION ERA

Martin Luther's Ninety-five Theses **1517**

1525 Katharina von Bora marries Martin Luther

John Calvin's *Institutes* **1536**

Chapter 4 discussed how medieval nuns and anchoresses contributed to the mission of the church through their exemplary lives, prayers, book production, and service to those on the margins of society. From the 1180s onward, thousands of women throughout Europe began to develop new ways to live lives committed to God and neighbor. Some of them lived in Belgium, where they were called "beguines," others lived in Italy, where they were called "Humiliati," and others lived in France and Germany. Whereas earlier monasteries had been only for women of the nobility and aristocracy, in this new religious movement, rich women, poor women, and even formerly prostituted women lived together. They adopted a life of chastity, poverty, prayer, study, and service. Their life was similar to that of nuns, but women in this new movement had more flexibility. Their vows were not permanent, and they had more freedom of movement rather than being cloistered. Many of them also worked to support themselves financially rather than depending on income from donors or land, as nuns did.[1]

This chapter explores the dynamics of the women's religious movement and traces some of the obstacles these women faced, most notably forced claustration in the thirteenth century.[2] It also explores the flowering of mysticism that unfolded in the midst of forced claustration. Through their visions of Jesus and the Eucharist, visionary women helped cause a shift in medieval piety from an emphasis on Christ's kingship to an emphasis on his bodily humanity and suffering.

The Women's Religious Movement

The beguine movement was "the only movement in medieval monastic history that was created by women and for women—and not affiliated with, or supervised by, a male order."[3] Sometimes these beguines and the other new communities of women lived in the home of one of the women, and sometimes

---

1. Petroff, *Medieval Women's Visionary Literature*, 171.
2. Claustration meant that instead of being able to wander around as they liked, these women had to stay cloistered—that is, behind the walls of the convent.
3. Simons, *Cities of Ladies*, 143.

they moved to a new location on the outskirts of town. If these women had children, they made sure that others could care for them. Many times these communities of women found a place to live that was located in proximity to sick people, such as those with leprosy, so that part of their new life together could involve caring for these needy people daily.

Some communities were as small as two or three women, and other communities grew to be as large as a hundred women. Sometimes entire walled communities developed, with wealthier members of the community occupying nicer homes and poorer women living in more modest dwellings. But both the smaller communities and the larger "cities of ladies" were composed of women who wanted to dedicate themselves more fully to God and who felt that doing so was best achieved in a community of like-minded women.[4]

Sometimes these communities sheltered women who were trying to avoid an unwanted marriage. They also educated young girls and orphans. Sometimes the women supported themselves by making and selling baskets or spinning wool or silk; other times they received support in the form of gifts from the surrounding community.[5] A woman who joined the community might stay for the rest of her life, or she might choose to leave to become an anchoress or to take a formal vow as a nun in a different order.

So many aspects of the women's religious movement were remarkable. Rich women were willing to surrender their status and move in with poor women and women who had formerly worked as prostitutes.[6] The surrounding townspeople not only supported these communities but actually celebrated these women and at times made their lives possible through patronage (donations of land, funds, and services). Even more remarkable, the church establishment didn't immediately forbid this organic spirituality. Instead, women in this movement, through their exemplary devotion and outreach, contributed to the growth and health of the medieval church.

Beguines as Exemplars and Teachers of the Religious Life

Why were wealthy women willing to surrender their status and take on lives of service to poor people? Why did these women want to live with people with leprosy on the margins of society instead of living with a husband and children at the center of society? In part, these women did so because they were tired of the responsibilities and angst of their socioeconomic position.

4. Simons, *Cities of Ladies*, 62.
5. T. Miller, *Beguines of Medieval Paris*, 65–71.
6. Lester, *Creating Cistercian Nuns*, 75.

Between the eleventh and the thirteenth century, people in Europe became more prosperous. Due to good weather, improved farming techniques, and a decrease in outside invasions, the population of Europe doubled. A bigger population meant that not everyone was needed to help with life on the farms. Some people could move to the towns and become artisans and tradespeople. As they developed new goods, people from other regions came to buy those goods and to bring other goods to sell. The towns grew richer, a new bourgeois class developed, and the gap widened between rich and poor people. Those who were among the new bourgeois class had a higher standard of living than their ancestors and had more luxury goods. However, some of them felt uneasy about the rising disparity between themselves and those with less. They felt a growing discomfort with the urban emphasis on profit and the vices of greed and envy that so often accompanied the market economy. When they went to church or when they heard preachers in the streets, they heard stories from the Bible about the rich man and Lazarus (Luke 16:19–31) and about it being harder for a rich person to enter the kingdom of heaven than for a camel to fit through the eye of a needle (Matt. 19:24). These stories made some men and women wonder if God was perhaps displeased with their family's wealth. Moreover, bourgeois families often worried about losing their wealth. It seemed that nothing could assuage this anxiety, and they wondered if the new wealth was even worth it. Some of them decided to simply give it up. As Anne Lester notes, "Escape from the burdens of family and business transactions pervades the conversion narratives of many holy women."[7]

Many of the women who chose to give up their wealth deliberately entered into a state of repentance when they did so. They felt convicted about having played a part in the profit-driven economy of their time. Taking on a life of poverty and service was their way of living out their repentance. It was a way of apologizing to God for themselves and their families and replacing vices like greed and envy with virtues like generosity and humility.

Women and men who chose to live this way were said to be living the *vita apostolica* (apostolic life), imitating the poverty, repentance, and service of the early church. Francis of Assisi lived out his repentance by wandering around preaching and begging for food. Other men lived out their public repentance by going on a crusade to the Holy Land. Women did not typically become itinerant preachers or crusaders (though this did happen occasionally).[8] The quintessential way that women lived out their repentance was by caring for poor people and sick people. They believed that as they suffered with others

7. Lester, *Creating Cistercian Nuns*, 76.
8. Remember Hildegard, Rose, Umiltà, and Catherine in chap. 4.

and attended to their needs, they became more Christlike. The notion of imitating Christ was central to the spirituality of the time. Bernard of Clairvaux, an influential twelfth-century monk, once said, "As the Son of God used his humanity to save the world, so ordinary men and women could use their humanity to imitate His divinity and so save themselves and others."[9] Those who lived the *vita apostolica* believed that people who were poor or sick had a special place in God's heart. By caring for such people, they believed that they were moving closer to God's heart. Moreover, by making themselves poor, they were making themselves into people who were especially beloved of God. They also found that becoming literally poor had a way of cultivating an inner humility.

These women also believed that serving "the least of these" was a way of serving Christ. Matthew 25:35–36 was real for these women and for the wider society in which they lived.[10] When they gave food to hungry people, drink to thirsty people, shelter to strangers, clothing to naked people, and care to sick and imprisoned people, they envisioned Christ as the recipient of their care.

As towns developed hospitals and houses for those with leprosy, it was overwhelmingly women who took care of these people. Women were essential to this important caring ministry of the church. Moreover, during the thirteenth century, there was a close connection between caring for physical ailments and caring for spiritual ailments. Thus, it would not be appropriate to think of these women as doing only "social justice work" as opposed to "evangelism" (a dichotomy that occasionally divides mission work in evangelical communities today). Rather, the idea was that "hospitals, hospices, and leper houses were to be places that cared foremost for the soul." Therefore, these women were ministering simultaneously to the physical and spiritual needs of the individuals in their care.[11]

Bourgeois women who moved to the margins of society to care for "the least of these" gave up their social privilege, but in doing so they gained a new kind of social prestige. These women began to be viewed by others as exemplars of faith. Just as Jesus lifted up as exemplary the Canaanite woman and the woman who anointed his feet with perfume (Matt. 15:21–28; 26:6–13), so medieval townspeople lifted up the holy women in their midst. They viewed

9. Quoted in Lester, *Creating Cistercian Nuns*, 145.

10. Matt. 25:35–36 says, "For I was hungry and you gave me something to eat, I was thirsty and you gave me something to drink, I was a stranger and you invited me in, I needed clothes and you clothed me, I was sick and you looked after me, I was in prison and you came to visit me." The phrase "the least of these" occurs in v. 40 as a summary of those in need and has become a shorthand reference to this passage.

11. Lester, *Creating Cistercian Nuns*, 126.

these women as holy because they pursued lives of poverty, chastity, and service to poor people and because they spent more time than ordinary people in prayer and fasting. Their commitment to prayer was often not as regulated as that of their male and female counterparts in more formal monastic communities, but it was still a significant part of their life together. And unlike cloistered nuns, beguines could move about in society, encouraging people to come to church, hear a sermon, or make a confession. Indeed, it was their constant outreach in the community that made Robert of Sorbon urge the students at his college to look to the beguines as models of religious life in the world.[12] He was impressed by their love, humility, and strength to withstand criticism for their countercultural way of life. He also knew that they did important work facilitating the reception of male preaching.

In addition to their outreach in the community, the theology and passion of the Paris beguines also proved inspirational to the student priests and professors at the Sorbonne. A preaching manual was prepared in 1272 by a Paris priest named Raoul. It included a series of sermons preached by the head of the beguines to her community in Paris and was kept in the Sorbonne library.[13] Students at the Sorbonne were influenced by beguine theology through this text and through the questions beguines asked them after they preached at the beguine chapel. Students were also impacted by stories about beguine piety, stories that they would often weave into their own sermons. According to one story, a professor of theology came upon a beguine "weeping in a church out of love for Christ."[14] The professor was so impressed by this woman's piety that he asked her to help him feel a similar level of passion for Christ.

Beguines were also instrumental in creating devotional materials for the increasingly literate laity.[15] Many beguines chose to compose and circulate devotional materials in their native language instead of Latin. These materials then became some of the first vernacular literature in their communities and facilitated the religious instruction of the laity.

Forced Claustration

Many people respected the beguines and were grateful for their contributions to society, but others found fault with these and other women who had dedicated their lives to the service of God. Some monks and priests complained

12. T. Miller, *Beguines of Medieval Paris*, 88–94.
13. T. Miller, *Beguines of Medieval Paris*, 121.
14. T. Miller, *Beguines of Medieval Paris*, 99.
15. T. Miller, *Beguines of Medieval Paris*, 104.

that women were disobeying proper procedure because, instead of consulting male priests about creating religious communities, these women were acting on their own initiative. In France, Cistercian monks complained about some women who had taken to wearing a white habit, which was the official uniform of the Cistercian order. Many Cistercians didn't want more women in their order, and they certainly didn't want women claiming to be in their order when in fact they were not. These women may have worn the white habit, but they didn't stay cloistered within convent walls, which was standard procedure for Cistercian nuns. Instead, they wandered about whenever they pleased. They also didn't follow the formal Cistercian Rule. Some monks and priests also didn't like the amount of spiritual authority the women had gained in the community. They seem to have thought that spiritual authority was a zero-sum game, meaning that if more women held the seats of religious honor in the community, their own seats of honor would be diminished.[16] They also viewed women's sexuality as a problem. As the church continued to insist that all priests be celibate, many priests took out their frustration on nuns and beguines. As Penelope Johnson says, "In response to the chafing demands on them, the clergy insisted on rigid claustration of nuns, which served two purposes: strict enclosure made these tempting women as inaccessible as possible to protect men from the pollution of arousal, and it allowed the clergy to vent frustration by punishing nuns as the scapegoats for male sexual feelings."[17]

Throughout the thirteenth century, numerous monks, priests, and popes insisted on claustration for nuns, beguines, and other women religious. During this time, Pope Innocent III also declared that all these women religious had to follow a formal rule. He wanted to tighten official control of women. No longer could women decide on their own whom to minister to, how to pray, where to live, what to wear, when to go out. They were to stay enclosed within the walls of their convent.[18] Their communities were incorporated into formal orders like the Cistercians and the Dominicans and were given more permanent buildings and funds.[19]

At first glance, better buildings and more money seem like benefits, not problems. However, part of the religious life these women had chosen for themselves included poverty and, in some cases, begging. Such a life, they believed, kept them humble, kept them close to the heart of God, and enabled them to live out their vocation of service to poor people. While new church rulings still enabled them to live in proximity to poor people and to serve those

16. Lester, *Creating Cistercian Nuns*, 44.
17. Johnson, *Equal in Monastic Profession*, 162.
18. For variations on this ruling, see Hamburger, *Visual and the Visionary*, 38–43.
19. Lester, *Creating Cistercian Nuns*, chap. 3.

with leprosy, they did not enable the women to remain poor themselves. The point of giving the women better buildings and more money was to ensure that their communities would be more permanent and self-supporting so that the women wouldn't need to beg.[20]

While forced claustration was for the most part a major drawback for women, there were a few benefits. One benefit was that these women were now less likely to be deemed heretics. Several women of this period who had chosen a life of autonomy, poverty, prayer, and imitation of Christ had been burned at the stake as heretics. Being in an established monastic order, following a formal rule, and being sheltered behind convent walls largely protected women from being deemed heretics.

Not all priests enforced the claustration rule. Beguines in Belgium, for example, continued to form noncloistered communities over the course of the thirteenth century and even won the explicit blessing of the pope to do so. They were also encouraged in their vocation by some priests, who were so impressed with them that they wrote their *Vitae* for the inspiration of the faithful.

Additional Obstacles Faced by Beguines and Nuns

Beguines and nuns faced similar obstacles in the twelfth and thirteenth centuries, even though the structure of their lives was slightly different. First, the growing emphasis on claustration meant that nuns couldn't join monks and priests in processions through towns on holy days. It also meant that women religious couldn't join monks and priests in the growing universities throughout Europe. Some women religious stopped learning Latin. They began to fall behind men in both learning and financial support. Because they weren't as visible in society as men, people began to think less about them and less about the important roles they played in society. And because Francis of Assisi and his followers were starting to be seen as the holiest of monastics, townspeople began giving their alms to Francis and the friars instead of to the nuns and beguines.[21]

The elevation of the priesthood was another factor that began to obscure the work of beguines and nuns. During the twelfth and thirteenth centuries, there was a growing emphasis on the sacraments of the church and a growing

20. Some women still decided to break the claustration rule in order to return to the streets to beg. But the beguines in Belgium and the Humiliati in Italy were not as concerned about absolute poverty as some of their counterparts in France and Germany. Lester, *Creating Cistercian Nuns*, 116; Simons, *Cities of Ladies*, 69.

21. Johnson, *Equal in Monastic Profession*, 251–53.

push to permit only ordained men to officiate these sacraments. People began to revere the Eucharist more than they used to. They wanted to take it more often, so priests were in demand to lead eucharistic services. People were also supposed to confess their sins to a priest at least once a year, so priests were in demand to hear people's confessions. Beguines and nuns were part of this growing trend, so they also needed more priests to hear their confessions and lead their eucharistic services.

If you asked a beguine or a nun in the late Middle Ages whether the growing emphasis on the priesthood was obstructing her own mission or clouding her sense of her place in the world, she probably would not have seen it that way. The growing prestige of the male priesthood was part of the reform of the church, and most women religious supported such reform. They favored clerical celibacy. They, like male reformers, didn't want priests having concubines. They wanted the church to be more attuned to virtues like humility and love instead of caught up in vices like pride and greed. Nevertheless, looking back at the history, it is evident that even though nuns supported reform, the elevation of the priesthood did cause some nuns to lose a sense of their role in the mission of the church. As Johnson says, with "the growing importance of being a priest, the nun's self-definition as an integral part of the social fabric started to unravel."[22]

Mysticism: A Predominantly Female Phenomenon

At the very time that beguines and nuns were experiencing these obstacles, some of them began to have mystical visions. The mystics were kind of like modern-day charismatics. They would "see" or "hear" a word from God. Sometimes it was a quick vision, a little glimpse of light or the presence of the Christ child by the altar when the priest was serving the Eucharist. Other times a mystic would be entranced for hours, and when she came to, she would tell others what she had seen and heard. "Again and again mystics emphasize that their experience is in no way the result of any effort or preparation, but comes to them suddenly, unexpectedly," says Paul Mommaers, an expert on mysticism.[23]

Mysticism, especially visions centered on the Eucharist and the baby Jesus, was a predominantly female experience.[24] There were male mystics during this period too, but according to Caroline Bynum, "For the first time in Christian

22. Johnson, *Equal in Monastic Profession*, 246.
23. Mommaers, *Hadewijch*, 85.
24. Bynum, *Jesus as Mother*, 172.

history we can document that a particular kind of religious experience [mysticism] is more common among women than men. For the first time in Christian history certain major devotional and theological emphases emanate from women and influence the basic development of spirituality."[25]

Three of the most famous medieval mystics lived together in a convent in Helfta, Germany. Two of them were named Mechtild, and one was named Gertrude. The older Mechtild (1207–1282)—named Mechtild of Magdeburg after her town—started having visions long before she came to Helfta. These visions started when she was twelve years old and continued after she became a beguine at age twenty-three.[26] Mechtild recorded her visions in her native language, German, in a piece called *The Flowing Light of the Godhead*, which she wrote before moving to Helfta in 1270. *The Flowing Light of the Godhead* reads like a love poem to God, complete with sexual imagery. "Lord! Now am I a naked soul," wrote Mechtild, "And Thou a God most Glorious! / Our two-fold intercourse is Love Eternal."[27]

Mechtild also had profound experiences of separation from Christ, which she interpreted as a way of purging her sin and identifying with Christ's suffering. She also experienced through visions the pain of other people's separation from God and spent much of her time praying for these people. She also spoke out about the ways in which the contemporary church had strayed from God.

Mechtild of Hackeborn (1240–1298) and Gertrude (1256–1301) were a generation younger than Mechtild of Magdeburg. Unlike Mechtild of Magdeburg, who came to Helfta in her later years, these nuns entered the convent when they were young. They had beautiful visions of Christ as their spouse, but they also had visions of Christ as king, judge, protector, emperor, prince, craftsman, teacher, counselor, brother, and friend.

For these mystics and others, the Eucharist was central to their visions and was associated with union with Christ. Mechtild of Hackeborn once had a vision of union with Christ in which Christ said to her, "I in you and you in me" and then gave her his heart as a token of his love, only the heart was shaped like a cup. On the cup were the words "By my heart you will praise me always; go, offer to all the saints the drink of life from my heart that they may be happily inebriated with it."[28] The strange phrase "happily inebriated" was a reference to Acts 2, which describes the apostles receiving the Holy Spirit at Pentecost and speaking in tongues. It seems the vision may have been a way

25. Bynum, *Jesus as Mother*, 172.
26. Bynum, *Jesus as Mother*, 228.
27. Mechtild of Magdeburg, *Flowing Light of the Godhead* (Petroff, 220).
28. Mechtild of Hackeborn, *Liber specialis gratiae* 1.1.7–10, quoted in Bynum, *Holy Feast and Holy Fast*, 232.

of encouraging Mechtild to share her visions with others, that they might become filled with joy as well.

Hadewijch of Brabant (1200–1248) was a Flemish (Belgian) mystic, poet, and leader of a beguine community. One year at Pentecost, Hadewijch had a vision of the Christ child when preparing to take the Eucharist. Before her eyes, the Christ child then transformed into the man Jesus, who came to her and served her Communion. Not only that, but Jesus also embraced her and she experienced union with Christ. Here is how she describes it: "After that he came himself to me, took me entirely in his arms, and pressed me to him; and all my members felt his in full felicity, in accordance with the desire of my heart and my humanity. . . . But soon, after a short time . . . I saw him completely come to nought and so fade and all at once dissolve that I could no longer recognize or perceive him outside me."[29] Hadewijch found this experience of union with Christ incredibly satisfying, but she also realized that this feeling of bliss was rare and worried that her intense desire for God could never be satisfied.[30] She began to realize that what she really wanted was to enjoy the sweetness of God without suffering.[31] She instructed her followers not to chase after bliss—the kind of "spiritual high" that one receives after being caught up in a vision. Instead, Hadewijch instructed them to chase after devotion to God, being eager to obey him even in suffering.[32]

Hadewijch wrote poems in Dutch about her love for God. Using French courtly love poetry as a model, she wrote of herself as a knight pining away for *Minne*, her name for both God and her experience of love. In one of her poems, she wrote:

> Valiant souls who have come so far
> That they endure unsatisfied Love
> Shall in all ways, toward her,
>   Be bold and undaunted,
>   And ever ready to receive
>   Be it consolation, be it blows,
> From Love's mode of action.[33]

In compositions like this one, Hadewijch conveyed that one should serve God valiantly, whether one felt the love of God or not. By combining courtly love

---

29. Hadewijch, "Vision 7," 64 (Hart, 281).
30. Mommaers, *Hadewijch*, 125–26.
31. Mommaers, *Hadewijch*, 127–28.
32. Mommaers, *Hadewijch*, 123.
33. This excerpt is from Hadewijch's poem 5, "Love's Mode of Action" (Hart, 139–40).

poetry with Christian faith, Hadewijch created a new genre of poetry, that of "mystical love lyric."[34]

Mysticism: An Avenue of Power and Authority for Women in the Church

Hadewijch, Gertrude, the two Mechtilds, and the other mystics didn't keep their visions to themselves. They told other people about them and wrote them down to give others comfort and inspiration. People began to view mystics as people who were particularly close to God and could therefore offer sage advice. As a result, nuns, beguines, monks, priests, and townspeople began to ask mystics for spiritual counsel.

Mystics were seen as bridges to God. They became "direct channels of God's power."[35] Interestingly, at this very time, being a bridge to God and channeling God's power were increasingly thought of as actions associated with male priests, who administered the sacraments. Mystics did not challenge the priestly office. On the contrary, through their visions of the Eucharist, they reinforced this growing emphasis on the priesthood. And yet in a way, these women were also being given the very same power and authority that priests had. Through their visions of the Eucharist and through sharing these visions with others, mystics were able to become many of the things that priests were: "mediators, preachers, touchers of God, vessels within which God happened."[36] So although they didn't see themselves as challenging the authority of the priesthood, they actually were creating another avenue to many of the things thought to be the sole prerogative of priests. Furthermore, many monks and priests not only permitted nuns and beguines to share their visions but also celebrated the mystical avenue for God's power and authority.

But sadly, mystics faced opposition from some in the church. Mechtild of Magdeburg, for example, faced persecution and suspicion. She had to resort to a tactic that Hildegard of Bingen had used a century earlier. She referred to herself as a "poor maid" and emphasized that it was only because of her weakness and absolute unworthiness that God had deigned to reveal himself to her in visions.[37] This posture was enough to assure the church that she was not out to challenge priestly authority, and it enabled her to continue teaching and admonishing others. But some other mystics were not tolerated. For

34. Mommaers, *Hadewijch*, 1.
35. Mommaers, *Hadewijch*, 181.
36. Mommaers, *Hadewijch*, 258.
37. Mechtild of Magdeburg, *Flowing Light of the Godhead* 2.4 (E. Anderson, 39).

example, fellow beguine Marguerite Porete (?–1310) was executed because the church was convinced that she was teaching false doctrine, was a threat to priestly authority, and would lead the laity astray.[38] One reason that Mechtild of Magdeburg and Marguerite were persecuted was that they were beguines. By contrast, Mechtild of Hackeborn and Gertrude were protected from suspicion in part because they belonged to a well-established monastery. Indeed it was likely this fact that made Mechtild of Magdeburg leave her beguine community to become a nun at Helfta in 1270.

Despite opposition, mystics contributed to the mission of the church. Although they were not priests, they did some of the things priests did. They were counselors and teachers. They served as mediators, bringing people's concerns to God in prayer and bringing the concerns of God back to the church. They inspired the faithful to revere the majesty, glory, kindness, and judgment of God. Some of them composed prayers and songs, and others translated Scripture and the church fathers from Latin into vernacular languages. People looked at them as women whose holiness was so powerful that others could participate in it. Mystics used the gifts God gave them to serve God's people, and they did so "with power and serenity."[39]

Mystics Shaped Theology and Responded Creatively to Cultural Constraints

Mystics' role in the mission of the church went beyond counseling, prayer, and virtuous living. These women also shaped theology. During the early Middle Ages, the dominant conception of Christ was as king, but by the late Middle Ages, Christ's humanity and his suffering had become much more important to theology and popular piety. Women mystics played a major role in this shift. Their visions of the infant Christ, the Eucharist, Christ's body on the cross bleeding for humanity, and marriage to Christ helped to shift the emphasis from Christ's kingship to Christ's bodily humanity and suffering. Crucifixes, which showed Jesus on the cross, started replacing bare crosses in churches during this period and demonstrated the growing attention to Christ's suffering.

38. Marguerite Porete wrote a book called *The Mirror of Simple Souls* sometime between 1296 and 1306. Although three church authorities approved of her book, many more said it taught antinomianism (lawlessness) and she should therefore stop disseminating it. She disagreed, saying she was not in favor of antinomianism. She kept disseminating the book and in 1308 was brought before the Inquisition. She was imprisoned for almost a year and a half and was then condemned and executed in 1310.

39. Bynum, *Jesus as Mother*, 227.

One of the reasons women were particularly interested in Christ's human-ity and Christ's suffering was that women were seen in their culture as more bodily than men. Theology since the early church had associated women with flesh and men with spirit. Experiences like menstruation gave medieval women insight into what it means to have a body and what it means to suffer in the body. As medieval piety began to center on imitating the suffering Christ, women—through their own suffering—could readily resonate with Christ.

Mechtild of Magdeburg, Catherine of Siena, and other mystics took their contemplation of Christ's humanity a step further. They had visions of mar-rying Christ, cuddling Christ as a baby, and nursing the infant Christ. They fasted to feel in their bodies the physical suffering of Christ. Denying food to their own bodies, they gave their food instead to poor people, imitating the way Christ denied himself and suffered so as to save human beings. Their identity as women was tied to food. Women nursed infants; women prepared and distributed food to their families. Women in the Middle Ages often did not have power and authority to give up for the sake of Christ. But women did have food. And so they gave up food for the sake of Christ. Food became central to their spirituality, a fact explained by Caroline Bynum in *Holy Feast and Holy Fast*: "To religious women food was a way of controlling as well as renouncing both self and environment. But it was more. Food was flesh, and flesh was suffering and fertility. In renouncing ordinary food and directing their being toward the food that is Christ, women moved to God not merely by abandoning their flawed physicality but also by becoming the suffering and feeding humanity of the body on the cross, the food on the altar."[40]

Bynum says that medieval religious women accepted their presumed bodily nature and made use of it to aid their spiritual growth. She argues that since women understood themselves to be more bodily, they could more readily identify with the incarnate Christ than men could. Women in medieval cul-ture were seen as weak and dependent, as feeders and nurturers, so when medieval religious women took the Eucharist, they simply "became a fuller version of the food and flesh they were assumed by their culture to be."[41] Men, however, had to engage in some gender gymnastics. Because the male form was associated with spirit, men had to somewhat surrender their maleness and take on "feminine" physicality in order to more readily identify with the incarnate Christ. According to Bynum, while men were weighed down by the paradoxes of gender, women could embrace their gender and even move beyond it. "Religious women . . . saw in their own female bodies not

---

40. Bynum, *Holy Feast and Holy Fast*, 5.
41. Bynum, *Holy Feast and Holy Fast*, 289.

only a symbol of the humanness of both genders but also a symbol of—and a means of approach to—the humanity of God."[42] Since women considered their bodiliness representative of humanity, their bodiliness gave them an identity that transcended gender. Bynum concludes, "They saw themselves as human beings—fully spirit and fully flesh."[43]

Nuns and beguines faced many cultural constraints in the thirteenth and fourteenth centuries and found ways to creatively respond to them. One obstacle they had not yet had to face, however, was opposition to their choice to be celibate. Since the earliest days of the church, virgins had been honored and celibacy had been seen as a sign of one's commitment to Christ. All of that was about to change with the Protestant Reformation.

The Protestant Reformation and the Rejection of Celibacy

In 1517 the Reformer Martin Luther nailed his Ninety-Five Theses to the church door in Wittenberg. Like other reformers before him, many of whom had been monks and nuns, Luther was unhappy with abuses he saw in the church, like simony, indulgences, and misuse of power. Luther, however, became convinced that monasteries were part of what was wrong with the church. Thus, in 1523 he helped a group of nuns leave a convent. Luther found husbands for all the nuns who wanted to marry except one, Katharina von Bora, so she became his wife. He called her Katie, and they had six children together.

Martin and Katie's vision for married life was admirable. Married people, they believed, "can do no better work and do nothing more valuable either for God, for Christendom, for all the world, for themselves, and for their children than to bring up their children well."[44] Marriage, believed the Luthers, was a place where spouses and children were nurtured in the ways of God. The ordinary, day-to-day affairs of the household—raising children, growing food and producing meals, caring for sick and dying people—offered the best opportunities for growing in holiness.

For the Luthers to arrive at such a celebration of married life after a millennium of the church's preference for celibacy was remarkable. Many married people in the sixteenth century welcomed this abrupt change of emphasis. Interestingly, comparing the day-to-day lives of wives and mothers before and after the Protestant Reformation shows there are few differences. Women

42. Bynum, *Holy Feast and Holy Fast*, 196.
43. Bynum, *Holy Feast and Holy Fast*, 296.
44. Luther, "Sermon on the Estate of Marriage," 635.

cared for children and households before the Reformation, and they did so after it. However, the way Reformers spoke of the significance of marriage and parenting in the mission of the church likely changed women's experience of their domestic tasks. Before the Reformation, wives and mothers would have looked upon nuns, beguines, and mystics as the ones most capable of honoring God. After the Reformation, wives and mothers in the Western church could see their own lives as being just as capable of honoring God.

The role of the pastor's wife also became a new ministry opportunity for women. The early and medieval church had long taught that since celibacy was the ideal, the clergy should be celibate. Thus, Protestant pastors' wives had to chart new territory. Whereas the medieval church had often depicted women as temptresses, eager to draw honorable men away from the celibate life, the Protestant clergy saw their wives as partners in ministry. The role of the pastor's wife would continue to develop into the seventeenth century, particularly among the Puritans. Many Puritan clergy wives were literate, well versed in the Scriptures, and committed to the task of training up other women and children in the faith. They were true partners in ministry.

However, in their affirmation of marriage and parenthood, Luther and other Reformers came to denigrate celibacy. Luther called celibacy a "papal innovation contrary to God's eternal Word."[45] Many who joined the Protestant cause began to see "freeing the nuns" as a way of fighting for Protestantism. And sadly, the way these Protestants went about fighting for their cause was often not very Christlike. Some of these men and women harassed nuns and verbally and physically tried to force these women to abandon the celibate life and the Catholic faith with it.

Clearly, then, the Protestant emphasis on marriage was a mixed bag. On the one hand, married people could more fully conceive of their domestic life as being sanctified and integral to the mission of the church. On the other hand, nuns faced persecution and sometimes even exile and physical harm. Throughout the sixteenth century, Protestants continued to oppose monastic life, and Catholics continued to support it. Women could find in Protestantism a hearty embrace of their roles as wives and mothers, but if they felt called to a celibate life, there was no place for them. For several hundred years, single women in the Protestant world with a missional calling had no opportunity to exercise that calling. This situation finally began to change with the women's missionary movement of the nineteenth century. Chapter 8 discusses the stories of missionary women, but for now, this chapter closes with some reflections on the contributions beguines and mystics made to the church.

45. Luther, "Exhortation to All Clergy," 40.

Conclusion

During the thirteenth century, there was a great flourishing of options for religious life, and women found many new opportunities for religious leadership. A central concern of church reformers in the Middle Ages was imitating Christ and living like the apostles. Many in the women's religious movement embraced this *vita apostolica*. They gave away their personal belongings and took up a life of serving sick people and those with leprosy. "Whatever you do for the least of these, you do for me" was constantly on their lips. However, some priests and monks were uncomfortable with beguines and other women religious wandering around town outside a convent, so claustration was increasingly enforced in the thirteenth century. Beguines in Belgium retained their freedom, but other women throughout Europe were integrated into established religious orders. For some women, this severely hampered their ability to pursue the mission they believed God had called them to. Moreover, with the growing emphasis on the priesthood and the rise of the Franciscan friars, some women religious saw their own prestige and authority in society wane.

Even though claustration made some previous forms of mission impossible, women found new ways of devoting themselves to God and serving their neighbor. Some began to see food as a way to honor their call to poverty. They fasted, gave away their food, and developed even deeper dependence on the spiritual food of the Eucharist. Some women began to have visions and to write about these visions, often in their mother tongue rather than in Latin. Their writings formed some of the first vernacular literature in their regions. Priests who served them shared their visionary writings with others, promoting them as a way of encouraging the faithful.

Mysticism in this period was a predominantly female phenomenon and became an important avenue for women's religious leadership. It enabled women to serve as counselors, teachers, mediators, and theologians. Moreover, the theological shift in emphasis from Christ's kingship to his bodily humanity was stimulated in large part by women's visions of the Eucharist, the Christ child, and the man Jesus.

PART 3

WOMEN'S LEADERSHIP

SINCE THE

REFORMATION

6

Women Preachers
in America

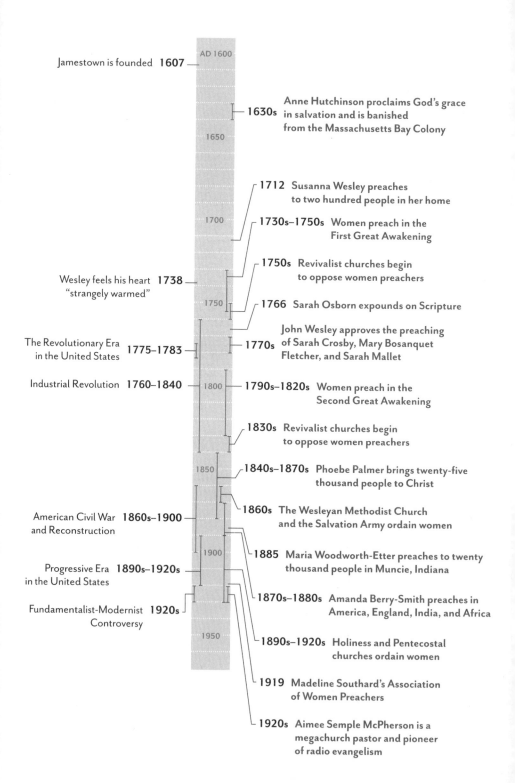

Jamestown is founded **1607**

AD 1600

1630s Anne Hutchinson proclaims God's grace in salvation and is banished from the Massachusetts Bay Colony

1650

1712 Susanna Wesley preaches to two hundred people in her home

1700

1730s–1750s Women preach in the First Great Awakening

1750s Revivalist churches begin to oppose women preachers

Wesley feels his heart **1738** "strangely warmed"

1750

1766 Sarah Osborn expounds on Scripture

The Revolutionary Era in the United States **1775–1783**

1770s John Wesley approves the preaching of Sarah Crosby, Mary Bosanquet Fletcher, and Sarah Mallet

Industrial Revolution **1760–1840**

1800

1790s–1820s Women preach in the Second Great Awakening

1830s Revivalist churches begin to oppose women preachers

1850

1840s–1870s Phoebe Palmer brings twenty-five thousand people to Christ

1860s The Wesleyan Methodist Church and the Salvation Army ordain women

American Civil War **1860s–1900** and Reconstruction

1900

1885 Maria Woodworth-Etter preaches to twenty thousand people in Muncie, Indiana

Progressive Era **1890s–1920s** in the United States

1870s–1880s Amanda Berry-Smith preaches in America, England, India, and Africa

Fundamentalist-Modernist **1920s** Controversy

1950

1890s–1920s Holiness and Pentecostal churches ordain women

1919 Madeline Southard's Association of Women Preachers

1920s Aimee Semple McPherson is a megachurch pastor and pioneer of radio evangelism

So far this book has described women's leadership in the early and medieval church. This chapter turns to women in the United States who took up the public ministry of preaching. As various religious awakenings swept the country, new opportunities for public preaching appeared for women. Between 1740 and 1845, there were over a hundred women preachers in America and twice that many in England.[1] Thousands more have followed in their footsteps. This chapter tells the stories of a number of these women and their contributions to the spread of the gospel, ending with a discussion of Aimee Semple McPherson, one of America's first megachurch pastors. Throughout American history, women preachers have encountered gender-based obstacles, particularly the accusation of being "Jezebels." Faced with cultural opposition and their own self-doubt, many nineteenth-century women compared themselves to Jonah, fleeing God's call. Ultimately, however, through prayer and reliance on Scripture, they found the confidence and courage to answer God's call to preach.

Women in the Colonial Era

The earliest Puritan settlers of the American colonies required women to keep silent in church but allowed women to teach in their homes. The idea of spiritual equality at home led some women to question their silent position in church. Although they did not call themselves ministers, these women did claim spiritual authority that drew listeners to their home-based religious meetings. Most of these women were wealthy and educated and perhaps felt their elevated social status afforded them leverage to speak out on what they perceived as inconsistencies or problems in the church. Anne Hutchinson (1591–1643), the most famous of these women, hosted large groups in her home in the 1630s and expounded on Scripture. The wife of a wealthy merchant, Hutchinson was bold enough to challenge aspects of Puritan doctrine, which she claimed were too legalistic and works-based, and to proclaim the role of God's grace in salvation. Moreover, she claimed

1. Brekus, *Strangers and Pilgrims*, 3, 133.

that God had spoken to her in a personal revelation. Her behavior was too much for colonial officials. They brought her to trial, excommunicated her, and banished her from the Massachusetts Bay Colony. Hutchinson, her husband, and some of her followers established a community in what later became Rhode Island.[2]

After the excommunication of Hutchinson, the Puritan church began to draw "even sharper divisions between the clergy and the laity."[3] The laity, both men and women, saw their capacity to speak, exhort, or testify in church severely diminished. The clergy held almost total power over religious services and discipline cases.

The Quakers—in part because they did not have a separate class of clergy—more readily accepted that women could be called by God to expound on Scripture. The Quaker church service was a quiet gathering of believers. If anyone had received a word from God, they were supposed to stand up and tell the congregation what God had revealed to them. Women as well as men could receive a message from God. However, the Quakers were viewed as radicals and faced heavy opposition, and their view on women speaking in church was a minority view.[4]

Increased Opportunities for Women in the First Great Awakening

The First Great Awakening was a religious revival movement that swept across England and the US colonies starting in the 1730s. Women played a huge role in the movement. As Catherine Brekus says, "For the first time in American history, large numbers of evangelical women tried to forge a lasting tradition of female ministry. Ultimately they failed, but for a few brief years during the 1740s and 1750s, it almost seemed possible to imagine a church where women as well as men would be free to speak in public—a church where there would be 'neither male nor female.'"[5] Women were present at the camp meetings, where they testified and exhorted in front of large groups of men and women. "As defined in the eighteenth century, an 'exhorter' was an informal evangelist who publicly admonished or encouraged others to repent."[6]

Because of the revival emphasis on religious experience, individuals, no matter their level of education, could claim spiritual authority based on the encounters they had with God. Sarah Edwards, wife of the revivalist preacher

2. Brekus, *Strangers and Pilgrims*, 28–32.
3. Brekus, *Strangers and Pilgrims*, 33.
4. Brekus, *Strangers and Pilgrims*, 29.
5. Brekus, *Strangers and Pilgrims*, 26.
6. Brekus, *Strangers and Pilgrims*, 48.

Jonathan Edwards, described her personal conversion experience as being "overcome" by God to the point that she felt liberated from her fears, anxieties, and even her identity as a woman. All that mattered was her identity in Christ.[7] Once revivalists began valuing an individual's experience with God, social distinctions of race, class, and sex began to melt away. Brekus writes, "Middle class merchants, poor farmers, free blacks, slaves, and Native Americans all mixed in the church pews."[8] With this emphasis on a common and equal identity in Christ, women found more opportunities for church leadership.

Obstacles for Women in the Revolutionary Era

Most of the American women who publicly testified and exhorted during the First Great Awakening belonged to denominations that considered themselves "called out" from the wider American culture, such as the Strict Congregationalists (called Separates) and the Baptists. These churches viewed their vocal women as one important sign that they were, in fact, distinct from the surrounding culture. During the 1750s, '60s, and '70s, however, the Separates and the Baptists didn't want to be thought of as fringe communities anymore. They wanted social approval, they wanted their pastors to be educated, they wanted to draw a sharper distinction between the clergy and the laity, and they wanted to show that they were orderly and respectable. Those desires took a heavy toll on women's leadership. Vocal women began to be seen as "disorderly women" who kept the church from its goal of social respectability.[9] "In a pattern that would appear over and over again in American history, evangelical women lost their public voice as a struggling, marginal sect matured into a prosperous denomination with all of the trappings of respectability, including a well-educated male clergy."[10]

Even during this time of curtailed opportunities, however, some women found ways to "rise to positions of unofficial leadership."[11] Sarah Osborn (1714–1796) was one such woman. In 1766, between 350 and 500 people—women, men, and children—flocked to her Rhode Island home each week to hear her expound on Scripture.[12] Osborn had begun holding informal prayer meetings for women, but news of her skillful teaching spread. Clergy

7. Brekus, *Strangers and Pilgrims*, 42.
8. Brekus, *Strangers and Pilgrims*, 37.
9. Juster, *Disorderly Women*, 1–2, 128–29.
10. Brekus, *Strangers and Pilgrims*, 66.
11. Brekus, *Strangers and Pilgrims*, 75.
12. Brekus, *Strangers and Pilgrims*. See also Brekus, *Sarah Osborn's World*.

were uncomfortable with Osborn's instruction of adult men, but Osborn insisted she did not preach; she only humbly answered whatever questions men asked her.

Women Preachers in the Second Great Awakening

At the turn of the nineteenth century, America experienced another series of revivals known as the Second Great Awakening. During this time, industrialization and economic prosperity eroded the shared labor of subsistence farming. This economic change helped form a developing concept of "separate spheres" for men and women. According to separate spheres ideology, men's roles were performed chiefly in public institutions, such as politics and business, while women's roles were limited to domestic duties in the home.[13]

The gendered division of labor, and women's resultant separation from what society perceived as impure or "worldly" affairs, gave rise to the notion of women's moral superiority over men. This shift represented a massive change from the view of women that had dominated most of church history—namely, that women were "daughters of Eve" and were more susceptible to temptation. In the nineteenth century, women began to be thought of as naturally chaste, pure, submissive, and not interested in sex. They were seen as "angels of the house" who promoted and protected their families' virtue by caring for their well-being, educating children, and improving society through positive moral influence.[14] Because Queen Victoria reigned during this time in England (1837–1901), this vision of womanhood is often described as Victorian.

Some White evangelical women embraced society's view of themselves as mothers in order to justify their public preaching. These women argued that just as they instructed children in virtue at home, so they could also instruct congregants in virtue at church. Whereas women in the First Great Awakening had often felt their feminine identity fading away through revival experiences, women in the Second Great Awakening deliberately embraced their gender. These women called themselves "Mothers of Israel."[15]

Women's participation in churches was typically more welcome in the North than it was in the South, largely because the practice of slavery reinforced the subordination of women. In proslavery arguments, Southern ministers argued that just as God ordained that man was the head of woman, so God ordained that a master was the head of his slaves. A man was endowed

13. Ryan, *Cradle of the Middle Class*, 189–91.
14. Bloch, *Gender and Morality*, 143–49.
15. Brekus, *Strangers and Pilgrims*, 152–53.

with the responsibility to restrain the sinful and impulsive natures of his wife and slaves.[16]

In the North, the White churches most open to the leadership of women were the Freewill Baptists, Christian Connection, and Methodists.[17] Among Methodists, there was precedent for women's leadership in America because John Wesley had welcomed women to serve as class leaders in England; he had even allowed Sarah Crosby, Mary Bosanquet Fletcher, and Sarah Mallet to preach in the 1770s.[18] In 1712, Wesley's own mother, Susanna, had developed a spontaneous preaching ministry for two hundred people when her husband was out of town, and she welcomed neighbors to join the Wesley evening prayer time.[19] As the Methodist movement continued to expand in America, women found a space for leadership.

In Methodist, Baptist, and Christian Connection churches, "the distinctions of race, class, and sex were less important than whether or not one had been 'saved.'"[20] These churches considered themselves family and promoted sibling-type relationships of "brother" and "sister" to guide their interactions. Abigail Roberts (1791–1841) was an impressive preacher during this period. "So many converts came to her meetings that she eventually organized four new Christian Connection churches."[21] Rebecca Chaney Miller (1814–1844) traveled as a preacher in Ohio, Pennsylvania, and Virginia. "When she died in 1844 at the age of forty, she was memorialized in the Christian press as a devoted female laborer who had enthralled 'thousands' with her 'flow of eloquence.'"[22]

16. McCurry, "Two Faces of Republicanism," 1253.

17. "The churches that were established by law, or only recently disestablished, tended to be the most opposed to female preaching [i.e., Episcopalian, Dutch Reformed, and Congregationalist churches]. In other words, the most wealthy, powerful, and 'respectable' churches were the least likely to allow women to speak publicly." Brekus, *Strangers and Pilgrims*, 125.

18. "Classes" were small groups of people that would meet weekly so members could encourage one another in the pursuit of holiness. Each class had a class leader who would direct the conversation and serve as a role model for the others.

19. She explains the situation in a letter to her husband:

This was the beginning of my present practice. Other people's coming and joining with us was merely accidental. [One] lad told his parents: they first desired to be admitted; then others that heard of it begged leave also: so our company increased to about thirty, and it seldom exceeded forty last winter. . . . With those few neighbors that then came to me, I discoursed more freely and affectionately. I chose the best and most awakening sermons we have. And I spent somewhat more time with them in such exercises, without being careful about the success of my undertaking. Since this, our company increased every night; for I dare deny none that ask admittance. Last Sunday I believe we had above two hundred. And yet many went away for want of room to stand. February 6, 1711/1712. (Wesley, *Works of John Wesley*, 1:385–86)

20. Brekus, *Strangers and Pilgrims*, 11.

21. Brekus, *Strangers and Pilgrims*, 196–97.

22. Brekus, *Strangers and Pilgrims*, 142.

The story of preacher Elleanor Knight (1799–?) is especially moving. When Knight began exhorting in her church, her husband grew "increasingly resentful of her spiritual authority" and ordered her to stop.[23] She complied, even though she knew she would be "quenching the Spirit." In 1830, a series of tragedies convinced Knight that God was punishing her for her refusal to preach. Shortly after giving birth to her fourth child, Knight discovered that her husband was having an affair. Then her newborn and her two-year-old son died. Knight continued to attend church for consolation, but in 1832 a male deacon rebuked her for attempting to exhort the congregation. After these trials, Knight finally left her abusive, alcoholic husband and her church to find a new congregation. She discovered a Freewill Baptist congregation, where she began leading weekly meetings. She would go on to preach throughout Massachusetts, Connecticut, New Hampshire, and Vermont.

Most nineteenth-century women preachers were from the lower or middle class, but Harriet Livermore (1788–1868) was from the upper class. In 1827, Livermore preached to the US Congress. "Preaching without notes for more than an hour and a half, she admonished, instructed, and beseeched her listeners until many of them began to weep."[24] But President John Quincy Adams cruelly accused her of preaching out of "vanity and love of fame."[25]

Black women preachers faced even more obstacles than White women. Rebecca Jackson (1795–1871) encountered threats of physical violence because of her race. A group of Methodist ministers once described to her the various ways they could kill her: by stoning, burning, or throwing her in a barrel driven through with spikes and rolling her down a hill. Jackson received visions from God that gave her strength and peace in the midst of danger.[26]

Jarena Lee (1783–1864) was the first woman authorized to preach in the African Methodist Episcopal (AME) church. In 1811, Lee confessed to founding bishop of the AME Richard Allen that she believed God had called her to preach, but Allen told her that God did not accept women preachers. Several years later, Lee noticed that a new minister was stumbling in his sermon, and he grew so nervous that he stopped preaching. Lee advanced to the pulpit and picked up where he had ended, delivering a sermon so powerful that Allen, who was in attendance, could not deny her gifts. With Allen's blessing, Lee began her career as a "traveling exhorter," speaking to both Black and White audiences.[27]

23. Brekus, *Strangers and Pilgrims*, 163.
24. Brekus, *Strangers and Pilgrims*, 2.
25. Quoted in Brekus, *Strangers and Pilgrims*, 3.
26. Brekus, *Strangers and Pilgrims*, 184.
27. Andrews, *Sisters of the Spirit*, 6; Collier-Thomas, *Daughters of Thunder*, 45.

Zilpha Elaw (1790–1873) also experienced a clear call from God to preach and, like Jarena Lee, didn't answer that call immediately. When she got sick, she interpreted her sickness as a warning from God. She heeded the warning and set off as a traveling evangelist. She was a free Black woman, and she risked being kidnapped and enslaved as she traveled through the South to preach to enslaved people.

Preaching as a "Cross to Bear"

It was not easy to be a woman preacher in the early nineteenth century. These women were accused of being "Jezebels," for why else, argued their detractors, would they put their bodies and voices on display for onlookers? Critics also accused them of being vain and seeking attention. Yet the women themselves had experienced a call through the Spirit's prodding or through a divinely sent dream. These women didn't want to be preachers. They knew they would face ridicule. They had self-doubt. They didn't answer the call immediately. They often compared themselves to Jeremiah, "who resisted his call to preach because he was just a 'child,'" or Jonah, who "fled from the presence of the Lord" and later was so distraught that he just wanted to die.[28] But then they experienced some form of suffering that convinced them that they were "quenching the Spirit" by refusing to preach and that this was displeasing God. "Unanimously, female preachers testified that they had suffered either physical ailments or 'severe mental suffering' because of their sinful attempts to quench the spirit."[29] After such an experience of suffering, they obeyed God's call and began preaching.

The women who preached in the early nineteenth century were not rebels. They were faithful women who experienced a call from God and depended on God to sustain them through their preaching ministry, which many of them viewed as "a cross to bear."[30] Many of them used spiritual autobiography to counter social criticism.[31] In their autobiographies, they referred to Phoebe, Priscilla, Deborah, Miriam, and Esther in order to defend their call to preach. They were captivated by Jesus's interactions with the woman at the well, and they reveled in the fact that in making Mary Magdalene the first witness of the resurrection, God also made Mary Magdalene the first Christian preacher.

Women preachers of the Second Great Awakening found precedent in Scripture for their role as preachers, yet they were largely unaware of women in

28. Brekus, *Strangers and Pilgrims*, 172, 86.
29. Brekus, *Strangers and Pilgrims*, 190–91.
30. Brekus, *Strangers and Pilgrims*, 166.
31. Brekus, *Strangers and Pilgrims*, 166.

the First Great Awakening who, like them, had struggled with a divine call to preach in the midst of cultural opposition. "Cut off from their collective past, women struggled to defend their right to preach without ever realizing that others had fought the same battles before them."[32]

Backlash toward and Erasure of Women Preachers in the Mid-nineteenth Century

Just as women were squeezed out of leadership roles following the First Great Awakening, so too their voices were silenced following the Second Great Awakening. The same pastors who had supported women only a few years earlier turned against these women so that "by 1830 . . . not a single female preacher remained in the Methodist Episcopal Church."[33] What happened? First, these churches wanted to distance themselves from the women's rights movement, a movement that was pushing for women's suffrage, which the revivalist churches opposed. Supporting women's preaching seemed too close to supporting women's suffrage. Second, revivalist churches began to require clergy to be educated, and opportunities for women's education were limited. Third, the churches wanted to be socially respectable, and women preachers weren't considered respectable.

Sally Thompson suffered backlash when the Methodist church began to turn against women. She had been preaching for nine years, but when she moved from Massachusetts to New York, the clergy in her new town said she was too "masculine" and asked that she step down from itinerant preaching. When she refused, they succeeded in getting her "excommunicated from her church on the grounds of insubordination. . . . Despite Thompson's popularity in the pulpit, she had become an outcast."[34] When Thompson later wrote her memoir, she quoted Matthew 5:11, "Blessed are ye, when men shall revile you, and persecute you, and shall say all manner of evil against you falsely for my sake."[35]

As church leaders turned against the women preachers in their midst, they also began to rewrite their own history. They erased references to women preachers in their memoirs and church documents. "For example, when David Marks published the first edition of his memoir in 1831, he mentioned meeting some of the most popular female preachers of his time, including Susan Humes, Clarissa Danforth, Almira Bullock, Dolly Quinby, and 'Sister' Wiard. Yet in 1846, when

32. Brekus, *Strangers and Pilgrims*, 15.
33. Brekus, *Strangers and Pilgrims*, 295.
34. Brekus, *Strangers and Pilgrims*, 271.
35. Quoted in Brekus, *Strangers and Pilgrims*, 305.

his wife, Marilla, published a posthumous edition of his memoir, she removed all the references—no matter how small—to the women her husband had once defended."[36] Another minister, Jabez King, published a memoir in which he pretended that he and a male colleague had been the sole people responsible for a revival in New York, even though Nancy Cram (1776–1816) had been the one to invite them after she had already led hundreds to Christ. It was because she couldn't baptize these new believers that she had asked King to come. When King first wrote about this experience, he included "sister Nancy" in the story line. "By 1845, however . . . he took full credit for the revival she had led."[37]

During this same period, Black women preachers banded together to try to get the African Methodist Episcopal church to license women preachers. But the bishops repeatedly turned down their requests.[38]

When their churches opposed them in the 1830s and 1840s, women preachers often became missionaries or Sunday school teachers or married a clergyman or a missionary in order to continue their ministry.[39] Others turned to motherhood, and still others just kept on preaching despite the obstacles. "In total, at least thirty-six women continued to labor as local or itinerant preachers during the 1830s."[40]

Women Preachers in the Holiness Movement

Just as the First and Second Great Awakenings had prompted women to preach in America, so too did the Holiness movement, which was a renewal movement that developed out of American Methodism. Holiness Christians were deeply committed to social justice, and many "also defended the equality of women and their right to public ministry."[41] Phoebe Palmer (1807–1874) was "the leading theologian of the Holiness movement" and one of its most gifted preachers.[42] Palmer taught that entire sanctification—which John Wesley had said could happen over time—could in fact take place in an instant. Through this theological development, she, "more than any other, created the Holiness Movement out of Wesleyan Methodism."[43] Palmer and her sister held Tuesday prayer meetings, at which Palmer taught her ideas of holiness

36. Brekus, *Strangers and Pilgrims*, 296.
37. Brekus, *Strangers and Pilgrims*, 297.
38. Brekus, *Strangers and Pilgrims*, 296.
39. Brekus, *Strangers and Pilgrims*, 300.
40. Brekus, *Strangers and Pilgrims*, 302.
41. "I Received My Commission."
42. Knight, *From Aldersgate to Azusa Street*, 59.
43. Spickard and Cragg, *Global History of Christians*, 290.

to other women. Pretty soon men started coming to the Tuesday meetings as well. Hundreds of people crowded into her sister's house to hear Palmer expound on the Scriptures during the 1840s.

Palmer's skill as a revivalist preacher has been compared to that of Charles Finney.[44] In 1857 she went on a preaching tour through Canada and Britain. She inspired Catherine Booth, cofounder of the Salvation Army, to become a preacher and to write a book in favor of women's preaching called *Female Ministry*.[45] When Palmer died in 1874, "she was credited with having brought some 25,000 people to Christ for salvation."[46] Many other women in the Holiness Movement also drew people to Christ through their preaching.

What was it about the Holiness movement that led to an increase in women's preaching? For one thing, both men and women could experience entire sanctification and were called to testify about their experiences. Second, Holiness Christians believed that sanctification redefined who a person was. No longer were sanctified people primarily marked by sin, their past, or the norms of society. Rather, their identity in Christ was what mattered. This emphasis on sanctification and the death of self relativized the gender norms of American culture and empowered women preachers in the Holiness tradition. Holiness Christians also highlighted passages of Scripture that displayed women in ministry, and they believed that the Holy Spirit continued to be poured out on both "sons and daughters," just like on the day of Pentecost.[47]

Amanda Berry Smith (1837–1915) was one of the many women who experienced entire sanctification and went on to testify about it. Her story is remarkable. She was born into slavery. Her father worked hard to free his family from slavery, and her parents instilled in her a love for God. By the end of her life, Smith had become a globe-trotting evangelist, preaching throughout America, England, India, and Africa. "I often say to people that I have the right to shout more than some folks," Smith said. "I have been bought twice and set free twice, and so I feel I have a good right to shout hallelujah!"[48]

Overcoming Doubt through Prayer and Bible Study

Despite the support for women preachers in the Holiness tradition, individual women continued to struggle with their call to ministry, just as women had

44. Leclerc, "Phoebe Palmer," 93.
45. Hardesty, Dayton, and Dayton, "Women in the Holiness Movement," 233–34. Palmer herself also wrote a book defending women preachers called *The Promise of the Father*.
46. Tucker and Liefeld, *Daughters of the Church*, 263.
47. S. Stanley, *Holy Boldness*, 7.
48. Quoted in Hannula, *Radiant*, 207.

in the Second Great Awakening. They still had to face the reality in the surrounding culture that women preachers were seen as improper. Sometimes
their fellow Christians and family members tried to sabotage their preaching.[49]
Understandably, many women internalized this widespread opposition in the
form of self-doubt. Mary Cole (1853–1940) responded to her call with excuses:
"Lord," she prayed, "I am not talented; my education is so meagre; there is
no one to go with me; and, besides, I have a stammering tongue." Cole heard
the Lord assure her, "I will go with you myself."[50] Even after she accepted her
call and went on to become an effective preacher and one of the founders of
the Church of God, people continued to reject her. Some threw eggs at her
head and burned hot peppers near where she was preaching.[51] One time Cole
encountered an angry mob that fired shots at her.[52]

Lucy Drake Osborn (1844–1922) was able to counter opposition because
she had taken time to study Scripture. She had been raised in a family that
opposed women's preaching but became part of a Methodist community
that affirmed it. She wrote in her diary, "I want to understand more about
women speaking in meeting."[53] Osborn combed the Scriptures for references
to the work of women and asked for God's wisdom in interpreting them.
She wrestled with this conflict for six months before settling with "perfect
satisfaction" that "it was God's will that women should prophesy."[54] Osborn
wrote, "To question it again has never come to my mind. God had decided it
for me."[55] She went on to lead many to Christ and even to change her dad's
mind about women preachers. Although he had once opposed them, he later
declared that "the church must have been mistaken in its interpretation of
Paul's words about women's speaking; for certainly God would not convert
so many souls through them if they were working contrary to His will."[56]

Maria Woodworth-Etter (1844–1924) initially attended a church that opposed women's preaching, but she herself still experienced a call to preach. At
the same time, she worried that obeying this call "would subject me to ridicule
and contempt among my friends and kindred."[57] Ultimately, she turned to the
Bible, where she found "Miriam, Deborah, Hannah, Hulda, Anna, Phoebe,
Narcissus, Tryphena, Persis, Julia, and the Marys, and the sisters who were

---

49. S. Stanley, *Holy Boldness*, 116.
50. M. Cole, *Trials and Triumphs*, 51.
51. J. Stanley, "Reclaiming the Church of God."
52. S. Stanley, *Holy Boldness*, 148.
53. Osborn, *Heavenly Pearls*, quoted in S. Stanley, *Holy Boldness*, 116.
54. Osborn, *Heavenly Pearls*, 70.
55. Osborn, *Heavenly Pearls*, 70.
56. Osborn, *Heavenly Pearls*, 139.
57. Pope-Levison, *Turn the Pulpit Loose*, 105.

co-workers with Paul in the gospel."[58] These women in the Bible reassured her that God *was* calling her to preach, so she began to travel throughout the Midwest as an itinerant evangelist. Soon she was leading three services a day for weeks at a time in a tent that seated eight thousand. After a period of worship and prayer, she would deliver an hour-long sermon, punctuated by ecstatic gestures, clapping, and stomping. She ended her sermons with an emotion-charged appeal for people to repent, inviting them to the altar, where they experienced dramatic conversions. Over twenty thousand people traveled to see her preach outside Muncie, Indiana, in 1885. She accumulated such influence that she has been compared to Dwight Moody, and her ecstatic preaching style influenced the development of Pentecostalism.[59]

Maternal Martyrdom

Cultural opposition and self-doubt made many women hesitant to answer the call to preach, but several women also saw their love for their children as an obstacle to fulfilling God's call. Maria Woodworth-Etter wrote in her autobiography,

> Several ministers whom I had never seen before told me, at different times that God was calling me to the ministry, and that I would have to go. I said, "If I were a man I would love to work for Jesus." They told me I had a work to do which no man could do. . . . I said, "O Lord! I cannot take Willie [her son] with me, nor can I leave him behind." *Then the Lord saw fit to take him out of the way*; so he laid his hand on my darling little boy, and in a few days took him home to heaven.[60]

Five of Woodworth-Etter's six children died young. She came to believe that through their deaths God was paving the way for her to fulfill his call to preach. After their deaths, when only sixteen-year-old Lizzie remained, Woodworth-Etter said, "And now the great desire of my heart was to work for Jesus."[61] Occasionally, her old doubts about being ridiculed plagued her, but by relying on God, she was able to become a powerful preacher.

A similar connection between the death of children and fulfilling God's call to preach appears in the life of Phoebe Palmer. When she was a young

58. Pope-Levison, *Turn the Pulpit Loose*, 106.
59. Pope-Levison, *Building the Old-Time Religion*, 36–42.
60. Pope-Levison, *Turn the Pulpit Loose*, 99 (emphasis added).
61. Woodworth-Etter, *The Life and Experiences of Maria B. Woodworth*, quoted in Pope-Levison, *Turn the Pulpit Loose*, 99.

mother, three of her children died. As she mourned these children, she became convinced that God had taken them from her because she was too devoted to them. "After my loved ones were snatched away, I saw that I had concentrated my time and attentions far too exclusively, to the neglect of the religious activities demanded."[62]

Similarly, Elleanor Knight, who preached in the Second Great Awakening, interpreted the death of her two children as God's chastisement for her own disobedience to God's call to preach. She believed she had "quenched the spirit" and, like other nineteenth-century women, understood the tragedy that ensued as the result of her own disobedience. In telling this part of Knight's story, historian Catherine Brekus says that Knight's "reasoning was disturbingly simple. An angry God would never have taken away her children if she had been a more obedient Christian."[63] For Knight, however, the death of her children did end up catalyzing her obedience.

It is difficult to know what to make of these stories. Knight, Palmer, and Woodworth-Etter prayerfully came to the conclusion that at least one of the reasons God had taken their children from them was to free them for a life of preaching. Like Brekus, people today might find this reasoning "disturbingly simple." However, there was certainly precedent for this kind of reasoning. In the fourth century, Melania the Elder (see chap. 2) left her son, who was between the ages of twelve and seventeen, in the care of a guardian in Rome so that she could journey to Jerusalem, where she founded a monastery and lived for the next twenty-seven years. In seventeenth-century France, Marie de l'Incarnation (see chap. 8) left her son, age eleven, with guardians so that she could enter a monastery.[64] Both Melania and Marie were criticized by their contemporaries for abandoning their children, but Paulinus, a church father, praised Melania for her choice. According to Paulinus, Melania "loved her child by neglecting him and kept him by relinquishing him."[65] Or as Jesus says in Matthew 16:25, "Whoever wants to save their life will lose it, but whoever loses their life for me will find it."

Perhaps the best way to understand these women is to see them as martyrs, as people who experienced a death of self. Through that death of self, they came to believe that God was asking them to surrender what was most

---

62. Wheatley, *Life and Letters*, 26.

63. Brekus, *Strangers and Pilgrims*, 165.

64. Looking back on it, she wrote, "The interior voice that followed me everywhere said, 'Hurry, it's time; it's not good for you to be in the world any longer.' Putting my son in the arms of God and the holy Virgin, I left him, and my aged father also, who wept in lamentation." Davis, *Women on the Margins*, 63.

65. Paulinus, *Epistle* 29.9 (in *Letters of St. Paulinus*, Walsh, 109).

precious to them: their children. They came to believe that God could take better care of their children than they could. This realization freed them to put themselves completely at God's service, to do what he asked of them. They endured ridicule in their own day, and today people may still puzzle over their vision of God and his call. But it does seem clear that surrendering children to the care of God has been a form of maternal martyrdom throughout the history of the church.

In 1927, Methodist preacher Madeline Southard (1877–1967) articulated a theology of maternal martyrdom in her book *The Attitude of Jesus toward Woman*. She wrote, "Women should let nothing, not even their devotion to their offspring, come before their responsibility as persons to a personal God."[66] Jesus, said Southard, asked women "to subordinate their feminine interests to their interests as citizens of the kingdom of God."[67] But churches, just like the world of Jesus's first followers, still tended to idealize women as *mothers* rather than seeing them first as *persons*. Southard worked for women's rights in church and society. In 1919 she founded the interdenominational Association of Women Preachers. She was ordained in 1924 and "was in steady demand as a preacher and speaker throughout the Midwest."[68] Southard herself had chosen early on to turn away from marriage prospects and devote herself to doing something "great" for God.[69] Later in life, she struggled with an intense longing to be married and have children, so she knew firsthand what it was like to endure maternal martyrdom for the sake of Christ.

Aimee Semple McPherson

This chapter closes with Aimee Semple McPherson (1890–1944), one of the most significant preachers in American history. In the early 1920s, McPherson founded the Foursquare denomination, started a Bible college, pioneered the use of radio technology for evangelism, and launched the first megachurch, Angelus Temple.[70] Due to her musical and dramatic skills and her connections with Hollywood people, her Sunday services containing her "illustrated

---

66. Southard, *Attitude of Jesus*, 104.
67. Southard, *Attitude of Jesus*, 53. Southard elaborated on passages like Matt. 10:37 and Luke 14:26.
68. Du Mez, "Selfishness One Degree Removed," 21.
69. Du Mez, "Selfishness One Degree Removed," 17. Her longing for "greatness" and dedication to ministry are similar to how some nuns have approached their vocation. For example, see Prejean, *River of Fire*, 36.
70. Life Pacific College is still training men and women in a variety of fields and disciplines today.

sermons" could be quite theatrical.[71] Nevertheless, the focus was always on presenting a Bible story and preaching the gospel.[72] The fifty-three-hundred-seat church was filled every time the doors opened, three times each day, seven days a week. At one point, the church printed tickets and even reserved a section for first-time visitors to make sure those who had never heard the gospel would be able to get in.[73]

McPherson was the first woman to own and operate a Christian broadcasting network. She believed radio technology offered a way to get the gospel to people who couldn't come to church. Her voice became one of the most well known on the radio in her day.[74]

Another feature of McPherson's ministry was her insistence that inside the doors of Angelus Temple, there was to be no segregation by race or class; she expected Black, White, Latino/a, Asian, rich, and poor to sit, literally, side by side. Similarly, McPherson was deeply concerned for those whom society rejected. Recognizing struggles particular to women, she created a program that paired single pregnant women with older widows. Single mothers were social outcasts, and widows were often neglected. McPherson's approach provided care for both.[75] McPherson also organized and ran the largest food distribution in California during the Great Depression. Her church distributed more food than the government of Los Angeles.[76]

Despite the good work she was doing, McPherson faced opposition from some church and civic leaders who disapproved of her approach to ministry. People also smeared her reputation, in part because she was married three times. However, McPherson's first husband died when they were missionaries in China. Her second disapproved of her ministry, and when she wouldn't give it up, he sued for divorce on grounds of desertion.[77] Her third husband seems to have been an opportunist who took advantage of her loneliness and then divorced her when she "did not give him a large enough financial allowance" or a big enough role in the church.[78] The impact of her tragic marriages may be part of the explanation for why she loved to describe Christ as a perfect "husband" who would never desert his church.

McPherson became especially embroiled in controversy when she disappeared from Venice Beach in 1926 and reappeared in public five weeks later.

71. Maddux, "Feminized Gospel."
72. Sutton, *Aimee Semple McPherson*, 169.
73. Ambrose, "Aimee Semple McPherson," 109.
74. Sutton, *Aimee Semple McPherson*, 79.
75. Sutton, *Aimee Semple McPherson*, 63.
76. Sutton, *Aimee Semple McPherson*, 186–96.
77. Sutton, *Aimee Semple McPherson*, 58.
78. Sutton, *Aimee Semple McPherson*, 173.

She claimed she had been kidnapped, and her account of events never changed. Her church did receive multiple ransom notes, but people still accused her of making up the story for publicity or of having run away to have an affair.[79] However, no solid evidence for an affair has ever been found.

In some sense, there was no way McPherson could have lived a life without criticism. By being a woman with power, she stretched the bounds of what was considered socially acceptable. She may have intentionally chosen to preach on topics like servanthood and the church as the bride of Christ because these topics meshed well with her feminine identity, but preacher Robert Shuler and Los Angeles political leaders criticized her for being too emotional and seeking out fame. Kristy Maddux argues that in personifying the bride and the servant, McPherson was using "alternative personae" to the ones adopted by male fundamentalist preachers of the time, who "performed as sports heroes."[80] Her critics portrayed her as a "temptress" who lured gullible people away from the favored "masculine Christianity" of the day.[81] Had McPherson attempted to follow those masculine scripts, doubtless critics would have gone after her for breaking gender norms. Thus, argues Maddux, McPherson was caught in the same double bind that researchers have long noted exists for women: the double bind prevents women from being viewed as both good women and good leaders because the role requirements are mutually exclusive. Succeeding in one automatically means violating the other and opening oneself to criticism.[82]

Conclusion

McPherson's story illustrates several themes that have surfaced in this chapter. First, she faced opposition from civic leaders, other Christians, and even her own husband. Just as President John Quincy Adams had accused Harriet Livermore of preaching out of "vanity and love of fame," so Shuler accused

79. Sutton, *Aimee Semple McPherson*, 93, 99–100. In an incredible turn of events, rather than investigating the kidnapping, authorities quickly made McPherson the subject of a grand jury inquiry. She was accused of "criminal conspiracy" and bound over for trial. The charges were based primarily on one witness, who eventually turned out to be mentally unstable, and though the grand jury bound her over, the DA dropped the charges before the actual trial could start, stating he had been "duped" (Sutton, *Aimee Semple McPherson*, 136). McPherson's experience of becoming the target of attack when she herself had been the victim is known today as "testimonial injustice": some people's accounts of events are doubted because of their race or gender. See Fricker, *Epistemic Injustice*.
80. Maddux, "Feminized Gospel," 52.
81. Maddux, "Feminized Gospel," 60.
82. Dzubinski, Diehl, and Taylor, "Women's Ways of Leading," 236–37.

McPherson of the same.[83] And just like Elleanor Knight and other nineteenth-century preachers, McPherson faced opposition from her husband and was accused of sexual immorality.[84] She even faced physical threats, as earlier women preachers had.

Second, just like the nineteenth-century preachers who embraced society's view of them as "mothers" in order to justify their public preaching, McPherson used the gender scripts of the day to facilitate her ministry.[85] McPherson knew that her critics despised, for example, her marital history, yet she turned her marriage experience into a way to talk about the church as the bride of Christ, a relationship far superior to any human marriage. Her illustrated sermons allowed her to capitalize on her own natural dramatic flair, which her critics considered wholly unsuitable for church.[86] At the same time, the illustrated sermons were attractive to the people of Los Angeles, who were used to having Hollywood on their doorstep. Her ability to turn gender constraints into assets led her biographer, Matthew Sutton, to remark, "The methods by which McPherson's opponents attempted to discipline her, and the means she used to fight back, reveal how women in religious leadership have overcome seemingly insurmountable obstacles by transforming the very gender constructs that shackled them to patriarchy into keys for their liberation."[87]

McPherson was both an innovator and someone who was building on the work of women who preceded her. It is possible to trace a line of influence all the way from Phoebe Palmer (preacher-theologian of the Holiness movement) to Catherine Booth (cofounder of the Salvation Army) to Catherine's daughter Evangeline to Aimee McPherson. Palmer's preaching inspired Catherine Booth to answer the call to preach, and when McPherson was a little girl in southern Ontario, she likely witnessed the preaching of Evangeline Booth, who was a leader in the Canadian Salvation Army. At Angelus Temple, McPherson ended up using Salvation Army "lingo and maneuvers and exploited Evangeline Booth's notion of the illustrated sermon and the Army's custom of using dramas."[88] This lineage illustrates a theme demonstrated throughout this book. Whether they have been deacons, martyrs, patrons, or preachers, women have passed the baton of religious leadership from one generation to the next.

83. Quoted in Brekus, *Strangers and Pilgrims*, 3.
84. Brekus, *Strangers and Pilgrims*, 221.
85. Ambrose, "Aimee Semple McPherson," 111.
86. Maddux, "Feminized Gospel," 57.
87. Sutton, *Aimee Semple McPherson*, 149.
88. Blumhofer, *Aimee Semple McPherson*, 13.

Opinions regarding women's preaching remain divided in the United States today. In the late nineteenth and early twentieth centuries, many denominations began to allow women to preach and be ordained. The Wesleyan Methodists and the Salvation Army were the first to ordain women in the 1860s. Then came the Church of God, Evangelical Free Church in America, Pentecostal Holiness Church, Pilgrim Holiness Church, Pillar of Fire, Church of the Nazarene, Assemblies of God, and AME Zion Church in the 1890s and early 1900s. Some Baptist groups started ordaining women around this time as well. And of course, McPherson's Foursquare Church ordained women in the 1920s. Methodists and northern Presbyterians "gave women full ordination rights in 1956."[89] The Lutheran Church in America followed in 1970, and the Episcopal Church in 1976. Today, "about half of all American religious groups currently ordain women."[90] However, "the country's largest religious groups, the Catholic Church and the Southern Baptist Convention," do not.[91]

Whether ordained or not, women preachers have made substantial contributions to the spread of the gospel. Women found opportunities for preaching particularly in times of revival, like the First and Second Great Awakenings and the Holiness movement. The emphasis on religious experience and the movement of the Holy Spirit tended to relativize distinctions of race, class, and gender and to create opportunities for those on the margins to gain religious authority. When nineteenth-century women experienced the call to preach, nearly all of them "quenched the Spirit" for a time because of fear, uncertainty, or maternal obligations. Ultimately, however, the precedent of women's leadership in Scripture and the continual prodding of the Spirit in their hearts convinced them to fulfill God's call to preach.

89. Braude, *Sisters and Saints*, 99.
90. Braude, *Sisters and Saints*, 104.
91. Braude, *Sisters and Saints*, 104.

7

Social Justice
Activists

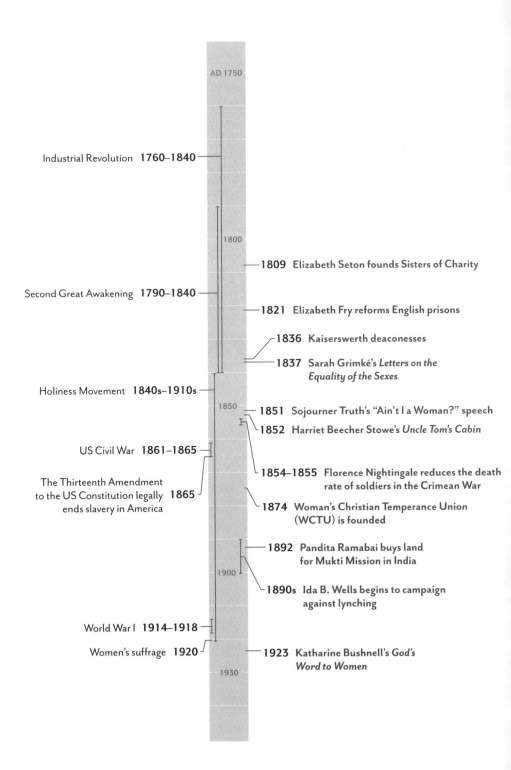

AD 1750

Industrial Revolution **1760–1840**

1800

1809 Elizabeth Seton founds Sisters of Charity

Second Great Awakening **1790–1840**

1821 Elizabeth Fry reforms English prisons

1836 Kaiserswerth deaconesses

1837 Sarah Grimké's *Letters on the Equality of the Sexes*

Holiness Movement **1840s–1910s**

1850

1851 Sojourner Truth's "Ain't I a Woman?" speech

1852 Harriet Beecher Stowe's *Uncle Tom's Cabin*

US Civil War **1861–1865**

The Thirteenth Amendment to the US Constitution legally ends slavery in America **1865**

1854–1855 Florence Nightingale reduces the death rate of soldiers in the Crimean War

1874 Woman's Christian Temperance Union (WCTU) is founded

1892 Pandita Ramabai buys land for Mukti Mission in India

1900

1890s Ida B. Wells begins to campaign against lynching

World War I **1914–1918**

Women's suffrage **1920**

1923 Katharine Bushnell's *God's Word to Women*

1930

As previous chapters have shown, women have always taken the lead in caring for people on the margins of society. In the early church, widows and deaconesses cared for sick people and distributed alms to poor people. In the medieval church, nuns and beguines helped develop hospitals and took care of people with leprosy. In some ways, then, the scores of nineteenth-century women who were active in caring for people on the margins of society were simply picking up the baton of women's religious leadership in caring for "the least of these."

But there were some major differences in the nineteenth and early twentieth centuries. First of all, colonialism and race-based slavery had created new disparities between various groups of people. In addition to the horrific ways that enslaved individuals suffered during this period, there were myriad other ways that the people in colonial lands suffered economically, politically, and culturally. They lost political sovereignty and were forced to trade away valuable natural resources. Western nations used social Darwinism—the theory that European races were superior to African and Asian races—to defend colonialism and to justify the imposition of Western culture in non-Western lands.

Another thing that made the nineteenth-century context different for women's relief work was that industrialization and urbanization brought new crowding to cities and exacerbated the gap between rich and poor. Just as some women whose families had benefited from economic advancement in the High Middle Ages felt a sense of guilt about their family's newfound wealth, so many nineteenth-century women felt obligated to use their wealth to help alleviate some of the pressing concerns of poor people living in urban centers. For some of these women, interest in social justice grew from religious conversion or from a desire to share with others the gospel healing they themselves had experienced. For others, interest in social justice flowed from personal tragedy or from the longing for God's will to be done "on earth as it is in heaven" (Matt. 6:10).

These women came from a variety of denominational backgrounds, social classes, and countries. Together, they formed what has been called a "global sisterhood." These women inspired one another in the various reforms they were pursuing, helped one another fundraise and brainstorm, and carried one another's stories across oceans. It would be impossible to tell all their stories in this chapter. What follows provides merely a window into the kinds of causes this global sisterhood pursued during the nineteenth and into the twentieth century.

The chapter starts by describing a few women who were active in education, prison reform, and nursing; then it looks at the temperance, social purity, and suffrage movements. Finally it examines abolition, anti-lynching, and the fight against racism. The following stories show how these women activists, like patrons, deacons, and nuns of earlier times, passed down the baton of religious leadership. Each generation built on the work of the previous generation in order to care for people on the margins of society.

Education, Prison Reform, and Nursing

Elizabeth Ann Seton (1774–1821) was the first American-born citizen to be canonized as a saint by the Catholic Church. She was raised as a high-society Episcopalian, but after her husband died, she became Catholic. In 1809 she accepted an invitation from a Catholic religious community in Maryland to start a school for girls. She also founded a community of nuns to care for poor people. Nuns had been at work in North America since the seventeenth century, but Seton's Sisters of Charity were the first community of nuns founded in America.

Nuns did a tremendous amount of work for the mission of the church in America. "In addition to their major work of teaching and nursing, nuns ran child-care facilities, orphanages, mental institutions, settlement houses, residences for working women and for single mothers, and homes for delinquent girls. Nuns oversaw an empire of interlocking institutions that constituted Catholic social services in most U.S. cities and towns."[1] Nuns in other countries did similar work in establishing schools and hospitals.[2]

Elizabeth Fry (1780–1845), a wealthy Quaker mother of eleven children, became known for her work to reform English prisons. When a friend told her about the horrible conditions in prison, she had to see for herself. She was appalled at what she found—those in prison sleeping on straw, women and children crammed into crowded prison cells. In 1817 she started a school for some of these children, and she began to teach some of the mothers to sew so they could have a way of supporting themselves when they got out

1. "In 1900, sisters operated 3,811 parochial (church-run) schools, 663 academies for girls (102 for boys), and 265 hospitals." Braude, *Sisters and Saints*, 72–73.
2. See chap. 8 of this book and Wall, *Into Africa*.

of prison. Other women joined her and formed the British Ladies' Society for Promoting the Reformation of Female Prisoners. When Fry noticed the horrible conditions prisoners faced while being transported to prisons, she worked to improve these conditions as well. Ultimately, her work led to new laws protecting prisoners in England.

A Lutheran couple in Germany named Theodore (1800–1864) and Friederike (1800–1842) Fliedner were inspired by the way Elizabeth Fry and the British women were caring for prisoners in England. The Fliedners wanted to give German women a similar opportunity to serve, but they also wanted to find a way for the German women to live in community while they were serving. What they ended up doing was reinventing the early church office of deaconess. They had traveled to Holland and had seen Mennonite deaconesses at work there. They had also seen Elizabeth Seton's Sisters of Charity caring for poor and sick people throughout Germany. With all these influences percolating within them, the Fliedners established a complex of institutions (a hospital, schools, an orphanage) in their town of Kaiserswerth, Germany. They also built a home for the deaconesses to live in while they were serving as teachers and nurses. The Kaiserswerth deaconesses prayed together every morning and evening. Many of them came from the peasant class, and all of them lived together in community. But rather than taking lifelong vows like Catholic nuns did, the Kaiserswerth deaconesses committed to serving for five years, and even during those five years, they were free to leave to get married.[3] Germans were generally opposed to unmarried women working in the public mission of the church. It may be that the distinctive uniform of the Kaiserswerth deaconesses—dark blue dresses and white bonnets—facilitated their acceptance in society, particularly because their bonnets were "soon out of style and may have made them less attractive to men."[4]

The deaconess community at Kaiserswerth grew quickly. "Within three decades, Kaisersworth was sponsoring more than four hundred deaconesses and served some one hundred outstations throughout the world."[5] By the 1880s, "there were at least 50 motherhouses in the Kaiserswerth Union with over 14,000 deaconesses."[6] There were also deaconesses unaffiliated with

3. Another difference between nuns and deaconesses is that deaconesses did not take a vow of poverty. They could keep their personal belongings. Deaconesses were also not as strictly cloistered as medieval nuns and could leave the motherhouse to nurse a parent, if need be. Olson, *Deacons and Deaconesses*, 231.

4. Olson, *Deacons and Deaconesses*, 203.

5. Tucker and Liefeld, *Daughters of the Church*, 253.

6. Olson, *Deacons and Deaconesses*, 210. As Methodists and Baptists heard about Lutheran deaconesses, they began to institute the office too.

Kaiserswerth who served in France, Switzerland, and the Netherlands.[7] Many of the founders of these communities saw themselves as picking up the baton of religious leadership from Elizabeth Fry.

In England, William and Catherine Booth (1829–1890) founded the Salvation Army, and Ellen Raynard (1810–1879) established the Raynard Mission, both of which trained women to be evangelists and to serve the needs of poor people. Women in the Salvation Army were called "Hallelujah lassies," but they were strong, courageous women who often encountered not only verbal but also physical abuse from people who didn't approve of what they were doing.[8] Raynard's mission paid lower-class women to serve as "Bible women" who took the gospel and offered counsel to people in the poorest sections of town.[9] Bible women, Hallelujah lassies, deaconesses, and nuns "met needs in health and social welfare that governments had not yet fully addressed."[10] These women pioneered the professions of nursing and social work.

Florence Nightingale (1820–1910), an English Anglican, has been called the "founder of modern nursing." Women of her class were supposed to get married, but Nightingale sensed that God had other plans for her. Her father broke social norms in educating his daughter and later supported her financially so that she didn't need to get married. In 1850 she visited Kaiserswerth and was inspired by the deaconesses caring for poor and sick people. She returned to England to train a new generation of nurses, who transformed the care of sick people in England and abroad. She was also famous for improving the sanitation in British military camps and hospitals, which decreased the death rate.

Pandita Ramabai (1858–1922) was a brilliant Indian woman who established a school and other charitable institutions for child widows in India. She grew up as a high-caste Hindu, and her father broke social norms in allowing her to be educated and to read the sacred Hindu texts. Ramabai became so well versed in these texts that she was later given the title *Pandita*, "a Sanskrit word that means learned master."[11] Ramabai became interested in Christianity in her twenties when she observed nuns caring for people on the margins of society, but her husband didn't want her to become a Christian. Then her husband died. Ramabai decided to travel with her daughter to England to study medicine; while there, she became a Christian. Next she went to the United States in order to raise funds for her new venture: a boarding school

---

7. Olson, *Deacons and Deaconesses*, 221–25.

8. When the Salvation Army came to America, it was through the work of seven courageous women called "the Splendid Seven." Tucker and Liefeld, *Daughters of the Church*, 266–67.

9. Olson, *Deacons and Deaconesses*, 245.

10. Olson, *Deacons and Deaconesses*, 215.

11. Hannula, *Radiant*, 232.

for high-caste child widows in India. Such widows were rejected by Indian society and lived in poverty and shame. Many American Christians supported Ramabai's plan to build a school for these women. Hindu reformers also supported her because she promised her school would be secular. In the end, Ramabai's Christian faith was so contagious that many women at the school became Christians. The Hindu supporters pulled out, and Ramabai had to move her entire mission to Kedgaon, India. Her new Mukti ("Liberty") mission became even more extensive than the previous one. Along with a home and school for high-caste widows, there was also a home for elderly and sick people, a home for blind people, and a home for boys. Her mission had eighty-five staff women and two thousand residents.[12] Over the years, Ramabai became known as a *mahatma* (living saint). Late in life, she devoted herself to Bible translation, believing that the current Marathi translation, which was filled with Hindu terms, conveyed a sense of women's inferiority. By learning Hebrew and Greek and retranslating the Bible into Marathi, Ramabai saw herself as bringing women the roots of true liberation.[13] The work Ramabai started is still in operation today.[14]

Temperance, Social Purity, and Suffrage

In England and America, many Christian women dedicated themselves to temperance, a movement to get people to drink less alcohol, and to social purity, a movement to end prostitution. Women were particularly dedicated to these social justice causes because they saw that women were the ones who suffered most from the practice of prostitution and from the abuse and poverty brought about by male addiction to alcohol. "Wives and children of alcoholics were extraordinarily vulnerable because, in most states, women possessed no rights to the custody of their children, and all their property, including current wages, belonged to their husbands."[15] Decreasing alcohol consumption and prostitution was therefore a concrete way to promote the flourishing of women.

Nineteenth-century women knew there was a double standard when it came to sexual purity. Women weren't supposed to have sex before marriage, and they were to sleep only with their husband within marriage. Men were supposed to be chaste before marriage and faithful to their wife within

12. Frykenberg, "Pandita Ramabai," 182.
13. Frykenberg, "Pandita Ramabai," 190.
14. "Pandita Ramabai Mukti Mission."
15. Braude, *Sisters and Saints*, 77.

marriage, but society tended to turn a blind eye if a man decided to visit a sex worker. If a woman slept with someone besides her husband, she would be socially shunned, but if a man did, his behavior could be excused. In the 1830s, a group of evangelical women in America decided to expose this sexual double standard and shame the men who were visiting sex workers. So these women reformers "stood outside brothels waiting for the patrons to depart. When the men who had visited prostitutes emerged onto the street, the reformers recorded their names. Then they published the names in their magazine."[16] These women also met with sex workers to pray and share the gospel with them.

Josephine Butler (1828–1906), a wealthy English Anglican, was appalled at the sexual double standard and became a leader in the social purity movement. Her motivation to help others grew from the experience of personal tragedy. She had four children, the youngest of whom died after a forty-foot fall from the top banister of the Butler home. Butler mourned terribly and suffered a nervous breakdown. Eventually, however, she said she "became possessed with an irresistible urge to go forth and find some pain keener than my own, to meet with people more unhappy than myself."[17] The first people she helped were prostituted women who were near death because of venereal diseases. Butler and her husband invited the women to live with them. They discovered that prostituted women were often forced to be medically examined against their will. Butler called it "surgical rape." If a woman was found to have a curable disease, she was locked up until she was healthy. Butler was appalled. Men with venereal diseases weren't locked up, only prostituted women. Butler led the movement to oppose this sexual double standard. She also worked to end child prostitution. In 1880, she helped to see that a Belgian deputy and several brothel owners involved in the trafficking of English girls were put in prison. Through her efforts, more stringent laws against human trafficking in England were passed.

Katharine Bushnell (1855–1946), an American Methodist, carried on the work of Josephine Butler and successfully ended the forced medical examination of prostituted women in the British colony of India. She also exposed prostitution in the state of Wisconsin. She is even more famous, however, for her work in Bible translation. As a young medical missionary in China, she had seen that when Christian missionaries in China were translating the Bible into Chinese, they gave male names to Paul's female coworkers Euodia and Syntyche (Phil. 4:2–3). When she realized this error, Bushnell began

16. Braude, *Sisters and Saints*, 37.
17. Butler, *Recollections of George Butler*, 183.

to wonder how many other portions of Scripture had been mistranslated. Eventually, Bushnell completed her own translation of numerous scriptural passages about women and published it as *God's Word to Women* in 1923. Bushnell never doubted that the Bible was true. However, she did think that the Bible had been translated and taught in a way that disparaged women, and it was this false message that she sought to correct.[18]

Bushnell was a member of the Woman's Christian Temperance Union (WCTU), which at the time was one of the world's largest organizations of women. The WCTU started in 1873 when women in Hillsborough, Ohio, began entering saloons to pray and sing. Their actions made people so uncomfortable that tavern keepers agreed to stop selling alcohol. "Within a few weeks, nine of the thirteen businesses selling alcohol in Hillsborough had closed and the women in nearby towns had taken up the campaign to close saloons in their communities."[19]

The WCTU became an impressive international organization. Frances Willard (1839–1898), who has been called "the nineteenth century's most beloved and respected female leader," served as president of the WCTU from 1879 to 1898.[20] Under Willard's leadership, members of the WCTU didn't focus just on temperance; they also worked to end prostitution, improve conditions for people in prison and for children, and obtain the vote for women. Women's suffrage was considered a radical cause in the 1880s, but many of the WCTU women sensed God calling them to work for suffrage because it would help them bring about God's ideals for society.[21] WCTU women argued that "by voting for the prohibition of alcohol and for a host of other social reforms, women, like Christ, could lift humanity out of sin."[22]

The causes of suffrage and abolition (the movement to end slavery) were united in the life of Sojourner Truth (1797–1883), a woman who had been born into slavery and obtained her freedom in 1826. Her speeches are still renowned today, including the famous "Ain't I a Woman?" speech delivered to a women's rights gathering in 1851, where she testified to her resilience, dignity, and beauty as a Black woman.

> I want to say a few words about this matter. I am a woman's rights. I have as much muscle as any man, and can do as much work as any man. I have plowed

18. Du Mez, *New Gospel for Women*, 86. Bushnell's work can still be read today. See Bushnell with Francis, *God's Word to Women*.

19. Braude, *Sisters and Saints*, 69.

20. She is "the only woman to be enshrined in the United States Capitol's Statuary Hall." Hardesty, *Women Called to Witness*, 14.

21. Braude, *Sisters and Saints*, 79; Tucker and Liefeld, *Daughters of the Church*, 273.

22. Braude, *Sisters and Saints*, 80.

and reaped and husked and chopped and mowed, and can any man do more than that? I have heard much about the sexes being equal; I can carry as much as any man, and can eat as much too, if I can get it. I am as strong as any man that is now. As for intellect, all I can say is, if women have a pint and man a quart—why can't she have her little pint full? You need not be afraid to give us our rights for fear we will take too much, for we can't take more than our pint'll hold. The poor men seem to be all in confusion, and don't know what to do. Why children, if you have woman's rights, give it to her and you will feel better. You will have your own rights, and they won't be so much trouble. I can't read, but I can hear. I have heard the bible and have learned that Eve caused man to sin. Well if woman upset the world, do give her a chance to set it right side up again. The Lady [another speaker at the convention] has spoken about Jesus, how he never spurned woman from him, and she was right. When Lazarus died, Mary and Martha came to him with faith and love and besought him to raise their brother. And Jesus wept—and Lazarus came forth. And how came Jesus into the world? Through God who created him and woman who bore him. Man, where is your part?[23]

Truth's faith propelled her not only to preach but also to act. After the Civil War, free Blacks moved north, but instead of opportunity, many of them just found more hardship. Truth met these refugees in Washington, DC, and ministered to them. When she herself encountered racial discrimination, she challenged it. For example, even though horse-drawn streetcars were by law desegregated, conductors often refused to pick her up. "Once an angry conductor shoved Truth with such force that her shoulder was dislocated. She brought a lawsuit against the conductor. And she won."[24]

Abolition, Anti-lynching, and Fighting Racism

Like Sojourner Truth, many Christian women during this period felt compelled by their faith to engage in courageous acts to bring justice and freedom to Black Americans. Harriet Tubman (1822–1913) and Harriet Beecher Stowe (1811–1896) were two such women. Tubman escaped from slavery herself and then risked her life to help others escape. She was so successful that "she was dubbed *Moses* for her tireless efforts to set her people free, and she became the most noted 'conductor' on the Underground Railroad" (a network of homes where people fleeing slavery could stay on their journey north).[25] Stowe's home was one such stop on the Underground Railroad. The majority

23. Robinson, "Women's Rights Convention," 160.
24. Koester, "Sojourner Truth's Unfinished Business."
25. Tucker, *Extraordinary Women*, 130.

of White Christian women supported the status quo, but some, like Stowe, became active in the movement to abolish slavery. Stowe wrote the novel *Uncle Tom's Cabin* to expose the horrors of slavery. The book was tremendously popular and was influential in turning people in the North against slavery.

Ida B. Wells (1862–1931) was the most important anti-lynching activist in nineteenth-century America. She was born into slavery, but when she was three years old, the Thirteenth Amendment to the US Constitution legally ended slavery. However, in the post–Civil War era, new forms of oppression developed. For example, on her train ride to work, she usually sat in the "ladies' coach." One day in 1884, the conductor told her to move to the smoking car. She refused. The conductor tried to move her, and she held her ground. He came back with two others and forcibly removed her. She later wrote in her autobiography that the White people in the train car "stood on the seats so that they could get a good view and continued applauding the conductor for his brave stand."[26] Wells sued the railroad company. Amazingly, she won. But then the railroad company appealed, and she had "to pay out over two hundred dollars in court costs."[27] At that point, she wrote,

> I felt so disappointed because I had hoped such great things from my suit for my people generally. I have firmly believed all along that the law was on our side and would, when we appealed to it, give us justice. I feel shorn of that belief and utterly discouraged, and just now, if it were possible, would gather my race in my arms and fly away with them. O God, is there no redress, no peace, no justice in this land for us? Thou hast always fought the battles of the weak and oppressed. Come to my aid at this moment and teach me what to do, for I am sorely, bitterly disappointed. Show us the way, even as Thou led the children of Israel out of bondage into the promised land.[28]

Wells's faith compelled her to continue fighting for justice. In the late 1800s, she led the campaign to end lynching—the horrible practice whereby a mob would brutally kill a person without a trial, usually by hanging them. "From 1882–1968, 4,743 lynchings occurred in the United States," and 73 percent of the people lynched were Black.[29] In 1892, as editor of a newspaper, Wells wrote about three young Black men who had been lynched in Memphis. She criticized the White community for sitting idly by. The next thing she knew, "an angry mob wrecked her press and declared that they would have lynched her if she had

26. Wells, *Crusade for Justice*, 19.
27. Wells, *Crusade for Justice*, 20.
28. Entry for June 7, 1884, in the unpublished diary of Ida B. Wells. See Wells, *Crusade for Justice*, xvii.
29. "History of Lynchings."

been found."[30] Wells didn't back down. She went on to lecture across the United States and Europe, building momentum for the movement to end lynching.

Wells taught Sunday school for ten years at the Presbyterian church she attended with her family. She taught the eighteen- to thirty-year-old men. One day in 1908, three innocent Black men were lynched in nearby Springfield, Illinois. To Wells's shock and dismay, her Sunday school class didn't care. "We can't do anything about it," they told her. She proceeded to lecture them on their duty to do something, and three of her students decided that maybe they could do something. With Wells's urging, they formed the Negro Fellowship League.[31] A few months later, they established their headquarters in an impoverished part of town, hoping to support some of the oppressed of their own people and help them leave a life of alcoholism and crime.

Wells's faith was strong, and it was contagious. While visiting twelve Black men who had been wrongfully imprisoned for a crime they didn't commit, she urged the men to stop thinking about death and start praying to God. She told them, "God knows that you are innocent. . . . The God you serve is the God of Paul and Silas who opened their prison gates, and if you have all the faith you say you have, you ought to believe that he will open your prison doors too. . . . Let all of your songs and prayers hereafter be songs of faith and hope that God will set you free; that the judges who have to pass on your cases will be given the wisdom and courage to decide in your behalf."[32] The twelve men listened to her. They started to pray, and ultimately they were acquitted.

Wells was a well-known crusader for justice on the international stage, but many women whose names are now forgotten worked to bring about justice and freedom for African Americans. "Largely through the fund-raising efforts of these women, the black church [in America] built schools, provided clothes and food to poor people, established old folks' homes and orphanages, and made available a host of needed social welfare services."[33] White women were establishing these same institutions, but their institutions didn't serve Black people. Blacks also faced laws that forbade them from using "parks, libraries, restaurants, meeting halls, and other public accommodations," so the Black church became their community center.[34]

In 1900, Black women in the Baptist church formed the Woman's Auxiliary to the National Baptist Convention. The Woman's Auxiliary held annual

30. Duster, introduction, xix.
31. Wells, *Crusade for Justice*, 299–300.
32. Wells, *Crusade for Justice*, 403.
33. Higginbotham, *Righteous Discontent*, 2.
34. Higginbotham, *Righteous Discontent*, 7.

meetings and created a space for Black women to mourn the oppression caused by racism, to dream of a better world, and to redefine themselves in light of God's love for them. These women also experienced a call from God to be missionaries to White America. At their annual convention in 1905, the women stated, "The American people need help. They need missionaries to go to them and warn them of the awful sin that they are committing by allowing these lines of color, of race, of blood and of birth, to stand in the way of the onward march of religion and civilization. The greatest service that could be rendered to this country at this time would be to rid it of its prejudice that stands more formidable than the walls of Jericho."[35]

These women demonstrated an admirable resilience in the face of oppression. Not only did they have to deal with racism, but they also had to deal with sexism. As they began holding conventions, founding missionary societies, and raising and dispersing funds to build schools and hire teachers, some of the men in their churches began to resent them. Some thought the gender-separate women's conventions and missionary societies would make women want to dominate men in other arenas. Other men were uncomfortable with the amount of money these women controlled.[36] Sometimes men succeeded in shutting down women's conventions, but other times men realized how essential these women were to the liberation of Black people in America. In order to defend their right to have power and influence, the women argued that the Bible was full of strong, capable, divinely chosen women leaders like Deborah, Esther, Mary, Mary Magdalene, Phoebe, Priscilla, and Lydia.[37] Despite the opposition they faced, these women insisted that their gender-separate organizations helped them to do a better job of "religiously training the world."[38]

A Note on Racism, Classism, and Anti-Catholic Sentiment: Contesting the "Sisterhood"

Black women and White women, Catholic women and Protestant women were all active in working for social justice throughout the world during the nineteenth and early twentieth centuries. However, even though these women were doing similar work, they often did not see one another as allies. White

35. Higginbotham, *Righteous Discontent*, 185. Conventions like this one were attended by up to or even over a million women.
36. Higginbotham, *Righteous Discontent*, 68.
37. Higginbotham, *Righteous Discontent*, 120–43.
38. Higginbotham, *Righteous Discontent*, 68.

Protestants defined themselves in opposition to Catholics, many of whom had recently immigrated from Ireland, Italy, and Eastern Europe. Because many of the Catholic immigrants were poor, Protestants tended to see the Catholic faith "as a moral failing that had caused such poverty."[39] They were also shaped by long-standing anti-Catholicism. Protestants saw Catholics as beholden to the pope. They thought the celibacy of Catholic nuns was strange, possibly even evil. Since the days of Martin Luther, marriage had been lifted up among Protestants as the ideal. This clash between the ideal of celibacy among Catholics and the ideal of marriage among Protestants led Protestants to persecute nuns and accuse them of immorality. After Rev. Lyman Beecher preached an anti-Catholic sermon in 1834, a mob went and burned down a convent in Boston.[40]

Another sad story from this period is that White women often perpetuated racial injustice, either because they thought it would help them move their own cause forward or because they couldn't see how their actions were oppressive. Frances Willard told the Southern branch of the Woman's Christian Temperance Union (WCTU) that they didn't need to allow Black women to join; a segregated WCTU was just fine.[41] Willard also accepted the myth her Southern hosts told her about lynching—that lynching was necessary because Black men were raping White women.[42] Rather than speaking out against lynching, Willard spoke in an interview in 1890 about "great dark faced mobs" who were putting "the safety of women, of childhood, of the home" at risk.[43] This argument was a lie made up to justify the lynching of Black men. Willard, one of the most influential women of her time, had the chance to inspire White Christians to a deeper discipleship by challenging their race prejudice, but her own pragmatism and race prejudice prevented her from doing so.[44]

Eventually, Willard did speak out against lynching, but she remained unable to believe that White women would have consensual relationships with Black men, so the only way she could understand the offspring of such unions was that the White women had been raped.[45] When Ida B. Wells suggested that

39. Braude, *Sisters and Saints*, 74.
40. Braude, *Sisters and Saints*, 73. See also Higginbotham, *Righteous Discontent*, 113.
41. Wells, *Crusade for Justice*, 209.
42. Wells, *Crusade for Justice*, 136.
43. Wells, *Crusade for Justice*, 151–53.
44. Willard wasn't alone in condoning injustice in order to advance her own causes. The famous revivalist preacher Dwight L. Moody agreed to exclude Blacks from the audience when he traveled through the South.
45. Earhart, *Frances Willard*, 360–62. Another famous White woman reformer of the era, Jane Addams, also continued to see Black men as sexual predators rather than confronting the racism bound up in this claim. Schechter, *Ida B. Wells-Barnett*, 110–13, 125.

White women could feel sexually drawn to Black men, Willard took this as a slam against White women's virtue, for they were thought by Victorian society to be chaste, pure, and submissive; they were expected never to initiate sex.[46] Willard was unable or unwilling to shift her understanding of womanhood to accommodate what Wells told her. Other Black women were upset with Wells for criticizing Willard. They had worked hard to build bridges with White women, and even if they agreed with Wells, they didn't want to jeopardize the relationships that had taken decades to build.

Building bridges with White women was difficult for Black women. They, just like Black men, were up against a cruel stereotype. White society viewed Black women as dirty, poor, beastly, and ignorant. In order to prove that they were not these things, Black women had to be twice as clean and twice as thrifty. They had to hold their head twice as high, work twice as hard, and have flawless manners. And to have any chance of breaking the stereotype that was lodged in White minds, Black mothers had to drill these same virtues of cleanliness, thrift, dignity, and industriousness into their children. They had to prove that they and their children were respectable. Most of these Black women were already motivated by their Christian faith to instill virtue in their children, but the "politics of respectability"—the need to look respectable in the eyes of White people—drove them even harder to be virtuous.[47]

Middle-class White women during this period were given respect and authority because Victorian society considered them virtuous, but Black women and lower-class women had to prove that they were virtuous. In some ways, the perceived virtue of White women depended on the continued negative stereotyping of other women or of other races. Whether such women were the women whom White missionary women went to save in India or the lower-class women trapped in prostitution in the United States, less privileged women served to bolster the social status of White, middle-class women. By arguing that they were rescuing less fortunate women, White women were able to increase their own power.

White women in the nineteenth century talked a great deal about how their "global sisterhood" transcended race and class, but it was far easier for them to use their status to benefit their sisters than to question why they themselves had a higher status. Their faith encouraged them to help others, they had time for charity work, and they liked to feel useful. But it was difficult for them to recognize how their higher status came more from the history of imperialism, slavery, and industrialization than from their own actual virtue.

46. See the discussion of nineteenth-century "separate spheres" ideology in chap. 6.
47. Higginbotham, *Righteous Discontent*, chap. 7.

Conclusion

The women described in this chapter were dedicated to different causes and were from different races, classes, countries, and denominations, but they were all motivated to bring Christ's love and care to "the least of these." Nineteenth- and early twentieth-century women founded and joined numerous social justice organizations, which helped to heal some of the social dislocation and suffering people around the world were experiencing as a result of colonialism, slavery, industrialization, and urbanization. Temperance and social purity were two of women's most prominent social justice causes. Women also took the lead in establishing modern nursing, pushing for women's suffrage, reforming prisons, and founding societies to care for underprivileged members of society. Women were also leaders in the abolition and anti-lynching movements.

Women more than men staffed and supported the vast majority of the public ministries for children, those in prison, women caught up in prostitution, and people afflicted by poverty and sickness. In 1900, "forty thousand nuns [in America] outnumbered priests by four to one."[48] At the same time, the WCTU was growing into a membership of hundreds of thousands of women around the world, and three million Protestant women belonged to missionary societies (see chap. 8).[49]

Even though there were at times severe disagreements between women who were active in social justice work—for example, between Wells and Willard—the networks that held together the "global sisterhood" also allowed many women to inspire one another in good work and to pass the baton of religious leadership. Florence Nightingale was "one of the most renowned Western heroines in China at the turn of the twentieth century."[50] Nightingale herself had been inspired by the Kaiserswerth deaconesses in Germany. And the Fliedners, who founded Kaiserswerth, had been inspired by Elizabeth Seton's Sisters of Charity and Elizabeth Fry caring for prisoners in England. Each of these women and many others played an instrumental role in leading the church to care for people on the margins of society.

48. "The number of nuns reached its peak in 1966, when more than 180,000 American women served in Catholic orders" (Braude, *Sisters and Saints*, 76). It is largely thanks to nuns that the United States has the number of Catholic hospitals that it does. Wall, *Into Africa*, 22.
49. Robert, "Women in World Mission," 51.
50. Judge, *Precious Raft*, 65.

8

Denominational Missionaries and Bible Women

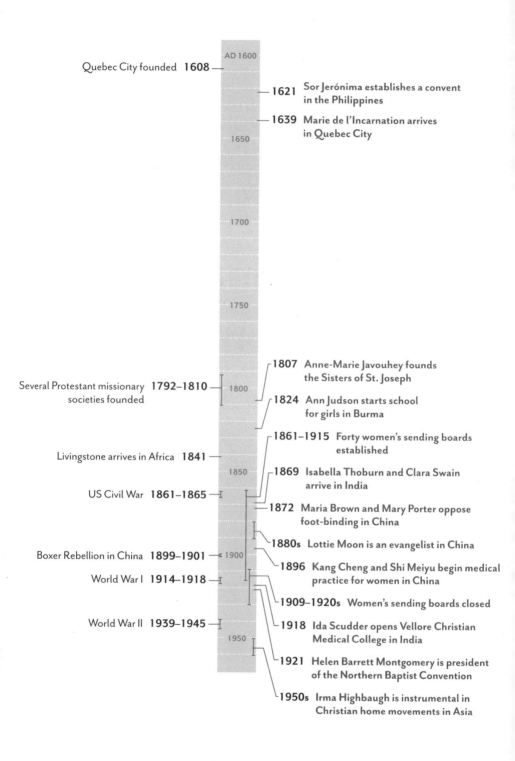

Quebec City founded **1608**

1621 Sor Jerónima establishes a convent in the Philippines

1639 Marie de l'Incarnation arrives in Quebec City

AD 1600

1650

1700

1750

1800

1807 Anne-Marie Javouhey founds the Sisters of St. Joseph

Several Protestant missionary **1792–1810** societies founded

1824 Ann Judson starts school for girls in Burma

1861–1915 Forty women's sending boards established

Livingstone arrives in Africa **1841**

1850

1869 Isabella Thoburn and Clara Swain arrive in India

US Civil War **1861–1865**

1872 Maria Brown and Mary Porter oppose foot-binding in China

1880s Lottie Moon is an evangelist in China

Boxer Rebellion in China **1899–1901** 1900

1896 Kang Cheng and Shi Meiyu begin medical practice for women in China

World War I **1914–1918**

1909–1920s Women's sending boards closed

World War II **1939–1945**

1918 Ida Scudder opens Vellore Christian Medical College in India

1950

1921 Helen Barrett Montgomery is president of the Northern Baptist Convention

1950s Irma Highbaugh is instrumental in Christian home movements in Asia

Women in every era of the church have engaged in cross-cultural mission, leaving their own home to journey to a new land. Think of Priscilla, who moved from Rome to Corinth to Ephesus, founding churches in each location (see chap. 1). Or Leoba, the eighth-century nun who left England and accompanied her cousin Boniface on a mission to Germany (see chap. 4). However, the number of women participating in cross-cultural mission rose substantially during the nineteenth century. This rise in women's participation was preceded by the fifteenth-century age of exploration and the European colonization of America, Asia, and Africa. At first, only male priests went abroad as missionaries to newly colonized lands, but gradually nuns went as well in order to establish monasteries and schools. The Protestant missionary movement began in the eighteenth century. Unlike Catholics, who sent single men and women to the mission field, Protestants sent families. In the mid-nineteenth century, Protestant women established their own missionary societies in order to send single women to the mission field. This chapter tells some of the stories of the first Catholic and Protestant cross-cultural missionaries in the modern era. It shows that women have brought both the gospel message and holistic care for women and girls to many parts of the globe.

Pioneer Catholic Missionary Women

Spain and Portugal sent nuns to their colonial empires to establish convents in the sixteenth century. In 1540, a convent was established in Mexico City.[1] In the 1550s, a convent was established in Santo Domingo in the Caribbean, and in the 1560s, another was established in Lima, Peru.[2] In seventeenth-century Japan, some nuns became catechists who "taught, preached, persuaded, baptized, catechized the neophytes, and provided pastoral care."[3] In 1621, Spanish nun Sor Jerónima (1555–1630) established a convent in the Philippines.[4] In

1. Owens, *Nuns Navigating*, 20.
2. Lundberg, *Mission and Ecstasy*, 8.
3. H. Ward, *Women Religious Leaders*, 31.
4. Owens, *Nuns Navigating*, 93–98.

both Mexico and the Philippines, there was controversy regarding who the convents would accept as novices. Would they admit native-born women, mixed-race women, and poor women or only the wealthy children of the Spanish conquistadors, merchants, and bureaucrats?[5] In Mexico City, a separate convent was created for native women in 1724.[6] In Manila, Sor Jerónima insisted on admitting native women, but the local authorities fought her. Nevertheless, a Japanese woman was allowed to join the community, and two Kapampangan (native Filipino) women were admitted shortly after Sor Jerónima's death.

The first French nun to become a cross-cultural missionary was Marie de l'Incarnation (1599–1672). In 1633, she began to have visions of herself as a missionary: "My body was in our monastery but my spirit, united to that of Jesus, could not remain shut up there. This apostolic spirit carried me . . . to every part of the inhabited world where there were human souls who belonged by right to Jesus Christ."[7] She was convinced that God was calling her to the mission field, even though many priests disapproved, and in 1639 she and two of her fellow nuns succeeded in getting permission to move to French Canada to join the male Jesuit missionaries already there. Marie founded the first school for First Nations girls in Canada, learned the Algonquian and Iroquois languages, and prepared books in these languages for the girls to read. Because Catholic doctrine required that nuns remain cloistered, Marie and her fellow nuns held classes for girls inside the convent.[8]

Anne-Marie Javouhey (1779–1851), another French Catholic missionary pioneer, also experienced a call to mission through a vision. She had just become a nun, and one night she woke up hearing voices and seeing children with "black skin, brown skin, [and] bronze skin" in her room, all of whom were smiling. She had never seen children like these before. In the middle of the room was a nun, who told her, "These are the children God has given you. He wishes you to form a new congregation to take care of them."[9] Javouhey established the Sisters of St. Joseph in 1807. The order founded schools, and its members became such expert educators that French colonial officials asked

---

5. Evangelisti, *Nuns*, 194–95.

6. Evangelisti, *Nuns*, 197. There is also evidence of earlier communities of indigenous women who, while they didn't take formal vows, still lived chaste lives and engaged in acts of charity. See O'Brien, "Catholic Nuns," 394.

7. Marie of the Incarnation, *Selected Writings*, 113–14.

8. "Though the Council of Trent limited female religious life to a contemplative and enclosed form, its decrees were not implemented everywhere. In some contexts, more active forms of female religious life continued and even thrived after the Council." Lundberg, *Mission and Ecstasy*, 31.

9. Kittler, *Woman God Loved*, 58.

Javouhey to send sisters to the West Indies and Senegal to establish schools there.[10] The sisters in Senegal staffed a hospital, and Javouhey joined them in 1822 to establish a school for girls. She also arranged for the education of young men who would become the first Senegalese priests.[11] By 1827, there were about five hundred nuns in Javouhey's order and she had become a kind of celebrity in France.[12]

But being a celebrity didn't save her from trials. In 1843 her bishop, wanting to increase his own power, claimed that he was the superior general of her order and that she would now need to run all her decisions by him.[13] When she left the diocese at the invitation of the French government to establish a colony in French Guiana (in South America), he saw it as an act of disobedience. Obedience to one's superiors was important to Javouhey. She required it of her nuns, and she required it of herself, but in this case, she was convinced that obeying the bishop would mean disobeying God. The bishop "retaliated by ordering her priest in Guiana to refuse her communion."[14] The two years she spent without Communion were very difficult, but ultimately she was vindicated and paved the way for generations of Catholic missionary nuns to establish schools and hospitals abroad.

Protestant Missionary Wives

During the early nineteenth century, the only way for a Protestant woman to get to the mission field was to marry a man who wanted to be missionary. Having a call to mission was a crucial qualification for both men and women, but the function of the call was different. Men were educated, supported, and sent to do ministry. Women needed both a calling and a husband in order to be sent. For many, the call to mission preceded and was stronger than the desire for marriage.[15]

Ann Hasseltine Judson (1789–1826) was one of the most productive American Baptist missionary wives. She and her husband, Adoniram, worked in Burma (now Myanmar). She opened a school for girls and encouraged other women missionaries to do likewise. In her eyes, education not only had the best chance of winning girls for Christ but also had the strongest potential for improving the physical lives of women. Although mission education was

10. Kittler, *Woman God Loved*, 89–92.
11. Kittler, *Woman God Loved*, 99–107.
12. Kittler, *Woman God Loved*, 147.
13. Kittler, *Woman God Loved*, 177.
14. Tucker and Liefeld, *Daughters of the Church*, 307.
15. Robert, *American Women in Mission*, 21.

her passion, Judson also evangelized, led Bible studies, wrote tracts and catechisms, held prayer meetings, and learned several languages to help her in these tasks. She and Adoniram translated parts of the Bible into Burmese, and her work on this project was especially important because she had learned the Burmese language better than Adoniram. For two years while Adoniram was imprisoned, she ran the ministry, brought him food in prison, and wrote letters to the government pleading for his release.[16] Although she died after only thirteen years in Burma, Ann Judson became a model for later missionary wives. Her husband married two more times. When his third bride set sail to join him in Burma, the *Boston Evening Transcript* ran an editorial protesting the ongoing sacrifice of women in this way.[17] Yet women, like men, continued to go.

Life on the mission field was hard. The strains and physical challenges of life on the field, coupled with childbearing, health problems, and the need to educate their children, meant that many wives were overburdened, and quite a number died very young. For example, William Carey, who is popularly known as the "father of modern missions," was a pioneer Baptist evangelist and Bible translator in India in the early 1800s. His wife, Dorothy, spent her last years in a mental institution, in part due to the toll that missionary work had taken on her.[18] William married twice more.

The Missiology of the Christian Home

Many missionary wives, like Ann Judson, were able to find satisfying roles for themselves on the mission field, but other wives were disappointed with what they were able to accomplish. For example, missionary wives in Hawaii went to the mission field hoping to be deeply involved in mission, but once they arrived, their domestic work took so much time that they had very little energy to devote to evangelism. Sybil Bingham (1792–1848) wrote, "My exhausted nature droops. . . . I sometimes grieve that I can no more devote myself to the language, & the study of my bible."[19]

Eventually, these exhausted women began to see that the work they were doing in caring for their families could be understood missiologically. Lucy Thurston (1795–1876) described in her journal how impressed the Hawaiian people were to see her newborn child wearing clothes: "There was the

16. Robert, *American Women in Mission*, 43–46.
17. Tucker and Liefeld, *Daughters of the Church*, 297.
18. Beck, "Missions and Mental Health," 9–10; Tucker and Liefeld, *Daughters of the Church*, 293–94.
19. W. Schenk, *North American Foreign Missions*, 124.

white infant, neatly dressed. . . . To witness home scenes and the manner in which we cherished our children seemed . . . to draw fore [*sic*] their warmest affections."[20] Women like Thurston began to see simple, daily tasks as a way to build relationships and communicate values. According to Dana Robert, the missiology of the Christian home "was adopted in Hawaii because it was effective and because it made a virtue out of necessity. By interpreting family life as a mission agency, the mission wives sacralized the myriad activities that ate up their strength and their days."[21]

As Christianity spread, women led the way in developing the missiology of the Christian home. In parts of Africa, missionary women and African Christian women began meeting weekly to sew, pray, read the Bible, and talk about their lives as wives and mothers. These "mothers' unions" also became a means for drawing other women into the faith, because some mothers' unions went out to evangelize and serve poor and needy people.[22] As Robert says, "The importance of mothers' prayer groups for African Christianity cannot be overestimated as a force for the spread of Christianity."[23]

At the 1938 meeting of the International Missionary Council, women from around the world presented strategies for shaping Christian homes.[24] In the 1950s, missionary Irma Highbaugh (1891–1973) traveled throughout Asia helping to establish and expand Christian home movements.[25] Christians in Asia, Africa, and the Caribbean packaged their Christian home theology in devotional books, magazines, and radio broadcasts.

In the 1950s and 1960s, Lutheran missionaries Walter (1923–1979) and Ingrid (1926–2007) Trobisch made the Christian home the center of their missionary message in Cameroon. An African pastor once told the Trobisches that their message about equal partnership in marriage was revolutionary: "It's bringing Christ into the marriage relationship!"[26] Most missionary couples who went abroad in the nineteenth and twentieth centuries believed that intimacy, love, and partnership were essential in marriage, even if they didn't always live this out. As people converted to Christianity and reflected on what

---

20. Thurston, *Life and Times*, 63. In the twenty-first century, her words may sound shocking because she seems to elevate her Western custom of dressing babies and to elevate the White baby. Her words have a racist and classist ring to them. However, it's important to remember that missionaries were embedded in a culture of colonialism and expansion. Expecting her not to sound like her time is unrealistic.

21. Robert, "Evangelist or Homemaker?," 10.

22. Gaitskell, "Devout Domesticity?"

23. Robert, *Christian Mission*, 131.

24. *Life of the Church*, 25–50.

25. Stasson, "Legacy of Irma Highbaugh."

26. Stasson, *Walter and Ingrid Trobisch*, chap. 4.

made Christian homes unique, many of them spread this companionate view of marriage. The perspective of Filipinos Jacob and Ermelinda Quiambao was typical. Jacob wrote, "The husband and the wife are partners, not master and slave; neither one is superior or inferior."[27] And Ermelinda wrote, "When husband and wife try to help each other to realize their best selves they become a source of mutual support."[28]

Throughout the history of the church, women's day-to-day work tending their homes, caring for their husbands, raising their children, and reaching out to their neighbors has contributed significantly to the mission of the church. During the nineteenth and twentieth centuries, women led the way in articulating how the Christian home was central to mission. Many Western missionaries inadvertently spread ideas about children and home life that had more to do with Western culture than with the gospel, and missionaries were often unable to see their own ethnocentrism. However, missionaries also helped to stimulate good, culturally sensitive discussions about what the Christian faith has to say about marriage and parenthood.

Women's Sending Boards and Single Women Missionaries

The challenges of juggling marriage, parenting, housework, and ministry roles plagued Protestant missionary women in the nineteenth century just as those challenges plague women today. For missionary women, the answer was to send single women to the mission field. Single women, they argued, would be less burdened with family responsibilities and more able to engage in mission work. In a handful of places, Protestant single women were already working.[29] But by and large, most male-led denominational sending boards refused to send single women overseas. In the mid-nineteenth century, women took matters into their own hands.

In 1861 Sarah Doremus (1802–1877) of New York founded the Woman's Union Missionary Society.[30] The Woman's Union was exactly what its name stated: an interdenominational union of women. In 1868 Congregational women formed their own sending board. That same year women in Chicago founded a sending board that included both Congregational and Presbyterian women.

27. J. Quiambao, *Manual on Marriage Counseling*, 31–32.
28. E. Quiambao, *Home and Family Life*, 9.
29. The New York Female Missionary Society of the Methodist Episcopal Church had sent out single women between 1819 and 1861, and the British Society for Promoting Female Education in the East began sending them in 1834. American Baptists had sent single women as missionaries to Native Americans as early as the 1820s and to Burma in the 1830s.
30. See Robert, "Doremus, Sarah Platt (Haines)."

The Woman's Foreign Missionary Society of the Methodist Episcopal Church (WFMS) was established in 1869 and went on to become the largest women's sending board in the United States. The organization began when two missionary wives, Mrs. William Butler and Mrs. Edwin Parker, were home in Boston on furlough from India. They spoke to a group of eight women, describing the needs of girls and women in India. The girls had virtually no education available to them. The women lacked health care because customs prevented them from being treated by male physicians. Within months, these eight women raised enough funds to send a teacher, Isabella Thoburn (1840–1901), and a physician, Dr. Clara Swain (1834–1910), to India. Thoburn founded a school with six young women; it became the first women's college in Asia. Isabella Thoburn College, located in Lucknow, India, is still training women today.[31] Swain started a hospital that became "the first hospital for women in Asia."[32] In addition to providing culturally appropriate health care for women and children, Swain also trained women physicians.[33] The Clara Swain Hospital is located in Bareilly, India, and still cares for people today.[34] The eight women in Boston who banded together to send these two women to India could hardly have imagined the long-term, far-reaching impact Swain and Thoburn would have. Swain was the first doctor to be sent abroad by a women's missionary society, and within forty years, 10 percent of "American women missionaries supported by Protestant women's mission societies were doctors or nurses."[35]

The Missiology of "Woman's Work for Woman"

Much of the impetus behind the creation of the women's sending boards had to do with the needs of women in unreached places and the necessity for women to evangelize women. India was a country with a clear need for a "woman's work for woman" missiology. Indian women were kept secluded from men and strangers through a system called "purdah," meaning "curtain" or "seclusion." The section of the house reserved for women was known as the "zenana." Although foreign women were still strangers, as women they had the possibility of entering the zenanas to meet Indian women. In 1880 the Zenana Mission Society of England was founded to send single women missionaries

31. See the website of Isabella Thoburn College, https://www.itcollege.ac.in/.
32. Wilson, "Swain, Clara."
33. "About Dr. Clara A. Swain."
34. See the website of Clara Swain Hospital, J.V, http://www.cshbareilly.com/.
35. Robert, *Christian Mission*, 132.

to India. Like Thoburn and Swain from the American board, women sent by the Zenana Mission Society worked to establish schools and offer health care to Indian women who otherwise had little access to such things.[36]

Dr. Ida Scudder (1870–1960) was an important American medical doctor in India and the granddaughter of the first male medical missionary to India. Born in India, Scudder and her family returned to the United States when she was seven years old. Her memories of India were painful, and she swore she would never go back. When she was thirteen, her parents returned to India but allowed her to stay in the United States to continue her schooling. A few years later, they summoned her because her mother was dying. While there she experienced what she later described as "three knocks in the night." In one night, three women, one of whom was a Muslim and two of whom were high-caste Hindus, died in childbirth. Three times someone came to her parents' house requesting a woman doctor to assist in delivery, and all three left disappointed because no woman doctor was available. Ida Scudder's heart changed, and she decided to return to India as a medical missionary.[37]

Scudder attended medical school at Cornell, where she was part of the first class open to women. Upon graduation, she returned to Vellore, India, and set up a medical practice in her father's bungalow. Eventually, she raised money from the United States to build a hospital, where she became a well-known surgeon, performing as many as forty thousand operations annually. Her next project was to train nurses. Her nursing school became India's first graduate nursing program and was later incorporated into Madras University. She also set up a system of public health visitation for villages in the area, providing medicine and consultations for thousands. That system eventually became Vellore's Rural Unit for Health and Social Affairs (RUHSA). She also established the Vellore Christian Medical College to train doctors and nurses. The hospital and RUHSA are still in operation today.[38]

Health care was also important for mission work among women in China. Chinese missionary doctors Kang Cheng (1873–1931) and Shi Meiyu (1873–1954) developed some of the first hospitals and nursing schools for women in China. Shi was a pastor's kid in Jiujiang, and Kang had been adopted by missionary Gertrude Howe. Howe taught the girls English, science, and history, and they attended the University of Michigan together.[39] After medical school, Kang and Shi returned to China as missionaries with the Women's Foreign Missionary Society (WFMS) to establish dispensaries and hospitals

36. Seton, *Western Daughters in Eastern Lands*, 80.
37. Wilson, "Scudder."
38. See the website of Friends of Vellore UK, https://friendsofvellore.org/.
39. Shemo, *Chinese Medical Ministries*, 36.

for women and children. Other nursing schools and medical schools were being established at this time, but only upper-class women had the prerequisite education, time, and money to attend. Kang and Shi made it possible for lower-class women to gain a nursing education. Education allowed women to avoid being "forced into marriage with undesirable partners or left completely destitute by the death or abandonment of a spouse."[40]

As Shi gained prestige as a doctor and took on more student nurses, she began to address aspects of missionary racism that she found in the WFMS. For example, missionary magazines portrayed Chinese workers as unreliable and selfish, so Shi wrote articles about her "beautiful, devoted" nurses who were willing to work for little pay and whose love for the patients was evident.[41] Missionary magazines also spoke of Chinese workers as lacking the competence and spiritual maturity to take on leadership roles in mission institutions. Shi countered this belief by giving her nurses lots of independence and by leaving the hospital in their competent hands when she needed to be absent.

Kang and Shi believed that Christ was central to China's flourishing, but when Chinese reformers wrote about Kang as a model for what the "new Chinese woman" could be, they downplayed her Christianity. Kang continued to insist that Christianity was central to her identity, and she wanted it to be part of China's future. As Connie Shemo says, "Christian evangelism was for Kang a profoundly patriotic activity."[42]

Kang and Shi saw themselves as Christian evangelists, Chinese nationalists, and—though they wouldn't have used the word—feminists. They believed that women's empowerment was central to the gospel and key to the flourishing of China. "Their example was instrumental in inspiring many Chinese women to become physicians themselves, and in opening the medical profession to Chinese women."[43]

Bible Women

Bible women were local women in Asia and Africa who were hired and trained by the Western women's boards and paid a modest wage to take the gospel from village to village. Bible women spent much of their time meeting with women in their homes, leading Bible studies. Sometimes they held prayer

40. Shemo, *Chinese Medical Ministries*, 89.
41. Shemo, *Chinese Medical Ministries*, 86.
42. Shemo, *Chinese Medical Ministries*, 108, 200.
43. Shemo, *Chinese Medical Ministries*, 1.

meetings or led Sunday school. "The role of Bible woman was the first independent ministry role available to Christian women in Asia and Africa."[44]

Some Bible women evangelized in public settings and spoke to audiences of both men and women. For example, a widow in 1930s India preached to a crowd of four hundred "prosperous Hindu farmers." The missionary who was present recorded the following: "For thirty-five minutes that preacher held the attention of her audience. Her sermon, in a language which the writer does not understand, was said to be logical, forceful and eloquent."[45]

There were so many Bible women in India that some of them formed their own mission society, linked to the Female Education Society (FES), which had trained them. Like the FES, this daughter organization was run completely by and for women and sought to raise the status of Indian women through education. By 1889, the FES had so many Indian partners in mission that it decided to include the names of these Indian women on the list of FES missionaries, published in each annual report. Even on the first published list, which the committee said "is not as complete as we hope it will be in future," the Indian missionaries outnumbered the British missionaries.[46] According to Dana Robert, women's mission organizations in the early twentieth century supported "three times as many indigenous women as evangelists as they did foreign missionaries."[47]

The earliest Bible women were simply trained by Western missionary women in their homes, but gradually the women's sending boards developed schools where they could train Bible women in Scripture, theology, history, evangelism, hymnody, and hygiene. "By 1900 there were forty female training schools in China alone. . . . In India there were more than thirty such schools."[48] Bible women began to teach other women who would themselves become Bible women.[49] Some Bible women were also trained in medicine.

By 1910, there were "5783 Bible women and native helpers" around the world.[50] Some of these Bible women worked very closely with missionaries, while others were independent. In South Africa, the ministry of Bible women was considered an "order," just like the orders of widows and deacons in the early church, and these South African Bible women were commissioned with a formal prayer.[51]

---

44. Robert, *Christian Mission*, 139.
45. Quoted in Tucker and Liefeld, *Daughters of the Church*, 343.
46. "Female Education Society Annual Report for 1889."
47. Robert, *Gospel Bearers, Gender Barriers*, xi, 13.
48. Tucker, "Role of Bible Women," 135.
49. Tucker, "Role of Bible Women," 139–40.
50. Montgomery, *Western Women in Eastern Lands*, 243–44.
51. Attwell, *Take Our Hands*, 79.

Often Bible women encountered obstacles, insults, and even personal injury and theft.[52] Ruth Tucker says that many Bible women in the early twentieth century were "paid an amount so small that it was barely enough to cover their expenses."[53] Then there was the issue of status. "The Bible woman, catechist or evangelist was the lowliest employee on the hierarchical ladder of the mission churches."[54] Even though everyone acknowledged that Bible women were doing important work and that the mission of the church would be greatly hampered without their participation, Bible women simply were not given the same respect as male evangelists or Western missionary women.

Racial Hierarchy, Ethnocentrism, and the "Savior Complex"

Western missionaries who traveled to foreign lands believed that Christ "made of one blood all nations" of the world (Acts 17:26 KJV). They thought of Christians around the world as their "brothers and sisters in Christ." However, they—like all of us—had a hard time making that universal brotherhood and sisterhood a reality. At some level, they still felt superior. At some level, there was still a distance between them and the new Christians, which they felt should be maintained.[55] Even when they became aware of the problem of racial prejudice and critiqued it, they struggled to live without prejudice.[56]

Nineteenth- and early twentieth-century missionaries also tended to equate evangelization with civilization and to view Western culture as superior to non-Western cultures. Missionaries of the time firmly believed that Christianity would bring social uplift to women who were oppressed by their own cultures and religions.[57] As Melody Maxwell says, "The gospel, in their thinking, contained truths that would liberate members of all societies from superstitions and pre-modern practices into a peaceful, forward looking Christian civilization."[58] Missionaries tended to see conversion to Christianity as being part and parcel of accepting Western culture. The idea that foreign cultures

52. Attwell, *Take Our Hands*, 81.
53. Tucker, "Role of Bible Women," 141.
54. Beaver, *American Protestant Women*, 121.
55. For example, in the mission periodicals, Bible women were generally referred to simply by first name, whereas Western missionary women were described as professionals and were named by first and last name. Semple, "Ruth," 564.
56. Du Mez, *New Gospel for Women*, 77.
57. Robert, *American Women in Mission*, 130.
58. Maxwell, *Woman I Am*, 27.

could be turned to Christ, that people could become "converts" instead of "proselytes," didn't come to dominate missionary thinking until the second half of the twentieth century.[59]

A related issue that plagued missionaries of the nineteenth century was what has since been named the "White savior complex."[60] Nineteenth-century missiological literature depicted women in places like India and China as victims without any access to medical care. The perceived need of these foreign women "became a powerful justification for medical education for women in the United States."[61] On the surface, there was nothing wrong with the fact that women's need abroad promoted women's medical education in the United States. However, the Western women who received medical training with the express purpose of going abroad to help foreign women tended to develop an attitude of racial superiority, and their education at times reinforced the tendency to elevate Western culture over non-Western cultures.

Even though the missiological literature of the day depicted foreign cultures as oppressive to women, many of the Western women who entered the missionary profession had stories of how their own culture had oppressed them. In some cases—for example, early twentieth-century India—"women missionaries found themselves in the ironic position of claiming rights for Indian women that they themselves did not possess in their churches back home."[62] Scholars have also pointed out that one way Western missionary women were able to transcend the gender limits of their own culture was by casting themselves as saviors of non-Western women.[63]

Drawing attention to the savior complex does not minimize the great good that was done by missionaries. Dana Robert notes that "by 1909 . . . American Protestant women were supporting eighty hospitals and eighty-two dispensaries around the world."[64] People around the world certainly benefited from the medical care and education provided by missionaries. However, it is important to be cognizant of the unintended consequences of this history and the ways in which the ideology of "rescue" had a way of reinforcing distinctions of race and class instead of breaking them down and helping people to live out the reality that "there is neither Jew nor Gentile, neither slave nor free" (Gal. 3:28).

59. Walls, *Missionary Movement*, 51–53; Walls, "Converts or Proselytes?," 2–6; Bosch, *Transforming Mission*, 420–32.
60. Bandyopadhyay, "Volunteer Tourism"; T. Cole, "White-Savior Industrial Complex."
61. Shemo, *Chinese Medical Ministries*, 5.
62. Khan, "American Women Missionaries," 142.
63. Shemo, *Chinese Medical Ministries*, 32–33.
64. Robert, *Christian Mission*, 132.

The Movement to End Foot-Binding in China

Women in China faced a specific cultural challenge for over a thousand years—the practice of foot-binding. In this practice, a girl's foot was broken and folded over, then wrapped in layers of bandages to prevent growth. The ideal of beauty was a three-inch foot. Marriage contracts could be dependent on a woman having bound feet. In rural areas, the practice may have also served an economic purpose, as young girls with bound feet were easier to keep still and engaged in weaving, sewing, and similar types of handwork.[65] Foot-binding was an entrenched social practice in the mid- to late 1800s, when many missionaries were first entering China. Yet few male missionaries recognized foot-binding as a significant missiological problem.

However, some women missionaries took a different perspective. In 1871 Maria Brown and Mary Porter (1848–1906) sailed for China as Methodist missionaries to open a school for girls. After deep, prayerful reflection, they decided to oppose foot-binding in their schools. First, they reasoned that foot-binding was painful and harmful to women. Second, because it crippled women and made it difficult for them to contribute to society, Brown and Porter concluded that the practice was bad for society as a whole. Third, and equally important, was the question of evangelism. How could a woman become an itinerant preacher or Bible woman after her conversion if she could not walk? So Brown and Porter decided that an admission requirement for their gospel-training schools would be unbound feet. Of course, this decision met some opposition. Teachers who had been in China longer than Brown and Porter believed that parents would not allow their daughters to study at a school that opposed such a long-cherished custom. However, Brown and Porter insisted; they believed that foot-binding was sinful, and they were compelled to oppose it.[66]

Six years later at an inter-mission conference in Shanghai, their ideas were presented to all the missionaries. Some of the men at the conference recognized that they had never considered foot-binding as a hindrance to spreading the gospel, and they joined the women in using moral persuasion to stop it when they could. At the same time, a growing Chinese movement was also pushing for the elimination of the practice. Gradually more and more missionaries and Chinese people became convinced that foot-binding was a harmful practice. In fact, in 1907, the Chinese government itself outlawed the practice. Brown and Porter's story is an excellent example of the mission theory of "woman's work for woman" that dominated this time period.

65. Bossen and Gates, *Bound Feet, Young Hands*, 139.
66. Hubbard, *Under Marching Orders*, 35.

Lottie Moon

The missiology of "woman's work for woman," though an apt strategy for many women, did not sit well with missionary Lottie Moon (1840–1912). Moon was passionate about evangelism, but because she was a woman, the Baptist mission board sent her to China in 1873 with an assignment to teach school. She briefly considered marriage and even got engaged to a missionary, but when he chose to take up an academic career in the United States, she broke off the engagement.[67] At a time when some mission boards were complaining that women's holistic ministry could distract from evangelism, Moon was developing into an extremely effective evangelistic preacher.

Moon found a creative way around the constraints placed on her. She made her women's meetings and messages so interesting that men could not resist coming to hear her as well. She also worked to train and support local male believers as quickly as possible so that they could take on pastoral roles among those who came to faith. That way she was not going against her Southern Baptist board by actively evangelizing men, yet she reached them all the same. To the members of her Southern Baptist sending board, she was outspoken in her insistence that missionary women receive the same voice, vote, and support as their male colleagues. She also called upon all Southern Baptist women to make a special monetary Christmas offering to mission work.

Moon was particularly frustrated by what she saw as a lack of commitment to mission work among American Southern Baptist churches. For years she regularly sent letters to the United States, begging, pleading, and eventually shaming people because not enough were coming to join her in the work. At one point she wrote, "It is odd that a million Baptists of the South can furnish only three men for all of China!"[68] She grew increasingly discouraged and frustrated by what she believed was a lack of obedience to the mission call. At the same time, she extended herself to the point of exhaustion in her efforts to meet the needs of those around her.

Moon died on Christmas Eve 1912 from starvation. She was seventy-two. Her region of China had been hit with a severe famine, and she had shared what little food she had with those around her. Today the entire Southern Baptist Christmas offering for mission work is named for her, which is ironic, because far more than money, she had desired workers for the spread of the gospel in China. Nevertheless, the money raised in her name continues to fund global mission work.

67. Tucker and Liefeld, *Daughters of the Church*, 304–5.
68. Tucker, *Guardians of the Great Commission*, 42.

Helen Barrett Montgomery

Helen Barrett Montgomery (1861–1934) was probably the single most influential person in the women's missionary movement of the late 1800s and early 1900s. Montgomery worked with Susan B. Anthony on women's rights; she also worked for education reform in New York and helped obtain admission for women to the University of Rochester. In 1899 she became the first woman elected to public office in Rochester, serving on the Rochester school board for ten years. The year 1910 marked her entrance into the women's missionary movement, with the publication of her book *Western Women in Eastern Lands*.

Montgomery's subsequent record of accomplishments is astonishing. In 1910–1911 she went on a national tour to promote women's mission work. She raised $1 million, most of which went to fund women's work in Asia. (In 2020 numbers, that would be about $27 million.) In 1913 the Federation of Women's Boards of Foreign Missions sent her to study and write a report on mission work around the world.[69] That report was published in 1915 as *The King's Highway*. It sold over 160,000 copies.[70]

In 1915 she and two other women founded a group called the World Wide Guild to encourage young women to become missionaries. She founded the guild while serving as president of the Woman's American Baptist Foreign Mission Society from 1914 to 1924. In her role as president, she sought to increase access to education and health care for women and children. Finally, in 1921 she was elected president of the Northern Baptist Convention—the first woman ever to hold the office of president for the denomination.[71]

Montgomery's commitment to education extended beyond the two books she wrote on mission topics. In 1924 she became the first woman to publish a translation of the Greek New Testament.[72] It was called *The Centenary Translation of the New Testament*, and her goal was to produce a readable version written in ordinary language. Her scholarship, her visionary leadership in mission, and her passion for women's work illustrate the many facets of "woman's work for woman" that dominated this period in history.

69. Benowitz, *Encyclopedia of American Women and Religion*, 378.
70. Such sales numbers are "bestseller" status. The Federation was a multidenominational association of women's sending agencies, with membership requirements and standing committees. Montgomery served as its president from 1917 to 1918.
71. Robert, *American Women in Mission*, 307.
72. Benowitz, *Encyclopedia of American Women and Religion*, 378.

Using and Challenging Cultural Ideals of Womanhood

Whether they were visiting zenanas, evangelizing, conducting Bible studies, or founding schools, orphanages, or hospitals, women missionaries often thought of their work in a gendered way. They did not think of their biological sex as an accident; they thought of it as an asset. Only women could bring the gospel to the zenanas; only women could treat sick women. Women used these gender-based arguments to justify the existence of their gender-separate missionary organizations.

Women also used gender-based arguments to showcase why their work was so important. "It is the influence of the female, the mother, the sister, the wife, that molds the character of a people," went the argument in one missionary publication.[73] "Only get the hearts of our women, and you will get the heads of the men" went another.[74] The women's missionary movement flourished during the Victorian era, when women were perceived to be more spiritual than men. They were believed to exert a strong moral influence on the men in their lives. The women involved in the women's missionary movement strategically used this cultural vision of womanhood to bolster their work.

It is interesting to note that even as women were using their culture's vision of womanhood, they were simultaneously undermining it. Women who ran the sending boards engaged in numerous activities that would in other circumstances have been reserved for men. They held positions of leadership and influence, controlled their own funds, and developed their own mission strategies. These women did not necessarily see themselves as breaking the bonds of their femininity; rather, they saw themselves as responding to the needs of uneducated, non-Christian women around the world. Nevertheless, by the sheer fact of running a society for themselves, they were challenging Victorian gender roles.

In a culture that thought of women as weak and delicate, the women's sending boards recruited women for their physical strength. For example, the FES in Britain cautioned missionary candidates, "Organic delicacy, constitutional taint, or predisposition to any mental or physical infirmity . . . should be truthfully and frankly stated, in order to prevent public money being wasted in sending out one who may prove unfit for the trials and anxieties of missionary work."[75] The FES also challenged the assumption that women were unsuited for theological discussion. Many of the questions given to female missionary candidates were explicitly theological in nature. Candidates were asked

73. "Female Education Society Annual Report for 1889."
74. "Light through Eastern Lattices."
75. "Female Education Society Annual Report for 1868," 8.

to articulate their view of the following doctrines: "The Trinity in Unity—Original Sin—The Atonement—Justification—Conversion—Sanctification—Devotedness to God—and a future state of rewards and punishment."[76] Candidates were asked, "What has been your method of studying the Scriptures? and what theological works have you chiefly read?"[77] These women missionaries had to be physically and emotionally strong as well as equipped with robust theological training.[78]

The women's missionary movement also challenged cultural conceptions of women abroad. Providing medical care for women, founding schools for women, and working to end foot-binding and female genital mutilation (see chap. 9) communicated a commitment to women's dignity and the flourishing of women's minds and bodies. This commitment to women's rights as human persons was not always welcomed. Yet the women persevered. In 1910 the women's sending boards celebrated their Jubilee, or fifty-year anniversary. But even in the midst of their celebrations, a major obstacle was looming.

The Demise of Denominational Women's Sending Boards

In the early twentieth century, some denominational leaders began a concerted effort to close down the women's sending boards and bring women's work under male control. According to Dana Robert, these men argued that "women diverted the attention of the denomination from the primary missionary task [of evangelizing], that women did not know how to handle money, and that single women missionaries caused trouble on the mission field. As the women's missionary societies became successful and incurred far less overhead than the general boards, arguments emerged that women were causing imbalance in the missionary effort, or that their successful fundraising was causing financial hardship for the general missionary board."[79] These complaints were not, generally speaking, factually accurate. The work that women did on the field was evangelistic. In some cases, they did direct evangelism even when male leaders were uncomfortable with women engaging in that type of work. In other cases, they addressed the needs of women

76. "Female Education Society Annual Report for 1883."
77. "Female Education Society Annual Report for 1883."
78. It is important to bring up the issue of class. Undoubtedly, the women who applied to the FES were some of the best and brightest of England. They had access to the privileges of education. The application specifically asked them, "What advantages of education have you enjoyed?" The FES was a middle- and upper-class society. It was among the middle and upper classes that separate spheres ideology developed and began to break down.
79. Robert, *American Women in Mission*, 305.

and girls for education and health care yet always with the goal of sharing the gospel with those they educated and cared for.

The argument that single women caused problems on the mission field was not substantiated, and the argument that women did not know how to manage money was simply untrue. The women's sending boards had maintained their regular contributions to the denominational work and had added their own work on top of their previous commitments.[80] They had been so successful in raising and managing money that many more missionaries had been sent to the field.

Still, women's board after women's board was closed. In 1909, the Brethren church dissolved its women's board. The Methodist Episcopal Church South followed in 1910, and the Disciples of Christ and Protestant Episcopal Church followed in 1919. The pattern of dissolution continued until practically all the women's sending boards had been dissolved and their work absorbed into the main denominational boards.[81]

The closing down of the women's boards was such a major shift that it could truly be called a "sea change." In some ways it is surprising that a change of this magnitude is virtually unknown less than a hundred years later. In other ways the "disappearing" of women's contributions and women's work is nothing new. It happened with the loss of leadership opportunities for women in the early church, the forced claustration of medieval nuns, and the suppression of women preachers. Women did resist the closure of their sending boards, but they simply were unable to prevent the closures from happening.[82] In many cases, women as laypeople had no say in denominational decisions; in other cases, they were able to reach compromises that only delayed the closures. Robert points out that the demise of the women's sending boards in mainline Protestant churches was followed quickly by a reduced emphasis on mission work overall.[83]

Conclusion

Women played a clear leadership role in modern mission history. As Catholic nuns, they went abroad to establish convents, schools, and hospitals. Protestant missionary wives served as teachers and evangelists and developed a missiology of Christian home life. Through modeling family life and engaging

80. Maxwell, *Woman I Am*, 45–46.
81. Robert, *American Women in Mission*, 303.
82. Robert, *American Women in Mission*, 304.
83. Robert, *American Women in Mission*, 306–7.

local women on topics from marriage to childcare to hygiene, Protestant missionary wives demonstrated how to bring Christ into conversation with everyday tasks and relationships. Women in the global church have continued to take the lead in developing the missiology of the Christian home.

In the mid-nineteenth century, Protestant women founded over forty gender-separate women's sending boards. As these boards sent thousands of single women to the field, the main denominational boards continued to send married women. By 1890, the foreign missionary force was more than 60 percent women, a number that has remained basically constant to this day.[84]

In the early twentieth century, more than three million women belonged to missionary societies.[85] More women in the United States belonged to missionary societies than to any other kind of society. These women and the missionaries they sent developed the missiology of "woman's work for woman" and supported "over 3,200 schools, including eleven women's colleges in Japan, China, Korea, and India."[86] Missionary women also trained and employed Bible women to serve as teachers, preachers, and health workers, and Bible women came to outnumber Western women on the field.

Women missionaries often worked to bring a Christian perspective to social ills that affected women and children. Sometimes, like Maria Brown and Mary Porter, they were able to show how certain practices that harmed women also harmed society and hindered the spread of the gospel. The degree to which missionaries ought to challenge local cultural practices is a persistent question, but too often practices that are harmful to women (and children) are the ones tolerated in the name of acculturation. In part because of women's willingness to follow Christ across cultural boundaries, the church has grown both in numbers and "in knowledge and depth of insight" (Phil. 1:9).

84. Reeves-Ellington, "Women, Protestant Missions," 190–206.
85. Robert, "Women in World Mission," 51.
86. Robert, *Christian Mission*, 137.

9

Faith Missionaries, Evangelists, and Church Founders

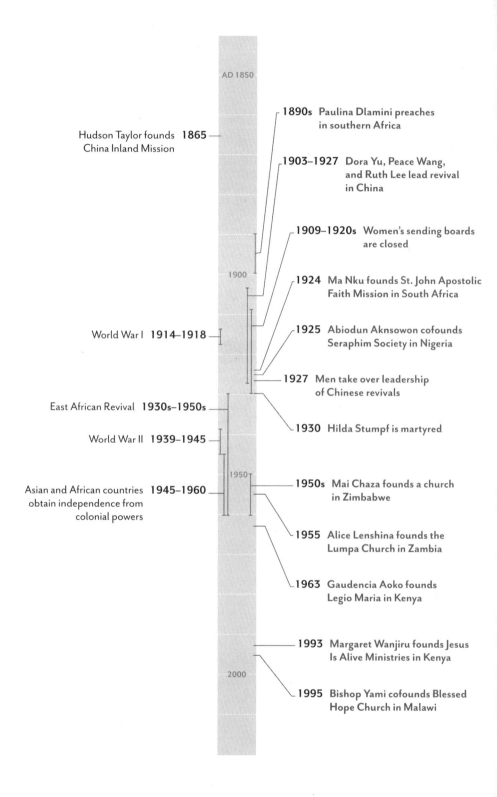

AD 1850

Hudson Taylor founds **1865**
China Inland Mission

┌ **1890s** Paulina Dlamini preaches
in southern Africa

┌ **1903–1927** Dora Yu, Peace Wang,
and Ruth Lee lead revival
in China

┌ **1909–1920s** Women's sending boards
are closed

1900

┌ **1924** Ma Nku founds St. John Apostolic
Faith Mission in South Africa

World War I **1914–1918**

┌ **1925** Abiodun Aknsowon cofounds
Seraphim Society in Nigeria

1927 Men take over leadership
of Chinese revivals

East African Revival **1930s–1950s**

1930 Hilda Stumpf is martyred

World War II **1939–1945**

1950

Asian and African countries **1945–1960**
obtain independence from
colonial powers

1950s Mai Chaza founds a church
in Zimbabwe

1955 Alice Lenshina founds the
Lumpa Church in Zambia

1963 Gaudencia Aoko founds
Legio Maria in Kenya

1993 Margaret Wanjiru founds Jesus
Is Alive Ministries in Kenya

2000

1995 Bishop Yami cofounds Blessed
Hope Church in Malawi

The previous chapter described women's leadership in the modern missionary movement. In the mid-nineteenth century, women founded their own gender-separate missionary societies to send single women to the mission field in order to address the needs of women and girls worldwide. Tragically, these societies were dismantled in the early twentieth century. This chapter shows that even as denominational women's boards were closing, there were still opportunities for American women in independent faith mission organizations. This chapter also features the remarkable Dora Yu (Yu Cidu), who founded the first Chinese faith mission and served as "the first cross-cultural Chinese missionary in modern times."[1] Yu and other Chinese women led a revival in early twentieth-century China. Through their preaching, future male evangelists Watchman Nee (Ni Tuosheng) and Witness Lee (Li Changshou) were converted. From China, the chapter turns to Africa, where women preachers, prophets, and healers were essential to the founding and growth of African Initiated Churches (AICs).

There are many stories of women's leadership in the twentieth-century global church. We chose the content of this chapter because it communicates particularly well the thesis of this entire book: that women have been integral to the mission of the church but have faced gender-based obstacles. The stories in this chapter show that women were initially leaders in faith mission organizations, Chinese revivalism, and AICs, but in each case, their leadership became contested because of their gender. The chapter ends by highlighting a few obstacles faced by women in mission today.

Women's Leadership in Western Faith Mission Organizations

Faith mission organizations were founded outside denominational lines and were often interdenominational. Missionaries with faith mission organizations had to solicit their own financial support. Many of the faith mission organizations that were founded during the late nineteenth and early

1. Wu, "Dora Yu," 85.

twentieth centuries were—at least initially and in name—open to women as full participants.

The earliest faith mission was China Inland Mission (CIM), founded in 1865 by Hudson Taylor. Taylor recruited and sent single women from the start. The first group to go to China consisted of Taylor, his wife and their four children, one married couple, and fourteen singles. Of the singles, five were men and nine were women.[2] A biographer commented, "There was something experimental, almost casual, about Taylor's recruitment of single women." And the same biographer reported Taylor explaining, "The younger they were, the sooner they would be fluent in Chinese."[3] Taylor also found that when a single woman was in charge, it was easier for a Chinese Christian man to take ownership of the work and engage in preaching, teaching, and discipleship. Taylor saw these partnerships as helping to develop a strong indigenous church that was less dependent on foreign ways.[4] The women of CIM were also the first to recognize the evangelistic value of the "wordless book," which used colors (black, red, white, and yellow) to tell the gospel message. Since Chinese culture already used color symbolically, the wordless book was particularly suited for the context.[5] Thus, Taylor's decision to include young single women in his group quickly became part of his overall mission strategy of acculturating to the local setting. His choice seems to have been pragmatic, and he was the first in a line of mission organizations that made similar decisions.

The Evangelical Missionary Alliance was founded in 1887 by Albert Benjamin Simpson. Now known as the Christian and Missionary Alliance, CMA went one step further than CIM: women were not sent as doctors, teachers, or caregivers aimed only at interaction with women and children. Instead, they were recruited as full, equal partners in the task of gospel proclamation to everyone.[6] Other agencies quickly followed suit. In 1890 Frederick Franson established the Evangelical Alliance Mission; he too recruited and sent single women from the start. So did the Gospel Missionary Union (1892), Sudan Interior Mission (1893), Africa Inland Mission (1895), and Worldwide Evangelistic Crusade (1913).

The faith mission movement represented a shift in missiology. The denominational women's sending boards had been using "woman's work for woman" as the rationale for sending single women to the mission field

2. Austin, *China's Millions*, 100.
3. Austin, *China's Millions*, 100.
4. Tucker, *Guardians of the Great Commission*, 47.
5. Austin, *China's Millions*, 168.
6. Robert, *American Women in Mission*, 200–202.

since the mid-nineteenth century. With the start of the faith mission movement, women's calling and ministry were recognized as valid on their own terms without requiring additional justification. According to Dana Robert, "Women joined nondenominational and faith missions because those organizations provided opportunity for their public recognition as evangelists."[7]

Yet the faith mission organizations' goal of sending single women to the field as full-fledged missionaries and evangelists alongside men floundered fairly quickly. In Africa Inland Mission (AIM), women like Anna Compton and Julia McClary, who had envisioned themselves as evangelists, were put to work caring for children by their male colleagues once they got to the field. Dr. Florence Newberry, another woman hoping to evangelize, "was appointed to do medical work."[8] Even though the initial vision of AIM in 1895 was to use the laity as evangelists, women's lay status as well as their gender predisposed the male leaders of AIM to place women in support roles. AIM continued to attract women who believed God was calling them to evangelism. However, there was also a clear need on the field for teachers and health workers. Women were assumed to be well suited for those roles, so those were the roles assigned to them.

Hilda Stumpf (1867–1930) was a well-educated woman who joined AIM in the early twentieth century. At the age of forty, she sailed from New York to Kijabe, Kenya. Although Stumpf had ample qualifications for mission leadership, she was treated as a relatively unimportant part of the mission team. Her colleagues saw her as "junior" in role and experience, and the local people considered her of low status because she was single. Similar to Maria Brown and Mary Porter, who had resisted foot-binding in China (see chap. 8), Stumpf believed that female genital mutilation (FGM) was harmful to women, was harmful to society, and hindered the spread of the gospel. Others, however, associated her with a Western, colonial empire that was forcing its beliefs on the Kikuyu people. In 1930, just a week shy of her sixty-third birthday, a man broke into her room, raped her, choked her to death, then mutilated her in FGM fashion. In some ways, Stumpf's death can be thought of as martyrdom.[9] Like the martyrs of the early church, she persevered in obedience to Christ even when that faithfulness led to her death.

7. Robert, *American Women in Mission*, 205.
8. Robert, *American Women in Mission*, 217.
9. Newell, *Martyr's Grace*, 103. Humanitarian workers and missionaries have often been targets for violence because of their perceived connection with Western imperialism. See Robert, *Christian Mission*, 97–98. For one missionary's response to this phenomenon, see Roseveare, *Living Sacrifice*, 20–22.

Women's Leadership in China

Dora Yu and the Leadership of Women Evangelists in China

At the same time that Western missionary women were joining the new faith mission organizations and hoping to serve as evangelists abroad, several Chinese women were leading a Christian revival in China. Dora Yu (1873–1931) was "the foremost female evangelist in twentieth century Chinese revivalism."[10] She grew up in a Christian family and in 1896 was one of the first graduates of Soochow Women's Hospital.[11] The next year she went to Korea as a missionary and became "the first cross-cultural Chinese missionary in modern times."[12] She was the only physician in the mission, and she also helped to establish a girls' school.[13] She wrote curriculum for the school, taught the girls how to make lace and embroider, and "translated a two-volume Chinese geography textbook into Korean."[14] She also served as a Bible woman and in one year alone visited 925 women and 211 children in their homes.[15]

Not surprisingly, after such a strenuous schedule, her health deteriorated, and she was forced to return to China in 1903. The next year she founded "the first Chinese faith mission" and began to lead prayer meetings, trusting God to tell her what to say.[16] "I took my Bible and went in fear and trembling; but God kept telling me, 'I will put my own word into your lips when the time comes.' But I said, 'Lord, the time has come, the bell has rung, and the people are gathering.' To my surprise, however, I did not seem to have any of my anticipated difficulties, and there was blessing in the meeting."[17]

Yu conducted prayer meetings in Chinese, English, and Korean, and many Chinese people came to faith through her work.[18] She also published what was probably the first Chinese Christian hymnal and became the first Chinese woman to establish a Bible school.[19] Yu continued to be a celebrated revivalist preacher throughout the 1920s, and she also traveled internationally to speak at Christian conferences.

Peace Wang (Wang Peizhen), Ruth Lee (Li Yuanru), and Christina Tsai (Cai Sujuan) were other prominent Chinese evangelists during this period. In

10. Wu, "Dora Yu," 85.
11. Wu, "Dora Yu," 89.
12. Wu, "Dora Yu," 85.
13. Li, "Yu, Dora."
14. Wu, *Dora Yu and Christian Revival*, 89.
15. Wu, *Dora Yu and Christian Revival*, 94.
16. Wu, "Dora Yu," 92.
17. Wu, *Dora Yu and Christian Revival*, 128.
18. Wu, "Dora Yu," 93.
19. Wu, "Dora Yu," 85; Wu, *Dora Yu and Christian Revival*, 142.

fact, Silas Wu argues that "the major Chinese revivalists before 1927 [were] predominantly women."[20]

Peace Wang (1899–1969?) became a Christian when Dr. Shi Meiyu (see chap. 8) preached at her school.[21] When Wang's family discovered that she was a Christian, her father pulled her out of school. Wang believed that she was called to serve God as an evangelist, but at this point, she was engaged and knew that backing out would bring disgrace on her family. Her father had even vowed to punish her with death if she did not comply. But the following Scripture kept resurfacing in her heart: "Anyone who loves their father or mother more than me is not worthy of me" (Matt. 10:37). Because her parents continued to resist her call, Wang locked herself in her room and fasted and prayed. Her parents feared that her hunger strike would end in suicide if they did not allow her to go to seminary.[22] Her father's anger finally abated, and he arranged for Wang's cousin to marry her fiancé instead. Wang enrolled in Jinling Theological College for Women in 1919.[23]

Upon finishing her education, Wang began her work as a traveling preacher. Many people were brought to the Lord by her preaching, including a young man named Witness Lee (Li Changshou), who later described how Wang led him to the Lord: "I attended her meeting, and I can testify that from that day to the present I have never seen preaching that was so prevailing. She preached to a crowd of over one thousand, not about sin or about hell, but concerning how Satan possesses and occupies people. She used the story of Pharaoh possessing the children of Israel as the basis of her message. I was immediately caught by the Lord."[24]

In 1926, Wang helped plant a church in Shanghai. The establishment of this church is usually credited to the male evangelist Watchman Nee (Ni Tuosheng), who did provide leadership over the project. However, without Wang and her friend from seminary, Ruth Lee (1894–1969?), the project would likely not have succeeded.

20. Wu, "Dora Yu," 86.
21. Wang reported that Shi's "every word touched [her] heart." Wu, *Dora Yu and Christian Revival*, 165.
22. Wu, *Dora Yu and Christian Revival*, 167.
23. Peace Wang's conversion story inspired many people, and Ruth Lee recorded her testimony in a 1919 issue of the *Spiritual Light* (Wu, *Dora Yu and Christian Revival*, 167). To stand firm against such familial pressure was a great act of courage and faith. On the day that Wang left her parents' house, her mother and father followed her to the door and wept, "My daughter! My daughter! You don't want your father and you don't want your mother; you only want your Jesus!" and Wang wept with them. This story is told in W. Lee, *Watchman Nee*, chap. 14, sec. 6.
24. W. Lee, *Watchman Nee*, chap. 14, sec. 6.

Navigating Gender Constraints in Chinese Revivalism

Peace Wang, Ruth Lee, Christina Tsai, and Dora Yu led revivals in China until 1927, but after that there was "a marked shift of gender selection in China's revival movement."[25] The movement "was taken over by a new generation of male evangelical revivalists such as Watchman Nee, Wang Mingdao, John Sung, and Leland Wang."[26] Watchman Nee himself was initially converted through the work of Dora Yu, but after he read John Nelson Darby's arguments against women's leadership, Nee decided that women should not teach men. He then convinced evangelists Ruth Lee and Peace Wang to stop teaching men.[27]

Ruth Lee and Peace Wang continued to be very active in Christian mission, but figuring out how to follow the Spirit's leading became more complicated. An example of how Ruth Lee tried to navigate faithfulness within this new constraint is evident in a letter she sent to male evangelists Watchman Nee and Witness Lee. In the letter, Ruth Lee shared her ideas about how to address several issues in the churches she was serving, but it seems she felt she lacked the authority to execute her plans. She labeled her concerns as matters that she wished "from now on the brothers would pay attention to." She wrote, "I am a sister, and in this letter I am simply conversing with you as a member of the family giving you a report of these matters."[28] Lee portrayed herself as an objective reporter, delivering the information to "the brothers" so that they could act as they saw fit—but at the same time, she encouraged them to act and told them what she thought was best.

Although Watchman Nee was against women's leadership, Ruth Lee's letter shows that women's roles may have been somewhat flexible in practice. Throughout the letter, Ruth Lee emphasized the significant contributions that women were making to their local churches. She explained that women and men should work together to build up the church in the unity and knowledge of Christ, though for the best results, she recommended that men minister to men and women minister to women.[29]

While Watchman Nee conversed with leading international theologians and wrote spiritual treatises, Ruth Lee talked one-on-one with new believers and offered practical strategies for improving local church leadership. In the early 1940s, she and Peace Wang rebuilt Nee's church in Shanghai after scandal

25. Wu, "Dora Yu," 86.
26. Wu, "Dora Yu," 86.
27. Wu, "Dora Yu," 98.
28. R. Lee, "Letter from Sister Ruth Lee," 278.
29. R. Lee, "Letter from Sister Ruth Lee," 278.

forced him to abandon it.[30] Yet these women have often gone overlooked. Most sources label them as supporters of Watchman Nee's ministry, but looking at their stories and their influence—Peace Wang's preaching that led to the conversion of Witness Lee, Ruth Lee's leadership in local churches, and the benefits that both Wang and Lee bestowed upon the community of Christian women in Shanghai—it seems that these women also had a ministry of their own.

Had Peace Wang been a man, it is likely that Witness Lee would have called her his mentor. He frequently sought her advice and looked to her for wisdom. However, because she was a woman, he said of her, "She always strongly *supported* me, and those with her always received her *help* and care."[31] Clearly, Peace Wang had significant ministry gifts, but Lee used gendered language to describe them. Several times Lee described Wang as "strong," but he never explicitly called her a "leader."[32] This omission is significant because the way in which people are described impacts how the church remembers them.

Peace Wang and Ruth Lee are remembered as "helpers" who "assisted" the male leaders, even though "coworkers" was the title that God had apparently suggested to Watchman Nee in a dream that he had prior to meeting Ruth Lee: "The night before her arrival, Watchman Nee was considering whether or not to join the reception, thinking that although she might be a good evangelist, since she was a female, she should not be too highly esteemed. However, during the night he had a dream. In that dream he and others met her at the pier. When he saw her in the dream, the Lord told him that she would be his co-worker."[33]

Ruth Lee and Peace Wang were arrested in 1956 by the Chinese government for their leadership in the Christian movement.[34] Both women died in prison. Like Dora Yu, these women's influence on the spread of Christianity in China was immense.

Women's Leadership in Africa

The East African Revival

As women in China were trying to fit their leadership into gendered constraints, women in the East African Revival of the 1930s, '40s, and '50s were

30. W. Lee, *Watchman Nee*, chap. 14, sec. 8. See also Doyle, "Watchman Nee."
31. W. Lee, *Watchman Nee*, chap. 14, sec. 8 (emphasis added).
32. He also says that she "stood firmly" and "was really a wall against the tide." W. Lee, *Watchman Nee*, chap. 14, sec. 7 and 8.
33. W. Lee, *Watchman Nee*, chap. 14, sec. 2.
34. W. Lee, *Watchman Nee*, chap. 14, sec. 2.

being urged by the church to break out of gender constraints. "The East African Revival [was] a large-scale movement of renewal institutionalized within the Protestant churches of Uganda, Kenya, Tanzania, Rwanda, and Burundi."[35] People associated with the revival were called *Balokole* (saved ones). The *Balokole* met regularly to pray and sing together. They confessed their sins in public and testified to the power of God in their lives. Because women could testify to the transforming power of God just as much as men could, the revival tended to create new egalitarian norms in churches that had previously minimized women's leadership. *Balokole* women "preached in groups or in mixed teams . . . [and] served as graphic evidence of the new status enjoyed by women in the Revival fellowship."[36] *Balokole* women also experienced new status within marriage, as couples were encouraged to make decisions together and to confess their sins to each other.[37]

Paulina Dlamini

Paulina Dlamini (1858–1942) was a member of the court of the Zulu king and went on to found churches among the Zulu people of southern Africa.[38] Civil war forced Dlamini to flee the court, and eventually she wound up working for a farmer named Gert van Rooyen. She became a Christian through a dream and began leading worship services in the van Rooyen home.[39] Her ministry was so effective that people began to call her *umPhositoli* (the Apostle). Each week she and van Rooyen would plan a sermon, and then she would preach "to the Blacks," and he would preach "to the Whites."[40] As congregations began springing up as a result of Dlamini's preaching, the German missionary overseeing the evangelization of the region sent male evangelists to lead the congregations. It is difficult to tell from the twice-redacted memoir how Dlamini felt about male evangelists taking over her work. But it is clear that Dlamini was highly satisfied by the work she was able to do as an evangelist. She took great pride in being able to preach to two of the wives of the new Zulu king, who then converted. And late in life she said she was "overjoyed" when the commander of the royal army became a Christian.[41] Dlamini decided to remain unmarried because, she said, "I wished to dedicate

35. Robins, "Conversion, Life Crises," 185.
36. Robins, "Conversion, Life Crises," 195.
37. Larsson, "Haya Women's Response," 188.
38. Her tombstone says that she "initiated the congregations at Lemgo and Esibongweni." Bourquin, *Paulina Dlamini*, 109.
39. Bourquin, *Paulina Dlamini*, 51.
40. Bourquin, *Paulina Dlamini*, 86.
41. Bourquin, *Paulina Dlamini*, 93.

my whole life to the service of the Lord and could achieve this best by remaining single."[42]

Women's Leadership in African Initiated Churches

Dlamini and the *Balokole* of the East African Revival worked within denominations that had been initiated by Western missionaries, but during this same time, a number of new African Initiated Churches (AICs) began to take off throughout the continent. Women played a major role in the establishment and growth of these AICs. Unlike mission churches, which took years to turn over leadership to Africans, AICs were governed entirely by Africans from the start. Women were so active in the AIC movement that it has been called "a woman's movement."[43] According to Marthinus Daneel, "AIC women comprise the bulk (in some instances up to 80%) of adult membership in these churches. . . . AIC women have remained essentially the unsung bearers of the Gospel good news in Africa."[44]

Women were especially attracted to AICs because these churches tended to focus on women's concerns more than did mission churches. For example, mission churches offered little help to women who were barren. AICs—particularly those founded by women—were known for welcoming barren women, praying over them, and healing them.[45] Women flocked to these new churches and healing centers because, whether healed or not, they found their burden lightened by the presence of the church community.[46]

Witchcraft was another issue that women in Africa faced and that mission churches were inept at addressing. Women could be accused of witchcraft for a plethora of reasons: "too much education or success, too many children, too few children, too readily influenced by her in-laws, too resistant to the family of her in-laws, etc."[47] Especially when an individual's success seemed to be at the expense of others, she was likely to be accused of witchcraft.[48] Some women who practiced witchcraft did so because they were unable to get pregnant or because they needed help with their business ventures. Other women were wrongfully accused of witchcraft. But in each case, these women experienced social isolation. For accused women, AICs became a place where they could find healing and community. Women founders of AICs preached

42. Bourquin, *Paulina Dlamini*, 10.
43. Daniel, "Role of Women," 136.
44. Daneel, "AIC Women," 312–13.
45. For case studies of healing, see Sackey, *New Directions*, chap. 6.
46. Daneel, "AIC Women," 326.
47. Eck and Jain, introduction, 73.
48. Amoah, "Women, Witches and Social Change," 85.

against witchcraft and performed exorcisms in churches, homes, and healing centers. Some even had their entire congregations spend time during the
service confessing sins associated with witchcraft.[49]

Abiodun Akinsowon (1907–1994) was one of the first women to found an
AIC. She grew up as an Anglican in Nigeria. When she was fifteen, she "fell into a
trance that lasted seven days."[50] Her uncle called a holy man, Moses Orimolade,
to come to her bedside, and she awoke from the trance. She talked about seeing
angels and the heavenly city. "Soon people were traveling great distances to visit
Abiodun and hear about her visions. She and Orimolade began holding regular
prayer sessions, and by September 1925 they had formed an interdenominational
prayer group called the Seraphim Society."[51] Their gatherings soon became a new
church. As more people flocked to the church, Abiodun and Orimolade incorporated Bible classes on Sunday afternoons, and Orimolade appointed a group of
men to be his "Praying Band."[52] Abiodun, because of her powerful preaching,
became known as Captain Abiodun. "She has been credited with founding the
Society's branches in most of the important centers in Yorubaland."[53]

Sadly, in 1929 power struggles fractured the society. Abiodun alleged that
the men of the Praying Band were trying to push her out of the society.[54]
Orimolade insisted that he was the sole founder and ruler of the society.[55] In
actuality, the differing personalities and giftings of Orimolade and Abiodun
had complemented each other in the early years of the society, but then strife
drove them apart and they chose not to be reconciled to each other. Abiodun
tried to reconcile with the men of the Praying Band, but while the men were
willing to grant her authority over women in the society, they would not
recognize her as cofounder of the society. Abiodun's argument "was that
if England could tolerate Queen Victoria as their ruler and the Bible could
contain examples of prophetesses, there was no reason why she should not
be honored as the Living Founder of the Society."[56] According to Joseph
Akinyele Omoyajowo, who has chronicled the history of the society, "Perhaps if Abiodun had been a man, her significance in the history of the whole
movement . . . would have paved the way for a probable union of all the Lagos
sections—possibly under her leadership."[57]

49. Phiri, "African Women in Mission," 273.
50. Sheldon, "Emmanuel, Christiana Abiodun," 298.
51. Sheldon, "Emmanuel, Christiana Abiodun," 298.
52. Peel, *Aladura*, 75.
53. Omoyajowo, *Cherubim and Seraphim*, 59.
54. Omoyajowo, *Cherubim and Seraphim*, 190.
55. Omoyajowo, *Cherubim and Seraphim*, 68.
56. Omoyajowo, *Cherubim and Seraphim*, 80.
57. Omoyajowo, *Cherubim and Seraphim*, 201.

Another AIC founder, Christinah Nku (1894–1980), experienced a call to ministry in South Africa in the 1920s. Ma Nku, as people called her, worked in the slums and invited people back to her home for prayer and healing multiple times a day.[58] In 1924, she had a vision that she was supposed to build a church, so she did, calling it St. John Apostolic Faith Mission. It "became one of the largest indigenous churches in South Africa, attracting over fifty thousand members."[59] As she aged and it became time for a new leader to take over her church, Ma Nku hoped her son Johannes would be that leader. Instead, John Masango was elected. "Masango broke all ties with the Nku family and established himself as 'founder' of the church."[60]

Similar stories of women-initiated AICs across East Africa can be told. In Zimbabwe, Mai (Mother) Chaza (1914–1960) experienced a call to ministry after a series of personal crises. She established a church that, "at the height of its popularity . . . had nearly one million members."[61] Mai Chaza was a healer, particularly known for her ability to heal barren women. When she died, her church was taken over by a man from Malawi.[62]

A Catholic woman in Kenya, Gaudencia Aoko (1943–1988), was called to ministry through a series of dreams starting in 1963. She and a man by the name of Simeo Ondeto established an AIC called Legio Maria. In only a year, the church grew to one hundred thousand members, and it probably has more than a million members today.[63] Part of the reason Aoko broke away from the Catholic Church was that she believed God called both men and women to the priesthood. In the end, however, Aoko had to leave her own church because it developed a structure of male leadership "that excluded women from major leadership positions."[64]

Bishop Yami of Malawi (b. 1950) received a call to evangelism in 1978. Together with Pastor Lumwira, Yami started Blessed Hope Church, which focused on reaching people on the margins of society. Unfortunately, the partnership between Yami and Lumwira didn't last. "Lumwira wrote a letter to Bishop Yami informing her that it is not Biblical for a woman to become leader of a church. Therefore he asked that she should resign."[65] Yami left the church, but she continued to reach out to the marginalized, especially vision-impaired people, who were living in appalling conditions. She formed

---

58. Quinn, "Nku, Christinah."
59. Quinn, "Nku, Christinah."
60. A. Anderson, *African Reformation*, 110.
61. Muir, *Women's History*, 317.
62. Jules-Rosette, "Cultural Ambivalence," 92.
63. Kustenbauder, "Aoko, Gaudencia," 246.
64. Kustenbauder, "Aoko, Gaudencia," 246.
65. Phiri, "African Women in Mission," 286.

a church among them, but once again a male member of the church "started questioning the validity of having a woman leader of a church. He tried to divide and break the church but failed. He later left with ten members."[66]

The Significance of AIC Women

One of the reasons for the rapid growth of women-led AICs is that people, particularly women, experienced healing, community, and redemption in these churches. Women leaders of AICs spoke God's good news of healing into a myriad of situations, including "unemployment, poverty, sickness, stress, sin, housing, food, [and] family issues."[67] Like Jesus and the Israelite prophets, AIC women prophets were directed by the Spirit to preach "good news to the poor" (Luke 4:18). By depending on the Spirit, they were able to heal sick people and cast out demons, to welcome those whose deepest needs the mission churches did not know how to address.

By focusing on barrenness and witchcraft, healing and exorcism, women founders of AICs accelerated the process of enculturating the gospel in Africa. Mission churches often regarded African religion as mere superstition, but because they didn't take witchcraft seriously and bring the gospel into real conversation with it, people ended up "living double lives; going to Church, receiving sacraments and during moments of life crises, reverting to their traditional religion."[68] By knowing just how real and deeply woven into society witchcraft was, and by demonstrating Christ's power over witchcraft through healing and exorcisms in Christ's name, AIC women prophets helped extend Christ's lordship over aspects of people's lives previously untouched by the Western presentation of the gospel.

Women in AICs contributed immensely to the mission of the church in Africa. They welcomed people on the margins of society. They preached, prophesied, healed, cast out demons, and paid attention to issues of concern to women. But men contested their leadership because of their gender. Churches founded by women were eventually taken over by men, in some cases after the death of the founder and in other cases while the founder was still alive.

Many AIC leaders who faced opposition to their leadership—just like the women featured in chapters 6 and 7—took great comfort in the Scriptures.[69] When asked to speak on "the role of women in African Initiated Churches," Dr. Lydia August, daughter of Ma Nku, spoke about how AIC women were

66. Phiri, "African Women in Mission," 287.
67. Mwaura, "Gendered Appropriation," 292.
68. Wirba, *Women and Inculturated Evangelization*, 80.
69. Oduyoye, *Daughters of Anowa*, 124.

inspired by the stories of the Virgin Mary and Mary Magdalene.[70] Margaret Wanjiru (b. 1961), the founder of Jesus Is Alive Ministries (an AIC), has taken comfort and inspiration from the story of the Virgin Mary and that of Nehemiah. After Wanjiru's conversion to Christianity, she had a vision in which God compared her to Mary and Nehemiah. She heard God say to her, "I chose Mary because she was God fearing and humble. Because you are obedient and humble, I will send you to restore my church."[71] She also heard God say, "You will bring souls and rebuild the church like Nehemiah." And indeed, she has.[72]

These are some of the most well-known founders of AICs, but hundreds of other women have founded smaller AICs and have ministered to people in need. Today fewer women who found AICs are asked to surrender their leadership to men.[73]

The Struggle for Ministry Opportunities Continues

The Shift from Female to Male Leadership in the Philippines and India

The pattern revealed in this chapter—female leadership giving way to male leadership—also occurred as Western missionary societies turned over their mission work to indigenous leaders in the Philippines and India in the early twentieth century.

In 1925, the American Women's Foreign Missionary Society "supported 138 missionaries and assistants and 250 Bible women" in the Philippines.[74] But then two things happened: denominational leaders in America closed down the separate women's boards, and Americans surrendered control of mission institutions to Filipinos. As Laura Prieto notes, "The transfer of the missions into Filipino hands meant the end of separatist woman's work for woman. . . . Male pastors, not Bible women, would become the vanguard of Protestant Christianity in the Philippines."[75]

A similar thing happened in India. In the 1920s, the American Madura Mission supported around a hundred Bible women.[76] However, as Americans turned over leadership to Indian pastors, Bible women were marginalized.

---

70. Daneel, "AIC Women," 255.
71. Mwaura, "Gendered Appropriation," 284.
72. Mwaura, "Burning Stick."
73. Sackey, *New Directions*, viii.
74. Prieto, "'Stepmother America,'" 360.
75. Prieto, "'Stepmother America,'" 361.
76. Heim, "'Standing behind the Looms,'" 47.

Indian Bible women working under American missionary women experienced a unique set of challenges, but at least their work was valued and American missionary women provided them with funding and moral support. Once Bible women came under the authority of Indian pastors, they lost a great deal of this funding and support.[77]

Obstacles for American and Korean Protestant Women in Mission

The "two-person career" is an ongoing struggle for Western missionary women and clergy wives. In a two-person career, the husband has the career with the accompanying title, responsibility, and pay, yet the work involved requires two people—the husband and the wife—to fulfill all the responsibilities.[78] The husband's employing organization directly benefits from the wife's so-called voluntary service. In keeping with the two-person career mentality, most faith mission organizations talk about their workers in terms of "units," with a unit being either a single missionary or a missionary couple. Single women don't fit the two-person norm, so they are often assigned support roles. Women in faith mission organizations have always faced the constraints of their wider religious culture. In the early twentieth century, faith missions were influenced by the fundamentalist movement, and in the late twentieth century, they were influenced by the "biblical manhood and womanhood" movement. The teachings promoted by those movements easily aligned with a two-person approach to mission work but struggled to find a place for single women's contributions.

In 1984, Joyce Bowers found that married American women missionaries typically assumed one of four roles: homemaker, background supporter, team worker, or parallel worker.[79] In 2003, M. Elizabeth Hall and Nancy Duvall found that women in the homemaker and background supporter roles were happier than women in team-worker and parallel-worker roles.[80] They were surprised by this finding because it was contrary to most research being done at the time with North American women. They suggested that the freedom to choose their role might be of greater importance to women than the actual role itself. A few years later, two other psychologists also studied missionary women's happiness related to the four roles proposed by Bowers. They suggested collapsing the four roles into two, direct worker and support worker, and found that women in direct worker roles were slightly more satisfied than

---

77. Heim, "'Standing behind the Looms,'" 58–59.
78. Papanek, "Men, Women, and Work," 852.
79. Bowers, "Roles of Married Women Missionaries," 6.
80. Hall and Duvall, "Married Women in Missions," 311.

women in support roles.[81] Two additional studies examined married women's marital happiness. The results were dismal, showing that married missionary women ranked lower than other expatriate women in marital satisfaction and long-term well-being but that they were still strongly committed to mission work and to filling their gendered roles.[82]

Leanne Dzubinski's study of the work practices of American missionary women in one organization found that women reported many hours invested in ministry work outside the home each week and that gender concerns were just as stressful as ministry concerns. The women felt they were not respected, not supported in using their gifts, not welcomed into leadership, and generally not taken seriously as mission practitioners.[83] The dissonance between women's actual experiences of working as missionaries and organizational messages that overlooked, ignored, or subsumed their work under a male husband or colleague created stress, yet the women, like women in previous times, remained committed to mission work and to their organization.[84]

Young Hertig's study of two female evangelists (*jeondosa*) in Korean-American churches found that these *jeondosa*, like American missionaries, remained committed to ministry but struggled with painful gender dynamics. One *jeondosa* talked about how she didn't fit into the stereotypes projected onto her. "My multifaceted background, *jeondosa*, a mother of two little children, doctoral candidate, is perceived as a liability rather than an asset in the Korean immigrant church simply because I am a woman."[85] As a married woman, she was also expected to participate in the ministry of her husband, an associate pastor at the church. Noting the same issue that has plagued American women, she said, "The church takes the two leaders under one person's salary while demanding two full workloads."[86] This issue of workload and compensation was also mentioned by the other *jeondosa*. Both *jeondosa* also struggled with a call to preach, which they felt keenly but had to stifle. Not only the male pastors but also the women in their congregations opposed them.[87] When Christianity first came to Korea, it "challenged Confucian gender scripts. . . . [It] counterculturally advocated women's education and leadership when Korean society did not allow these."[88] But today Christianity is largely aligned again with traditional gender scripts, which require women

81. Crawford and DeVries, "Relationship between Role Perception and Well-Being," 187.
82. Bikos et al., "First-Year Adaptation," 658; Rosik and Pandzic, "Marital Satisfaction," 3.
83. Dzubinski, "Portrayal vs. Practice," 83–88.
84. Dzubinski, "Portrayal vs. Practice," 88–89.
85. Hertig, "Without a Face," 190.
86. Hertig, "Without a Face," 190.
87. Hertig, "Without a Face," 190.
88. Hertig, "Without a Face," 189.

to be silent and obedient to male leaders.[89] Christian women in the pews tend to harbor what Hertig calls "internalized sexism," believing themselves to be inferior to men.[90]

Dzubinski has found that, like the *jeondosa* in Korean churches, women in executive leadership in Western evangelical mission agencies today also have to carefully navigate limited space allotted for them to lead. These agencies tend to hold relatively prescriptive views of gender roles for men and women. The women leaders mostly accept and follow the gender scripts while cautiously maneuvering those scripts to be able to fulfill their sense of God's calling.[91]

Conclusion

The rise of faith mission organizations signaled a new opportunity for women. At least initially, many of these organizations were willing to send women as evangelists in their own right rather than requiring them to serve as part of a two-person career with their husbands or to work in support roles. So many women participated in the global faith mission movement that historian Dana Robert has said, "Without women there would have been no faith missions."[92] The same statement could be made about revivalism in twentieth-century China: without women, there would have been no Chinese revivalism. And the same statement could be made about AICs.

Sadly, this chapter also demonstrated that just as male leaders of Western denominations took over women's missionary societies in the early twentieth century, so male leaders took over ministries initially led by women in China, Africa, the Philippines, and India. Dora Yu and the other Chinese evangelists paved the way for male leadership of Chinese revivals in the years after 1927. Paulina Dlamini and AIC women founded congregations, but then men took over. Bible women were marginalized in the Philippines and India when American women surrendered their mission work to Indian and Filipino men. And women's leadership, once a central component of Korean Christianity, is now discouraged.

In Western missionary societies today, women still struggle to be accepted as leaders. Their work is often subsumed under that of their husbands, and

89. Julia Ma, who writes from a Korean Pentecostal perspective, notes that while most Pentecostal churches in Asia ordain women, "often Asian women in general have been deprived of their calling and their potential because their culture has commonly failed to recognize women's leadership qualities and capabilities." Ma, "Asian Women and Pentecostal Ministry," 103.

90. Hertig, "Without a Face," 196.

91. Dzubinski, "Playing by the Rules."

92. Robert, *American Women in Mission*, 253.

they struggle within the constraints of approved gender scripts. Dzubinski's current research is working to understand the degree to which the challenges present-day women missionary leaders encounter are specific to a Christian organization or comparable to the challenges women leaders encounter in any realm of North American society. A study that included mission leaders and leaders from higher education found that the challenges were the same for both groups of women.[93] Another study included women leaders in the medical and law professions and again found that women in all realms reported strikingly similar challenges to their leadership.[94] Despite these obstacles, Christian women around the globe continue to experience a call from God to serve in the mission of the church.

93. Diehl and Dzubinski, "Making the Invisible Visible."
94. Diehl et al., "Measuring the Invisible."

CONCLUSION

Women's Leadership in the Church

This book has demonstrated that women have been integral to the mission of the church. In every era, women have occupied positions of leadership and have spread the faith through word and deed. In the second century, there were so many women leaders that pagan critics like Celsus used this point to discredit the church. In the fourth- and fifth-century deserts of Egypt and Syria, church father Palladius drew attention to the great numbers of ascetic women "with manly qualities, to whom God apportioned labours equal to those of men."[1] In late antiquity and the Middle Ages, Christian empresses, queens, and nuns facilitated the Christianization of Asia and Europe, and in the thirteenth century, there were so many women entering and creating new forms of religious life that scholars have referred to this movement as "the women's religious movement."[2] Women preached in the First and Second Great Awakenings, and women played a leading role in the Holiness movement. In the nineteenth and early twentieth centuries, over three million women joined the women's missionary movement, either as contributing members of sending boards or as missionaries and Bible women. Early twentieth-century revivals in China were led by women, and so many women founded and joined African Initiated Churches that African Christianity has been called "a woman's movement."[3] According to Dana Robert,

1. Palladius, *Lausiac History* 41.
2. Lester, *Creating Cistercian Nuns*, 21–28.
3. Daniel, "Role of Women," 136.

not just African but *world* Christianity could be called "a women's movement" since "women constitute the majority of active participants."[4]

Women Passing the Baton of Religious Leadership

Throughout Christian history, women leaders have passed the baton of religious leadership to successive generations. These baton passes have not been the formal passes of apostolic succession, but they have been no less significant. In the early and medieval church, virgins like Thecla, martyrs like Perpetua, patrons like Melania, scholars like Paula, and deaconesses like Olympias inspired successive generations of Christians each year when their stories were told on the anniversaries of their deaths. Empresses and queens understood their royal leadership in light of the precedent set by Helena, the first Christian empress. And Clotilda was the first in a series of Western queens who facilitated the conversion of their husbands and kingdoms to Christianity. The precedent of religious leadership set by women inspired future women and men to pick up the baton of religious leadership.

At many points in history, as women puzzled over their own place in the church, they turned to Scripture for instruction and inspiration. They found the Bible to be full of strong, capable, divinely chosen women leaders like Deborah, Esther, Mary, Mary Magdalene, Phoebe, Priscilla, and Lydia. The precedent set by these biblical women empowered many later Christian women to pick up the baton of religious leadership and carry it into their own contexts.

Dreams and visions also inspired women to pick up the baton of religious leadership. In the fourth century, Emmelia had a vision in which her daughter Macrina was called "Thecla." Like the second-century Thecla, Macrina went on to become a recognized leader in her community. Hildegard of Bingen and Catherine of Siena were two of the most famous visionaries in the Middle Ages, but many other visionary women also played a leadership role in the church as mediators, counselors, and teachers. Pioneer nuns Leoba, Anne-Marie Javouhey, and Marie de l'Incarnation experienced God's call through a dream or vision. Many preachers in America and almost all of the founders of African Initiated Churches described in chapter 9 experienced God's call through a dream or vision. Dreams and visions bolstered women's sense of authority and gave them confidence to say yes to God's call. Dreams and visions also imparted prestige to women in cultures that otherwise tended to limit women's leadership.

4. Robert, "World Christianity," 180.

Women in every generation have led the way in caring for poor people
and sick people. Widows and deaconesses, nuns and beguines, missionaries,
social activists, and Bible women "met needs in health and social welfare that
governments had not yet fully addressed."[5] Christian women pioneered the
professions of nursing and social work. In the nineteenth century, women
who were involved in social outreach were particularly aware of the fact that
they were building on the work of previous women. For example, Elizabeth
Seton's Sisters of Charity influenced the deaconess community in Kaiserswerth, Germany, in the 1830s. The Kaiserswerth deaconesses inspired Florence
Nightingale, who became the founder of modern nursing. Nightingale and
Chinese doctors Kang Cheng and Shi Meiyu inspired an entire generation of
nurses and doctors in China. In this way, women passed the baton of religious
leadership to the next generation.

Women have also been committed to education and caring for the needs of
women and children. In the medieval world, convents were places where widowed women and orphaned children were cared for and educated. Nuns have
continued to be active in education up until the present day. In the nineteenth
century, Anne-Marie Javouhey's Sisters of St. Joseph founded schools and
hospitals around the world. So did Ann Judson, Isabella Thoburn, and many
of the Protestant women who became cross-cultural missionaries. Schools
founded by missionary women gave many girls their first access to education,
which increased their well-being and their status in society.[6] Women missionaries in parts of Africa and China also led the way in opposing practices like
female genital mutilation and foot-binding, which damaged girls and women.
In America, women dedicated themselves to the temperance and social purity
movements in order to liberate women and children who were oppressed
by prostitution and male addiction to alcohol. And the women founders of
African Initiated Churches worked to heal women of barrenness and deliver
them from witchcraft.

Theological Contributions Made by Women

Women have made significant theological contributions over the course of
Christian history. For example, in the early church, women martyrs shaped
the church's theology of suffering and Christology. Women may not have written theological treatises, but their example spurred theological developments
nonetheless. For example, Blandina hung on a stake in a way that evoked

5. Olson, *Deacons and Deaconesses*, 215.
6. Robert, *Christian Mission*, 136.

Christ on the cross. She and other early martyrs showed what it looked like to imitate Christ. And as these women continued to be remembered on the anniversaries of their deaths, they continued to shape theology and church practices.

During the Middle Ages, women played a major role in causing a theological shift. Their devotion to the Eucharist and their mystical visions of the infant Christ and marriage to Christ helped to shift the emphasis of medieval piety from Christ's kingship to Christ's bodily humanity and suffering. Medieval nuns also helped stimulate a growing use of art in worship and devotion. Nuns used a theology of the incarnation to justify their use of art and were far more dedicated to the use of images in their devotional lives than were male monks, priests, and theologians. Their use of art in their own devotion helped lead others in the church to value images as aids to the spiritual life.

Medieval nuns also contributed to reform movements within the church. Herrad, Hildegard of Bingen and Catherine of Siena were particularly active in calling for church reform. Hildegard and Catherine also wrote such important theological works that the Roman Catholic Church named them Doctors of the Church. Their work, and the work of other medieval nuns, shaped the church's understanding of God's relationship with humanity and humanity's call to imitate Christ.

During the women's missionary movement, women developed two important theologies of mission. The missiology of the Christian home brought Christ into the marital relationship and into the domestic tasks that women typically performed. As a result, marriage, parenthood, and housework were imbued with missiological significance. The missiology of "woman's work for woman" dominated the nineteenth-century women's missionary movement. As women missionaries attended to the holistic needs of the world's women, they also created a justification for women's participation in mission.

Activist women and preachers of the nineteenth and twentieth centuries also developed theological arguments for their work. Phoebe Palmer and Catherine Booth wrote books that offered a theological rationale for women's preaching, and many of the lesser-known nineteenth-century women preachers wrote theological rationales into their autobiographies.[7] Katharine Bushnell and Madeline Southard did important early work in exegesis that exposed biblical foundations for women's leadership in the church.

Women founders of African Initiated Churches in the twentieth century helped to contextualize the gospel in Africa through their lived theology of witchcraft and deliverance ministries. Rather than viewing witchcraft

---

7. See S. Stanley, *Holy Boldness*, 251–53, for a list of these autobiographies.

as superstition, as many mission churches had done, AIC women preached that Christ was more powerful than witchcraft and could liberate people oppressed by it.

Limiting Women's Leadership

In the early days of the church, Christianity was a charismatic movement. It had not yet become bureaucratized. Scholars have long noted that the very process of bureaucratization often has the effect of limiting the leadership of women. In the earliest days of a Christian movement, women are often free to minister in the ways God has called them. But as the movement grows and it becomes necessary to institutionalize, women see their opportunities for leadership decrease.[8] As the second-century church grew, it reduced leadership opportunities for women in order to appear more respectable to Roman society and to distance the church from heretical movements with women leaders. Preaching and leading house churches—two tasks that Christian women had done—were increasingly reserved for male leaders of the church.

During the medieval period, women were deeply involved in monastic movements in times of renewal and had more control over their own religious lives, but as the spirit of renewal gave way to institutionalization, the church clamped down on women's freedom and leadership. For example, in the late twelfth and early thirteenth centuries, women's religious communities sprouted up organically throughout Europe. Some of these women wandered the streets to beg and dedicated themselves to serving poor people and people with leprosy, but over the course of the thirteenth century, the church insisted on claustration. St. Clare, inspired by St. Francis and blessed by the pope, was allowed to write and follow her own rule of absolute poverty, but as soon as she died, her community lost that privilege.

The pattern of early women's leadership followed by constraint continued to play out during the modern period. In the late eighteenth century, evangelical women preachers who had been celebrated during the First Great Awakening came to be seen as "disorderly women." Evangelical leaders wanting to appear respectable to a wider American society that disapproved of women's preaching began to limit preaching to the men in their churches. Similarly, after the Second Great Awakening, churches that had formerly supported women preachers dropped their support in order to gain respectability. These churches also changed their stance on women's preaching so as to distance themselves from the women's suffrage movement. Some people

---

8. Tucker and Liefeld, *Daughters of the Church*, 15.

even deliberately altered the church records to hide the voices of women in this period.

In the late nineteenth and twentieth centuries, the pattern played out again in the faith mission movement. At first, women worked as founders, preachers, and partners with men in mission. As faith mission organizations grew and established more bureaucratic, less visionary structures, women hoping to be evangelists were pushed into support roles as teachers and health-care workers. The pattern also played out in Chinese revivalism and African Initiated Churches, as women leaders were replaced by men. Yet again, in some cases, women as founders were contested, further contributing to the disappearing of women's leadership.

In the early and medieval church, some male leaders sought to limit women's leadership because they viewed women as more sinful than men and as temptresses trying to lure men off the spiritual path. Some people also accused women of sexual misdeeds in order to discredit their leadership. Nestorius used this tactic with Empress Pulcheria, and Reformers used the accusation of sexual deviance to justify violence against nuns. Nineteenth-century Americans described women preachers as "Jezebels," and Aimee Semple McPherson's achievements have long been overshadowed by the suspicion that she ran off to have an affair.

Women Have Turned Constraints into Assets

Through prayer, reflection, and partnership with others, women throughout church history have come up with strategies for fulfilling God's call in the midst of cultural gender constraints. During the Middle Ages, when women were expected to be weaker and less powerful than men, Hildegard of Bingen and Mechtild of Magdeburg emphasized their own weakness and unworthiness in order to protect themselves from criticism and enable the church to hear the message that they believed God had told them to share with the church. Hildegard spoke of herself as a "poor little woman" and as a "fragile human, ashes of ashes, and filth of filth."[9] Mechtild of Magdeburg referred to herself as a "poor maid" and emphasized that it was only because of her lowliness that God had deigned to reveal himself to her in visions.[10] This posture was enough to assure the church that she was not out to challenge priestly authority, and it enabled her to continue teaching and admonishing others. Simi-, larly, in twentieth-century China, Ruth Lee learned how to fit her leadership

9. Hildegard of Bingen, *Scivias*, 59.
10. Mechtild of Magdeburg, *Flowing Light of the Godhead* 2.4 (E. Anderson, 39).

within the gender norms that came to dominate her Christian community. She portrayed herself as an objective reporter, delivering the information to "the brothers" so that they could act as they saw fit—while at the same time encouraging them to act and telling them what she thought was best. *Jeondosa* in Korean churches and Western women in executive leadership today have also learned to carefully navigate the limited space allotted for them to lead.

When faced with gender-based obstacles, many women in history turned the constraints of their culture into assets for ministry and spiritual growth. During the late Middle Ages, when women were considered to be more fleshly and more tied to food than men, women embraced their presumed bodily nature and used their relationship with food to further their relationship with God. They paid attention to their bodies, they meditated on the relationship between their bodies and Christ's body, and they contributed to the growing medieval interest in Christ's humanity. Women fasted, they gave their food to poor people, and they became more and more devoted to the food of the Eucharist. Through their eucharistic devotion and through the visions God granted them, these women contributed to the growing elevation of the Eucharist during this period.

During the nineteenth century, Western culture shifted from thinking of White women as more fleshly and more sinful than men to thinking of them as more spiritual and more angelic than men. Society idolized mothers, who remained in the moral "private sphere" of the home while their husbands engaged in so-called worldly business dealings in the "public sphere." During the Second Great Awakening, some White evangelical women embraced society's view of them as virtuous mothers to justify their public preaching. These women argued that just as they instructed children in virtue at home, so they could instruct congregants in virtue at church.

In China, medical doctors Kang Cheng and Shi Meiyu used the same argument about the capacity of women to shape children in the home to build support for their medical and educational work, which could improve the health and knowledge of mothers, who could then raise better children to make a stronger China. Pandita Ramabai also used this argument in India. Chinese and Indian reformers blamed some of their countries' problems on the poor health and ignorance of Chinese and Indian women. Kang, Shi, and Ramabai seized this argument and used it to justify their medical and educational ministries for women. White women in the West who likewise believed they were called to activism used society's view of them as "angels" to expand their involvement in the public sphere. Laying claim to their "spiritual" nature and their capacity to reform men, Josephine Butler, Katharine Bushnell, and Frances Willard organized movements of social reform for the sake of improving society.

The motif of turning constraints into assets was also a bedrock principle of the entire women's missionary movement. Because of the strict sex segregation of upper-class Hindu culture, only women could bring the gospel to the zenanas and treat women patients in India. Western women used these gender-based constraints to justify the existence of their gender-separate missionary societies. Missionary wives, who found that their domestic responsibilities left them no time for preaching and teaching, likewise used the constraints of their situation to develop the missiology of the Christian home.

Aimee Semple McPherson used early twentieth-century gender scripts to facilitate her ministry. McPherson's first husband died, and her second and third husbands divorced her. Critics pointed to her failed marriages to discredit her ministry, but she turned her failed marriages into a sermon illustration about how Christ was the perfect "husband" who would never desert his church.

Women Have Persevered Even to Death

Women have shown their ability to remain faithful to Christ under every imaginable stress and strain. In the early church, women like Perpetua, Felicitas, and Blandina were put to death in the arena because they wouldn't deny their Christian faith. Now the church reveres these martyrs as saints. After Christianity became a legal religion, women chose lives of asceticism as the new form of martyrdom, dying to self. Missionary women in the 1800s continued to go to the mission field even though they knew the living conditions would be difficult and their life expectancy might be shortened. They died in childbirth, from illness, and from strain. Their deaths are not typically labeled "martyrdom," but perhaps they should be.[11] These women persisted in serving Christ to the point of death and did not shrink from their missionary calling despite knowing the cost. Hilda Stumpf was martyred because of her opposition to a cultural practice that damaged girls. Many other missionaries and health workers also lost their lives while working to bring Christ's healing to those on the margins. Preachers like Maria Woodworth-Etter, Phoebe Palmer, and Elleanor Knight experienced "maternal martyrdom." The loss of their children prompted them to further obedience, to preaching wherever God called them, despite ridicule, slander, and pain. Black women preachers in America faced even more obstacles than White women, but bolstered by dreams, visions, and their sense of God's call, they persevered. Many cultures

---

11. Dana Robert does describe how Harriett Newell, who died at age nineteen of illness in India, was "embraced . . . as the first American martyr to foreign missions." Robert, *American Women in Mission*, 41.

throughout the centuries have construed women as the "weaker sex," unable to bear the same kinds of hardships that men face. But these stories of women martyrs paint a different picture of women who are strong, courageous, and faithful, even to death.

Women Have Challenged Cultural Notions of Womanhood

Only a few women in the history of the church have made it their primary goal to challenge cultural notions of womanhood. However, simply by virtue of being Christians and by going where they believed Christ was leading them, many women *have* challenged ideologies of womanhood. In the early church, Perpetua's father expected her to give up her Christian faith in order to be a good Roman woman, honoring her father and raising her son to manhood. But Perpetua refused; her allegiance to Christ was more important than her allegiance to father, son, and country. Such faith rocked the social norms of the Roman Empire. Through the courage that Christ granted her in the arena, Perpetua also proved that women were not cowardly and weak, as society assumed them to be.

During the Middle Ages, when women were still thought of as weak, women like Hildegard and Mechtild used this trope to protect themselves from criticism, but ultimately they showed through their actions that weakness didn't define them. Yes, Hildegard did "feel fear and [was] timid in her works," as she says in her book *Scivias*, but she also had courage. She called the priests of her day "lukewarm and sluggish" for failing to teach the gospel as it should be taught.[12] And because they were not being faithful, sixty-year-old Hildegard herself set out on a preaching tour throughout Germany, clearly proving that "weakness" should not be the primary designator for "woman." Hildegard and other nuns in the Middle Ages showed that women could be rational, eloquent, hardworking, and theologically literate.

In the nineteenth century, women who formed missionary societies demonstrated that they were capable of holding positions of leadership, administering funds, and developing mission strategies, all of which were assumed to be male activities. And in the twentieth century, women in African Initiated Churches challenged the vision of womanhood that operated in mission churches.

In every period of church history, then, women have undermined their culture's vision of womanhood. These women did not necessarily see themselves as breaking the bonds of womanhood by taking on so-called masculine traits

12. Hildegard of Bingen, *Scivias*, 60, 67.

of courage, strength, rationality, authority, financial control, and intellectual thought. Rather, they primarily saw themselves as responding to the call of God and the needs of God's world. Nevertheless, by being faithful to God and filled with the Holy Spirit, they did challenge Roman, medieval, and Victorian gender norms.

Diversity of Vocations in the Kingdom of God

Different eras of the church have tended to favor particular vocations and marital states. The early and medieval church considered celibacy a higher calling than marriage. Martin Luther and the Reformers considered marriage the higher calling. Christian history is filled with women who contributed to the mission of the church through a diversity of vocations: married and celibate, active and contemplative, public and private. Many of these women reflected on whether marriage or celibacy would best enable them to serve Christ and his kingdom. Ann Judson and other American Protestants married male missionaries in order to live out their callings to mission. But in the late nineteenth century, more and more Western women (Clara Swain, Lottie Moon, Florence Nightingale, Katharine Bushnell, Frances Willard) decided to stay single in order to pursue mission and activism. In twentieth-century China, Dora Yu, Peace Wang, and Christina Tsai broke off marital engagements because they believed that remaining single would enable them to better serve God as preachers and evangelists. Similarly, Chinese medical doctors Kang Cheng and Shi Meiyu and African evangelist Paulina Dlamini chose never to marry in order to best pursue the work they believed God had called them to do. Still others, like Aimee McPherson and some women who became nuns in the Middle Ages, were married for some years and single for others. All of these women were cognizant of how their marital state related to serving Christ.

What Should We Do Now?

We hope that educators will take the stories of women in this book and share them with their students. We hope that pastors will look at this history and share it with their congregations. We hope that individual women who have felt silenced or dismissed by the church will take courage from the stories presented in this book. When Anneke asked her students, "What difference does it make to you to know this history?" one of them replied, "I feel like I'm uncovering a lie." This student hadn't grown up with any stories of women leaders, so she just assumed that women had never played a major role in the history of the church. When Leanne's teaching assistant returned the manuscript after reading it, she noted how inspirational it had been for her to learn of all these faithful women who were previously unknown to her.

Sex, gender, race, ethnicity, and class matter. They shape people's experience of the world. Stories of men and women, of Christians from different races and ethnicities, and of Christians from different social classes are part of the full story of Christianity. Without the full story, an understanding of how God works in the world is incomplete. Listening to a multitude of voices and perspectives is part of life in God's kingdom. As the apostle John wrote in Revelation, "There before me was a great multitude that no one could count, from every nation, tribe, people and language, standing before the throne and before the Lamb. They were wearing white robes and were holding palm branches in their hands. And they cried out in a loud voice: 'Salvation belongs to our God, / who sits on the throne, / and to the Lamb'" (7:9–10).

Let us celebrate the myriad contributions of women to the mission of the church. As patrons and martyrs, virgins and deacons, mothers and queens, nuns and mystics, preachers and activists, missionaries and church planters, women in church history have shown faithfulness, creativity, courage, and resilience. As we close this book, we remember the pithy words of theologian Dorothy Sayers:

> Perhaps it is no wonder that women were first at the Cradle and last at the Cross. They had never known a man like this Man—there never has been such another. A prophet and teacher who never nagged them, never flattered or coaxed or patronized; who never made jokes about them, never treated them either as "the women, God help us!" or "The Ladies, God bless them!"; who rebuked without querulousness and praised without condescension; who took their questions and arguments seriously; who never mapped out their sphere for them, never urged them to be feminine or jeered at them for being female; who had no ax to grind and no uneasy male dignity to defend; who took them as he found them and was completely unself-conscious. There is no act, no sermon, no parable in the Gospel that borrows its pungency from female perversity; nobody could possibly guess from the words and deeds of Jesus that there was anything "funny" about woman's nature.[13]

---

13. Sayers, *Are Women Human?*, 47.

BIBLIOGRAPHY

"About Dr. Clara A. Swain." Clara Swain Hospital J.V, 2015. http://www.cshbareilly .com/pages/about-us/history.html.

Akyeampong, Emmanuel K., and Henry Louis Gates, eds. *Dictionary of African Biography*. 6 vols. Oxford: Oxford University Press, 2012.

Allen, Prudence. *The Concept of Woman: The Aristotelian Revolution, 750 BC–AD 1250*. Vol. 1. Grand Rapids: Eerdmans, 1985.

Ambrose, Linda M. "Aimee Semple McPherson: Gender Theory, Worship, and the Arts." *Pneuma* 39 (2017): 105–22. https://doi.org/10.1163/15700747-03901005.

Amoah, Elizabeth. "Women, Witches and Social Change in Ghana." In Eck and Jain, *Speaking of Faith*, 84–94.

Anderson, Allan H. *African Reformation: African Initiated Christianity in the 20th Century*. Trenton, NJ: Africa World Press, 2001.

Anderson, Gerald H., ed. *Biographical Dictionary of Christian Missions*. New York: MacMillan, 1998.

Andrews, William L. *Sisters of the Spirit: Three Black Women's Autobiographies of the Nineteenth Century*. Bloomington: Indiana University Press, 1986.

Angelova, Diliana N. *Sacred Founders: Women, Men, and Gods in the Discourse of Imperial Founding, Rome through Early Byzantium*. Oakland: University of California Press, 2015.

Anson, John. "The Female Transvestite in Early Monasticism: The Origin and Development of a Motif." *Viator*, January 1, 1974, 11–16.

Apostolic Constitutions (Book III). In vol. 7 of *The Ante-Nicene Fathers*, edited by Alexander Roberts, James Donaldson, and A. Cleveland Coxe, translated by James Donaldson. Buffalo: Christian Literature, 1886. Revised for New Advent by Kevin Knight. https://www.newadvent.org/fathers/07153.htm.

Aristotle. *Politics*. Translated by Benjamin Jowett. Accessed on the Internet Classics Archive, Massachusetts Institute of Technology, October 21, 2020. http://classics .mit.edu/Aristotle/politics.1.one.html.

Attwell, Peggy. *Take Our Hands: The Methodist Church of Southern Africa Women's Auxiliary, 1916–1996*. Cape Town, South Africa: Methodist Church of Southern Africa Women's Auxiliary, 1997.

Augustine. *Confessions*. Translated by Henry Chadwick. Oxford: Oxford University Press, 1991.

Austin, Alvyn. *China's Millions: The China Inland Mission and Late Qing Society, 1832–1905*. Studies in the History of Christian Missions. Edited by Robert Eric Frykenberg and Brian Stanley. Grand Rapids: Eerdmans, 2007.

Bandyopadhyay, Ranjan. "Volunteer Tourism and 'the White Man's Burden': Globalization of Suffering, White Savior Complex, Religion and Modernity." *Journal of Sustainable Tourism* 27, no. 3 (2019): 327–43.

Bartlett, Anna Clark. "Holy Women in the British Isles: A Survey." In Minnis and Voaden, *Medieval Holy Women in the Christian Tradition*, 165–93.

Beach, Alison L. *Women as Scribes: Book Production and Monastic Reform in Twelfth-Century Bavaria*. Cambridge Studies in Palaeography and Codicology. Edited by David Ganz and Tessa Webber. New York: Cambridge University Press, 2004.

Beaver, Robert Pierce. *American Protestant Women in World Mission: A History of the First Feminist Movement in North America*. Grand Rapids: Eerdmans, 1980.

Beck, James R. "Missions and Mental Health: A Lesson from History." *Journal of Psychology and Theology* 21, no. 1 (1993): 9–17.

Bede. *A History of the English Church and People*. Translated by Leo Sherley-Price. Baltimore: Penguin Books, 1965.

Beeson, Trevor. *The Church's Other Half: Women's Ministry*. London: SCM, 2011.

Belleville, Linda L. *Women Leaders and the Church: Three Crucial Questions*. Grand Rapids: Baker Academic, 2000.

Benowitz, June. *Encyclopedia of American Women and Religion*. 2nd ed. Vols. A–Z. Santa Barbara, CA: ABC-CLIO, 2017.

Bikos, Lynette H., Michael J. Klemens, Leigh A. Randa, Alyson Barry, Thomas Bore, Renee Gibbs, and Julia Kocheleva. "First-Year Adaptation of Female, Expatriate Religious and Humanitarian Aid Workers: A Mixed Methods Analysis." *Mental Health, Religion & Culture* 12, no. 7 (2009): 639–61.

Bloch, Ruth H. *Gender and Morality in Anglo-American Culture, 1650–1800*. Berkeley: University of California Press, 2003.

Blumhofer, Edith L. *Aimee Semple McPherson: Everybody's Sister*. Grand Rapids: Eerdmans, 1993.

"The Book of Margery Kemp." British Library. Accessed October 21, 2020. https://www.bl.uk/collection-items/the-book-of-margery-kempe.

Bosch, David J. *Transforming Mission: Paradigm Shifts in Theology of Mission*. Maryknoll, NY: Orbis Books, 1996.

Bossen, Laurel, and Hill Gates. *Bound Feet, Young Hands: Tracking the Demise of Footbinding in Village China*. Stanford, CA: Stanford University Press, 2017.

Bourquin, S., ed. *Paulina Dlamini, Servant of Two Kings*. Compiled by H. Filter. Pietermaritzburg, South Africa: University of Natal Press, 1986.

Bowers, Joyce M. "Roles of Married Women Missionaries: A Case Study." *International Bulletin of Missionary Research* 8, no. 1 (1984): 4–7.

Braude, Ann. *Sisters and Saints: Women and American Religion*. Oxford: Oxford University Press, 2008.

Bray, Gerald L., ed. *Romans*. Ancient Christian Commentary on Scripture, New Testament 6. Downers Grove, IL: InterVarsity, 1998.

Brekus, Catherine A. *Sarah Osborn's World: The Rise of Evangelical Christianity in Early America*. New Haven: Yale University Press, 2013.

———. *Strangers and Pilgrims: Female Preaching in America, 1740–1845*. Chapel Hill: University of North Carolina Press, 1999.

Brown, Peter. *The Cult of the Saints: Its Rise and Function in Latin Christianity*. Chicago: University of Chicago Press, 2015.

Brown, Raymond E., Karl P. Donfried, Joseph A. Fitzmyer, and John Reumann, eds. *Mary in the New Testament: A Collaborative Assessment by Protestant and Roman Catholic Scholars*. Philadelphia: Fortress, 1978.

Bushnell, Katharine C., with Amy Francis. *God's Word to Women*. UK: Crowning Educational, 2016.

Butler, Josephine E. *Recollections of George Butler*. Bristol, UK: Arrowsmith; London: Simpkin, Marshall, Hamilton, Kent, n.d.

Bynum, Caroline Walker. *Holy Feast and Holy Fast: The Religious Significance of Food to Medieval Women*. Berkeley: University of California Press, 1987.

———. *Jesus as Mother: Studies in the Spirituality of the High Middle Ages*. Berkeley: University of California Press, 1982.

"The Canons of the Council of Chalcedon (451)." Early Church Texts. Accessed October 21, 2020. http://www.earlychurchtexts.com/public/chalcedon_canons.htm.

"Canterbury." World Heritage Site. Accessed December 9, 2019. https://www.worldheritagesite.org/list/Canterbury.

"Catherine of Siena." *Christianity Today*. Accessed October 21, 2020. https://www.christianitytoday.com/history/people/innertravelers/catherine-of-siena.html.

Clark, Elizabeth A. *Women in the Early Church*. Collegeville, MN: Liturgical Press, 1983.

Cohick, Lynn. "Motherhood and Martyrdom: Family and Faith in the Early Church." Regent College, Vancouver, BC, Summer 2018. Audio recording, 1:19. https://www.regentaudio.com/products/motherhood-and-martyrdom-family-and-faith-in-the-early-church?_pos=11&_sid=7a8f2f2c5&_ss=r.

Cohick, Lynn H., and Amy Brown Hughes. *Christian Women in the Patristic World: Their Influence, Authority, and Legacy in the Second through Fifth Centuries*. Grand Rapids: Baker Academic, 2017.

Cole, Mary. *Trials and Triumphs of Faith*. Anderson, IN: Gospel Trumpet, 1914.

Cole, Teju. "The White-Savior Industrial Complex." *Atlantic*, March 21, 2012. https://www.theatlantic.com/international/archive/2012/03/the-white-savior-industrial-complex/254843/.

Collier-Thomas, Bettye. *Daughters of Thunder: Black Women Preachers and Their Sermons, 1850–1979*. San Francisco: Jossey-Bass, 1998.

Constitutions of the Holy Apostles. In vol. 7 of *The Ante-Nicene Fathers*, edited by Alexander Roberts and James Donaldson. Grand Rapids: Eerdmans, 1996. Christian Classics Ethereal Library. http://www.ccel.org/ccel/schaff/anf07.ix.iv.ii.html.

Corrigan, Kevin. Introduction to *The Life of Saint Macrina*, edited by Kevin Corrigan, 5–17. Eugene, OR: Wipf & Stock, 2001.

Crawford, Nancy, and Helen M. DeVries. "Relationship between Role Perception and Well-Being in Married Female Missionaries." *Journal of Psychology and Theology* 33, no. 3 (2005): 187–97.

Daneel, Marthinus L. "AIC Women as Bearers of the Gospel Good News." In *African Christian Outreach: The African Initiated Churches*, edited by Marthinus L. Daneel, 1:312–27. Menlo Park, South Africa: South African Missiological Society, 2001.

Daniel, Kasomo. "The Role of Women in the Church in Africa." *International Journal of Sociology and Anthropology* 2, no. 6 (2010): 126–39.

Davis, Natalie Zemon. *Women on the Margins: Three Seventeenth-Century Lives*. Cambridge, MA: Harvard University Press, 1995.

Deen, Edith. *Great Women of the Christian Faith*. Uhrichsville, OH: Barbour Publishing, 1959.

Diehl, Amy, and Leanne M. Dzubinski. "Making the Invisible Visible: A Cross-Sector Analysis of Gender-Based Leadership Barriers." *Human Resource Development Quarterly* 27, no. 2 (2016): 181–206. https://doi.org/10.1002/hrdq.21248.

Diehl, Amy B., Amber Stephenson, Leanne M. Dzubinski, and David C. Wang. "Measuring the Invisible: Development and Multi-industry Validation of the Gender Bias Scale for Women Leaders." *Human Resource Development Quarterly* 31, no. 3 (2020): 249–80.

Doyle, G. Wright. "Watchman Nee." Biographical Dictionary of Chinese Christianity. Accessed October 21, 2020. http://bdcconline.net/en/stories/nee-watchman.

Drijvers, Jan Willem. *Helena Augusta: The Mother of Constantine the Great and the Legend of Her Finding of the True Cross*. Brill's Studies in Intellectual History. New York: Brill, 1992.

Du Mez, Kristin Kobes. *A New Gospel for Women: Katharine Bushnell and the Challenge of Christian Feminism*. Oxford: Oxford University Press, 2015.

———. "Selfishness One Degree Removed: Madeline Southard's Desacralization of Motherhood and a Tradition of Progressive Methodism." *Priscilla Papers* 28, no. 2 (2014): 17–22.

Dunn, James D. G. *Romans 9–16*. Word Biblical Commentary 38B. Edited by Bruce M. Metzger, David A. Hubbard, and Glenn W. Barker. Grand Rapids: Zondervan Academic, 2018.

Duster, Alfreda B. Introduction to *Crusade for Justice: The Autobiography of Ida B. Wells*, by Ida B. Wells, xiii–xxxii. Edited by Alfreda M. Duster. Chicago: University of Chicago Press, 1970.

Dzubinski, Leanne M. "Playing by the Rules: How Women Lead in Evangelical Mission Organizations." PhD diss., University of Georgia, 2013.

———. "Portrayal vs. Practice: Contemporary Women's Contributions to Christian Mission." *Missiology: An International Review* 44, no. 1 (2016): 78–94.

Dzubinski, Leanne M., Amy B. Diehl, and Michelle O. Taylor. "Women's Ways of Leading: The Environmental Effect." *Gender in Management: An International Journal* 34, no. 3 (2019): 233–50. https://doi.org/10.1108/GM-11-2017-0150.

Earhart, Mary. *Frances Willard: From Prayers to Politics*. Washington, DC: Zenger, 1944.

Eck, Diana L., and Devaki Jain. Introduction to Eck and Jain, *Speaking of Faith*, 1–15.

———, eds. *Speaking of Faith: Global Perspectives on Women, Religion, and Social Change*. Philadelphia: New Society Publishers, 1987.

Eisen, Ute E. *Women Officeholders in Early Christianity: Epigraphical and Literary Studies*. Collegeville, MN: Liturgical Press, 2000.

Evangelisti, Silvia. *Nuns: A History of Convent Life*. Oxford: Oxford University Press, 2007.

Fairbanks, Eve. "Behold, the Millennial Nuns." *HuffPost*, July 11, 2019. https://www.huffpost.com/highline/article/millennial-nuns/.

"Female Education Society Annual Report for 1868." Church Missionary Society Archive, section II, part 1, reel 9. Boston: Boston University School of Theology Library. Microform.

"Female Education Society Annual Report for 1883." Church Missionary Society Archive, section II, part 1, reel 10. Boston: Boston University School of Theology Library. Microform.

"Female Education Society Annual Report for 1889." Church Missionary Society Archive, section II, part 1, reel 9. Boston: Boston University School of Theology Library. Microform.

Fitzgerald, Kyriaki Karidovanes. *Women Deacons in the Orthodox Church: Called to Holiness and Ministry*. Brookline, MA: Holy Cross Orthodox Press, 1998.

"Five Factors Changing Women's Relationship with Churches." Barna Group, June 25, 2015. https://www.barna.com/research/five-factors-changing-womens-relationship-with-churches/.

Fletcher, Joyce K. *Disappearing Acts: Gender, Power, and Relational Practice at Work.* Cambridge, MA: MIT Press, 1999.

Forman, Mary. *Praying with the Desert Mothers.* Collegeville, MN: Liturgical Press, 2005.

Frend, W. H. C. *The Rise of Christianity.* Philadelphia: Fortress, 1984.

"Frequently Requested Church Statistics." Center for Applied Research in the Apostolate. https://cara.georgetown.edu/frequently-requested-church-statistics/.

Fricker, Miranda. *Epistemic Injustice: Power and the Ethics of Knowing.* New York: Oxford University Press, 2007.

Frost, Carie Frederick. *Maternal Body: A Theology of Incarnation from the Christian East.* New York: Paulist Press, 2019.

Frykenberg, Robert Eric. "Pandita Ramabai and World Christianity." In *Indian and Christian: The Life and Legacy of Pandita Ramabai,* edited by Roger E. Hedlund, Sebastian Kim, and Rajkumar Boaz Johnson, 155–92. Chennai: Mylapore Institute for Indigenous Studies, 2011.

Gaitskell, Deborah. "Devout Domesticity? A Century of African Women's Christianity in South Africa." In *Women and Gender in Southern Africa to 1945,* edited by Cherryl Walker, 251–72. Cape Town, South Africa: David Philip, 1990.

Gibson, Margaret Dunlop Smith, trans. *The Didascalia apostolorum in English.* London: Clay, 1903. Internet Archive. https://archive.org/stream/didascaliaaposto00 gibsuoft/didascaliaaposto00gibsuoft_djvu.txt.

González, Justo L. *The Story of Christianity: The Early Church to the Present Day.* New York: HarperCollins, 2001.

Gooder, Paula. *Phoebe: A Story.* Downers Grove, IL: IVP Academic, 2018.

Green, Joel. "Blessed Is She Who Believed: Mary, Curious Exemplar in Luke's Narrative." In *Blessed One: Protestant Perspectives on Mary,* edited by Beverly Roberts Gaventa and Cynthia L. Rigby, 9–20. Louisville: Westminster John Knox, 2002.

Gregory of Nazianzus. "Funeral Oration for His Father." In *Funeral Orations,* edited by Leo P. McCauley, John J. Sullivan, Martin R. P. McGuire, and Roy J. Deferrari, 119–56. Washington, DC: Catholic University of America Press, 1953.

Gregory of Nyssa. *The Life of St. Macrina.* Translated by Kevin Corrigan. Eugene, OR: Wipf & Stock, 2011.

———. *On the Soul and the Resurrection.* Translated by Catharine P. Roth. Crestwood, NY: St. Vladimir's Seminary Press, 1993.

Gregory of Tours. "The History of the Franks." In *Internet Medieval Sourcebook,* edited by Paul Halsall. Fordham University Center for Medieval Studies. 1997; last modified January 2, 2020. https://sourcebooks.fordham.edu/source/gregtours1.asp.

Gregory the Great. *Epistle 29.* In *The Nicene and Post-Nicene Fathers,* Series 2, translated by Philip Schaff and Henry Wace, 13.2:56–57. 14 volumes. Grand Rapids: Eerdmans, 1956.

Griffiths, Fiona J. *The Garden of Delights: Reform and Renaissance for Women in the Twelfth Century*. Philadelphia: University of Pennsylvania Press, 2007.

Hadewijch. *The Complete Works*. Translated by Mother Columbia Hart. Ramsey, NJ: Paulist Press, 1980.

Hall, M. Elizabeth Lewis, and Nancy S. Duvall. "Married Women in Missions: The Effects of Cross-Cultural and Self Gender-Role Expectations on Well-Being, Stress, and Self-Esteem." *Journal of Psychology and Theology* 31, no. 4 (2003): 303–14.

Hamburger, Jeffrey. *Nuns as Artists: The Visual Culture of a Medieval Convent*. Berkeley: University of California Press, 1997.

———. *The Visual and the Visionary: Art and Female Spirituality in Late Medieval Germany*. New York: Zone Books, 1998.

Hannula, Richard M. *Radiant: Fifty Remarkable Women in Church History*. Moscow, ID: Canon Press, 2019.

Hardesty, Nancy A. *Women Called to Witness: Evangelical Feminism in the 19th Century*. Nashville: Abingdon, 1984.

Hardesty, Nancy A., Lucille Sider Dayton, and Donald W. Dayton. "Women in the Holiness Movement." In *Women of Spirit: Female Leadership in the Jewish and Christian Traditions*, edited by Rosemary Ruether and Eleanor McLaughlin, 225–54. Eugene, OR: Wipf & Stock, 1998.

Hefele, Charles Joseph. *A History of the Councils of the Church from the Original Documents*. 9 vols. Edinburgh: T&T Clark, 1871.

Heim, Melissa Lewis. "'Standing behind the Looms': American Missionary Women and Indian Church Women in the Devolution Process." In Robert, *Gospel Bearers, Gender Barriers*, 47–62.

Herrin, Judith. *Unrivalled Influence: Women and Empire in Byzantium*. Princeton: Princeton University Press, 2013.

Hertig, Young Lee. "Without a Face: The Nineteenth-Century Bible Woman and Twentieth-Century Female Jeondosa." In Robert, *Gospel Bearers, Gender Barriers*, 185–200.

Higginbotham, Evelyn Brooks. *Righteous Discontent: The Women's Movement in the Black Baptist Church, 1880–1920*. Cambridge, MA: Harvard University Press, 1993.

Hildegard of Bingen. *Scivias*. Edited by Mother Columba Hart and Jane Bishop. Mahwah, NJ: Paulist Press, 1990.

"History of Lynchings." NAACP, 2020. https://www.naacp.org/history-of-lynchings/.

Hollis, Stephanie. *Anglo-Saxon Women and the Church: Sharing a Common Fate*. Martlesham, UK: Boydell Press, 1992.

Hubbard, Ethel Daniels. *Under Marching Orders: A Story of Mary Porter Gamewell*. New York: Wentworth Press, 1909.

"'I Received My Commission from Him, Brother': Women Preachers in the Methodist and Holiness Traditions." An exhibit from the Methodist collections of Drew
University Library. Curated by Jennifer L. Woodruff Tait. Spring and Summer 2004.

Irvin, Dale T., and Scott W. Sunquist. *History of the World Christian Movement:
Earliest Christianity to 1453*. Maryknoll, NY: Orbis Books, 2001.

Isichei, Elizabeth. *A History of Christianity in Africa: From Antiquity to the Present*.
Grand Rapids: Eerdmans, 1995.

John Chrysostom. *On the Priesthood (Book I)*. In vol. 9 of *The Nicene and Post-Nicene
Fathers*, Series 1, translated by W. R. W. Stephens, edited by Philip Schaff. Buffalo:
Christian Literature, 1889. Revised for New Advent by Kevin Knight. http://www
.newadvent.org/fathers/19221.htm.

Johnson, Penelope D. *Equal in Monastic Profession: Religious Women in Medieval
France*. Women in Culture and Society. Edited by Catharine R. Stimpson. Chicago:
University of Chicago Press, 1991.

Jones, Kathleen. *Women Saints: Lives of Faith and Courage*. Maryknoll, NY: Orbis
Books, 1999.

Judge, Joan. *The Precious Raft of History: China's Woman Question and the Politics
of Time at the Turn of the Twentieth Century*. Stanford, CA: Stanford University
Press, 2008.

Jules-Rosette, Bennetta. "Cultural Ambivalence and Ceremonial Leadership: The Role
of Women in Africa's New Religions." In *The Church and Women in the Third
World*, edited by John C. Webster and Ellen Low Webster, 88–104. Philadephia:
Westminster, 1985.

Juster, Susan. *Disorderly Women: Sexual Politics and Evangelicalism in Revolutionary
New England*. Ithaca, NY: Cornell University Press, 2018.

Karras, Valerie A. "Female Deacons in the Byzantine Church." *Church History* 73,
no. 2 (2004): 272–316.

Keener, Craig S. "Learning in the Assemblies: 1 Corinthians 14:34–35." In *Discovering
Biblical Equality: Complementarity without Hierarchy*, edited by Ronald W. Pierce
and Rebecca Merrill Groothuis, 161–71. Downers Grove, IL: InterVarsity, 2005.

Kempe, Margery. *The Book of Margery Kempe*. Translated by Barry A. Windeatt.
London: Penguin Books, 1985.

Kerber, Linda K. *Women of the Republic: Intellect and Ideology in Revolutionary
America*. Chapel Hill: University of North Carolina Press, 2014.

Khan, Susan Haskell. "American Women Missionaries and the 'Woman Question' in
India, 1919–1939." In Reeves-Ellington, Sklar, and Shemo, *Competing Kingdoms*,
141–66.

Kienzle, Beverly Mayne, and Pamela J. Walker. *Women Preachers and Prophets through
Two Millennia of Christianity*. Berkeley: University of California Press, 1998.

Kittler, Glenn D. *The Woman God Loved*. Garden City, NY: Hanover House, 1959.

Knight, Henry H., III, ed. *From Aldersgate to Azusa Street: Wesleyan, Holiness, and Pentecostal Vision of the New Creation.* Eugene, OR: Pickwick, 2010.

Koester, Nancy. "Sojourner Truth's Unfinished Business." Paper presented at the Conference on Faith and History, Grand Rapids, October 6, 2018.

Kustenbauder, Matthew. "Aoko, Gaudencia." In Akyeampong and Gates, *Dictionary of African Biography*, 1:245–47.

Labarge, Margaret Wade. *Mistress, Maids, and Men: Baronial Life in the Thirteenth Century.* London: Phoenix Press, 2004.

Lampe, Peter. *From Paul to Valentinus: Christians at Rome in the First Two Centuries.* Translated by Michael Steinhauser. Edited by Marshall D. Johnson. Minneapolis: Fortress, 2003.

Landon, Edward H. *A Manual of the Councils of the Holy Catholic Church.* 2 vols. Edinburgh: John Grant, 1909.

Larsson, Birgitta. "Haya Women's Response to the East African Revival Movement." In *The East African Revival: History and Legacies*, edited by Kevin Ward and Emma Wild-Wood, 119–42. Kampala, Uganda: Fountain Publishers, 2010.

Lawrence, C. H. *Medieval Monasticism: Forms of Religious Life in Western Europe in the Middle Ages.* 3rd ed. New York: Routledge, 2013.

Leclerc, Diane K. "Phoebe Palmer: Spreading 'Accessible' Holiness." In Knight, *From Aldersgate to Azusa Street*, 90–98.

Lee, Ruth. "A Letter from Sister Ruth Lee in Her Travels." In *The Collected Works of Watchman Nee: Collection of Newsletters and Watchman Nee's Testimony*, edited by Watchman Nee. Anaheim, CA: Living Stream Ministry, 1992. https://www.ministrybooks.org/books.cfm?xid=SRZVHXUIGQLW0.

Lee, Witness. *Watchman Nee: A Seer of the Divine Revelation in the Present Age.* Anaheim, CA: Living Stream Ministry, 1991. https://www.ministrybooks.org/index.cfm.

Lester, Anne E. *Creating Cistercian Nuns: The Women's Religious Movement and Its Reform in Thirteenth-Century Champagne.* Ithaca, NY: Cornell University Press, 2011.

Li, Yading. "Yu, Dora (Yu Cidu) (1873–1931)." In *Biographical Dictionary of Chinese Christianity*, translated by Connor McCarthy. Methodist Mission Bicentennial. Accessed October 21, 2020. https://methodistmission200.org/yu-dora-yu-cidu-1873-1931/.

The Life of the Church. The Madras Series 4. New York: International Missionary Council, 1939.

"Light through Eastern Lattices: A Plea for Zenana Captives by the Society for Promoting Female Education in the East; On the Occasion of Its Jubilee, 1884." Church Missionary Society Archive, section II, part 1, reel 10. Boston University School of Theology Library. Marlborough, UK: Adam Matthew, 1996. Microform.

Loritts, Bryan. *Insider Outsider: My Journey as a Stranger in White Evangelicalism and My Hope for Us All*. Grand Rapids: Zondervan, 2018.

Lundberg, Magnus. *Mission and Ecstasy: Contemplative Women and Salvation in Colonial Spanish America and the Phillipines*. Uppsala, Sweden: Swedish Institute of Mission Research, 2015.

Luongo, Thomas. *The Saintly Politics of Catherine of Siena*. Ithaca, NY: Cornell University Press, 2006.

Luther, Martin. "Exhortation to All Clergy Assembled at Augsburg, 1530." In *Career of the Reformer IV*, edited by Lewis W. Spitz and Helmut T. Lehmann, translated by Lewis W. Spitz, 3–62. Vol. 34 of *Luther's Works*. Philadelphia: Fortress, 1960.

———. "Sermon on the Estate of Marriage." In *Martin Luther's Basic Theological Writings*, edited by Timothy F. Lull, 630–37. Minneapolis: Augsburg Fortress, 1989.

Ma, Julie C. "Asian Women and Pentecostal Ministry." In *Asian and Pentecostal: The Charismatic Face of Christianity in Asia*, edited by Allan H. Anderson and Edmond Tang, 103–17. Eugene, OR: Wipf & Stock, 2011.

MacHaffie, Barbara J., ed. *Readings in Her Story: Women in Christian Tradition*. Minneapolis: Augsburg Fortress, 1992.

Maddux, Kristy. "The Feminized Gospel: Aimee Semple McPherson and the Gendered Performance of Christianity." *Women's Studies in Communication* 35 (2012): 42–67. https://doi.org/10.1080/07491409.2012.667520.

Malone, Mary T. *Four Women Doctors of the Church: Hildegard of Bingen, Catherine of Siena, Teresa of Avila, Therese of Lisieux*. Maryknoll, NY: Orbis Books, 2015.

Mara, Maria Grazia. "Marcellina." In *Encyclopedia of Ancient Christianity*, edited by Angelo Di Berardino, 670. Downers Grove, IL: IVP Academic, 2014.

"Marcellina (fl. 4th c.)." Encyclopedia.com. Updated July 16, 2020. https://www.encyclopedia.com/women/encyclopedias-almanacs-transcripts-and-maps/marcellina-fl-4th-c.

Marie of the Incarnation. *Selected Writings*. Edited by Irene Mahoney. New York: Paulist Press, 1989.

Marucci, Corrado. "History and Value of the Feminine Diaconate." In *Women Deacons? Essays with Answers*, edited by Phyllis Zagano, 30–56. Collegeville, MN: Liturgical Press, 2016.

Maxwell, Melody. *The Woman I Am: Southern Baptist Women's Writings, 1906–2006*. Tuscaloosa: University of Alabama Press, 2014.

Mbonu, Caroline N. *Handmaid: The Power of Names in Theology and Society*. Eugene, OR: Wipf & Stock, 2010.

McCabe, Elizabeth A. "A Reexamination of Phoebe as a 'Diakonos' and 'Prostatis': Exposing the Inaccuracies of English Translations." Society of Biblical Literature. https://www.sbl-site.org/publications/article.aspx?ArticleId=830.

McCurry, Stephanie. "The Two Faces of Republicanism: Gender and Proslavery Politics in Antebellum South Carolina." *Journal of American History* 78, no. 4 (1992): 1245–64.

McNamara, JoAnn. "Living Sermons: Consecrated Women and the Conversion of Gaul." In *Peace Weavers*, edited by Lillian Thomas Shank and John A. Nichols, 19–38. Kalamazoo, MI: Cistercian Publications, 1987.

McNamara, JoAnn, and John E. Halborg, eds. *Sainted Women of the Dark Ages.* Durham, NC: Duke University Press, 1992.

Mechtild of Magdeburg. *The Flowing Light of the Godhead.* In *Mechtild of Magdeberg: Selections from* the Flowing Light of the Godhead, edited by Elizabeth A. Anderson. The Library of Medieval Women. Cambridge: Brewer, 2003.

———. *The Flowing Light of the Godhead.* In Petroff, *Medieval Women's Visionary Literature*, 212–21.

Miller, Patricia Cox. *Women in Early Christianity: Translations from Greek Texts.* Washington, DC: Catholic University of America Press, 2005.

Miller, Tanya Stabler. *The Beguines of Medieval Paris: Gender, Patronage, and Spiritual Authority.* Philadelphia: University of Pennsylvania Press, 2014.

Minnis, Alastair J., and Rosalynn Voaden, eds. *Medieval Holy Women in the Christian Tradition, c. 1100–c. 1500.* Chicago: Brepols, 2010.

Minucius Felix. *Octavius.* In *Tertullian, Minucius Felix*, edited by G. P. Goold, 314–437. Loeb Classical Library. Cambridge, MA: Harvard University Press, 1931.

Mommaers, Paul. *Hadewijch: Writer-Beguine-Love Mystic.* Leuven, Belgium: Peeters, 1989.

Montgomery, Helen Barrett. *Western Women in Eastern Lands.* New York: Macmillan, 1910.

Morgan, Barbara. "Anthusa (c. 324/334–?)." Encyclopedia.com. Updated July 30, 2020. https://www.encyclopedia.com/women/encyclopedias-almanacs-transcripts -and-maps/anthusa-c-324334.

Muir, Elizabeth Gillan. *A Women's History of the Christian Church: Two Thousand Years of Female Leadership.* Toronto, ON: University of Toronto Press, 2019.

Mulder-Bakker, Anneke. "Holy Women in the German Territories: A Survey." In Minnis and Voaden, *Medieval Holy Women in the Christian Tradition*, 313–41.

Mwaura, Philomena Nieri. "A Burning Stick Plucked out of the Fire: The Story of Rev. Margaret Wanjiru of Jesus Is Alive Ministries." In *Her-Stories: Hidden Histories of Women of Faith in Africa*, edited by Isabel A. Phiri, Devakarsham Betty Govinden, and Sarojini Nadar, 202–24. Pietermaritzburg, South Africa: Cluster Publications, 2002.

———. "Gendered Appropriation of Mass Media in Kenyan Christianities: A Comparison of Two Women-Led African Instituted Churches in Kenya." In *Interpreting*

Contemporary Christianity: Global Processes and Local Identities, edited by Obgu Kalu and Alaine Low, 274–95. Studies in the History of Christian Missions. Grand Rapids: Eerdmans, 2008.

Newell, Marvin J. *A Martyr's Grace: Stories of Those Who Gave All for Christ and His Cause.* Chicago: Moody, 2006.

Newman, Barbara J. Introduction to *Hildegard of Bingen: Scivias*, edited by Mother Columba Hart, 9–54. Mahwah, NJ: Paulist Press, 1990.

Noll, Mark A. *Turning Points: Decisive Moments in the History of Christianity.* 3rd ed. Grand Rapids: Baker Academic, 2012.

O'Brien, Anne. "Catholic Nuns in Translational Mission, 1528–2015." *Journal of Global History* 11 (2016): 387–408.

Oduyoye, Mercy Amba. *Daughters of Anowa: African Women & Patriarchy.* Maryknoll, NY: Orbis Books, 1995.

Olson, Jeannine. *Deacons and Deaconesses through the Centuries.* St. Louis: Concordia, 1992.

Omoyajowo, J. Akinyele. *Cherubim and Seraphim: The History of an African Independent Church.* New York: NOK Publishers International, 1982.

Origen. *Contra Celsum, Book III.* In vol. 4 of *The Ante-Nicene Fathers*, edited by Alexander Roberts, James Donaldson, and A. Cleveland Coxe, translated by Frederick Crombie. Buffalo: Christian Literature, 1885. Revised for New Advent by Kevin Knight. https://www.newadvent.org/fathers/04163.htm.

Osborn, Lucy Drake. *Heavenly Pearls Set in a Life: A Record of Experiences and Labors in America, India and Australia.* New York: Revell, 1893.

Osiek, Carolyn, and Margaret MacDonald. *A Woman's Place: House Churches in Earliest Christianity.* Minneapolis: Augsburg Fortress, 2006.

Owens, Sarah E. *Nuns Navigating the Spanish Empire.* Albuquerque: University of New Mexico Press, 2017.

Palladius. *Dialogue on the Life of St. John Chrysostom.* Translated and edited by Robert T. Meyer. New York: Newman, 1985.

———. *Lausiac History.* Transcribed by Roger Pearse. 2003. http://www.tertullian .org/fathers/palladius_lausiac_02_text.htm.

"Pandita Ramabai Mukti Mission." Global Aid Network. Accessed October 21, 2020. https://globalaid.net/initiatives/women-children/mukti-mission.

Papanek, Hanna. "Men, Women, and Work: Reflections on the Two-Person Career." *American Journal of Sociology* 78, no. 4 (1973): 852.

The Passion of Perpetua and Felicity. Translated by Thomas J. Heffernan. Oxford: Oxford University Press, 2012.

Paulinus of Nola. *Letters of St. Paulinus of Nola.* Vol. 2. Translated by P. G. Walsh. Ancient Christian Writers 36. New York: Newman, 1967.

Peel, J. D. Y. *Aladura: A Religious Movement among the Yoruba*. Oxford: Oxford University Press, 1968.

Petroff, Elizabeth Alvilda, ed. *Medieval Women's Visionary Literature*. New York: Oxford University Press, 1986.

Phiri, Isabel A. "African Women in Mission: Two Case Studies from Malawi." In *African Christian Outreach: The African Initiated Churches*, edited by Marthinus L. Daneel, 1:267–93. Menlo Park, South Africa: South African Missiological Society, 2001.

Pliny. "Pliny to the Emperor Trajan." *Letters* 10.96–97. Accessed October 21, 2020. https://faculty.georgetown.edu/jod/texts/pliny.html.

Pope-Levison, Priscilla. *Building the Old-Time Religion: Women Evangelists in the Progressive Era*. New York: New York University Press, 2014.

———. *Turn the Pulpit Loose: Two Centuries of American Women Evangelists*. New York: Palgrave Macmillan, 2004.

Prejean, Helen. *River of Fire*. New York: Random House, 2019.

Prieto, Laura R. "'Stepmother America': The Woman's Board of Missions in the Philippines, 1902–1930." In Reeves-Ellington, Sklar, and Shemo, *Competing Kingdoms*, 342–66.

"Privilege/Class/Social Inequalities Explained in a $100 Race—Please Watch to the End. Thanks." YouTube video, 4:12, posted by Peter D, October 14, 2017. https://www.youtube.com/watch?v=4K5fbQ1-zps&t=188s.

The Protevangelium of James. Translated by Lily C. Vuong. Eugene, OR: Cascade Books, 2019.

Quiambao, Ermelinda. *Home and Family Life*. Manila, Philippines: Philippines Federation of Christian Churches, 1955.

Quiambao, Jacob S. *Manual on Marriage Counseling for Filipinos*. Manila, Philippines: Philippine Federation of Christian Churches, 1962.

Quinn, Frederick. "Nku, Christinah." In *Dictionary of African Christian Biography*. https://dacb.org/stories/southafrica/nku-christinah/.

Reeves-Ellington, Barbara. "Women, Protestant Missions, and American Cultural Expansion, 1800 to 1938: A Historigraphical Sketch." *Social Sciences and Missions* 24 (2011): 190–206.

Reeves-Ellington, Barbara, Kathryn Kish Sklar, and Connie Anne Shemo, eds. *Competing Kingdoms: Women, Mission, Nation, and the American Protestant Empire, 1812–1960*. Durham, NC: Duke University Press, 2010.

Robert, Dana L. *American Women in Mission: A Social History of Their Thought and Practice*. The Modern Mission Era, 1792–1992: An Appraisal. Edited by Wilbert R. Schenk. Macon, GA: Mercer University Press, 1997.

———. *Christian Mission: How Christianity Became a World Religion*. Malden, MA: Wiley-Blackwell, 2009.

———. "Doremus, Sarah Platt (Haines)." In G. Anderson, *Biographical Dictionary of Christian Missions*, 183–84.

———. "Evangelist or Homemaker? Mission Strategies of Early Nineteenth-Century Missionary Wives in Burma and Hawaii." *International Bulletin of Missionary Research* 17, no. 1 (1993): 4.

———, ed. *Gospel Bearers, Gender Barriers: Missionary Women in the Twentieth Century*. Maryknoll, NY: Orbis Books, 2002.

———. "Women in World Mission: Controversies and Challenges from a North American Perspective." *International Review of Mission* 93, no. 3 (2004): 50–61.

———. "World Christianity as a Women's Movement." *International Bulletin of Missionary Research* 30, no. 4 (2006): 180–88.

Robins, Catherine. "Conversion, Life Crises, and Stability among Women in the East African Revival." In *The New Religions of Africa*, edited by Bennetta Jules-Rosette, 185–202. San Diego: University of California Press, 1979.

Robinson, Marius. "Women's Rights Convention: Sojourner Truth." *Anti-slavery Bugle*, June 21, 1851.

Roseveare, Helen. *Living Sacrifice*. Minneapolis: Bethany House, 1979.

Rosik, Christopher H., and Jelena Pandzic. "Marital Satisfaction among Christian Missionaries: A Longitudinal Analysis from Candidacy to Second Furlough." *Journal of Psychology & Christianity* 27, no. 1 (2008): 3–15.

Rudman, Laurie A., and Peter Glick. "Prescriptive Gender Stereotypes and Backlash toward Agentic Women." *Journal of Social Issues* 57, no. 4 (2001): 743.

Rudman, Laurie A., and Julie E. Phelan. "Backlash Effects for Disconfirming Gender Stereotypes in Organizations." *Research in Organizational Behavior* 28 (2008): 61–79.

Rudolf of Fulda. "Life of Leoba (c. 836)." In *Internet Medieval Sourcebook*, edited by Paul Halsall. Fordham University Center for Medieval Studies. 1997; last modified January 2, 2020. https://sourcebooks.fordham.edu/basis/leoba.asp.

Ryan, Mary P. *Cradle of the Middle Class: The Family in Oneida County, New York, 1790–1865*. Cambridge: Cambridge University Press, 1983.

Sackey, Brigid M. *New Directions in Gender and Religion: The Changing Status of Women in African Independent Churches*. Lanham, MD: Lexington Books, 2006.

Sanidopoulos, John. "Saint Emmelia, Mother of Saint Basil the Great." *Mystagogy Resource Center* (blog), May 30, 2017. https://www.johnsanidopoulos.com/2017/05/saint-emmelia-mother-of-saint-basil.html.

———. "Saint Nonna of Nazianzus, Mother of Gregory the Theologian." *Mystagogy Resource Center* (blog), August 5, 2016. https://www.johnsanidopoulos.com/2016/08/saint-nonna-of-nazianzus.html.

———. "Saints Emmelia, Nonna and Anthousa—Mothers of the Three Hierarchs." *Mystagogy Resource Center* (blog), February 7, 2016. https://www.johnsanidopoulos.com/2016/02/saints-emmelia-nonna-and-anthousa.html.

Sayers, Dorothy L. *Are Women Human? Penetrating, Sensible, and Witty Essays on the Role of Women in Society*. Grand Rapids: Eerdmans, 1971.

Schechter, Patricia Ann. *Ida B. Wells-Barnett and American Reform, 1880–1920*. Chapel Hill: University of North Carolina Press, 2001.

Schenk, Christine. *Crispina and Her Sisters: Women and Authority in Early Christianity*. Minneapolis: Fortress, 2017.

Schenk, Wilbert R., ed. *North American Foreign Missions, 1810–1914: Theology, Theory, and Policy*. Grand Rapids: Eerdmans, 2004.

Schulenburg, Jane Tibbetts. *Forgetful of Their Sex: Female Sanctity and Society, ca. 500–1100*. Chicago: University of Chicago Press, 1998.

Semple, Rhonda. "Ruth, Miss Mackintosh, and Ada and Rose Marris: Biblewomen, Zenana Workers and Missionaries in Nineteenth-Century British Missions to North India." *Women's History Review* 17, no. 4 (2008): 561–74.

Seton, Rosemary. *Western Daughters in Eastern Lands: British Missionary Women in Asia*. Santa Barbara, CA: Praeger, 2013.

Sheldon, Kathleen. "Emmanuel, Christiana Abiodun (1907–1994)." In Akyeampong and Gates, *Dictionary of African Biography*, 2:298.

Shemo, Connie Anne. *The Chinese Medical Ministries of Kang Cheng and Shi Meiyu, 1872–1937*. Bethlehem, PA: Lehigh University Press, 2011.

Simons, Walter. *Cities of Ladies: Beguine Communities in the Medieval Low Countries, 1200–1565*. Philadelphia: University of Pennslvania Press, 2001.

Smith, Julia M. H. "Radegundis peccatrix: Authorizations of Virginity in Late Antique Gaul." In *Transformations of Late Antiquity: Essays for Peter Brown*, edited by Philip Rousseau and Manolis Papoutsakis, 303–26. New York: Ashgate, 2009.

Southard, M. Madeline. *The Attitude of Jesus toward Women*. Stroudsburg, PA: International Association of Women Ministers, 1999.

Spickard, Paul R., and Kevin M. Cragg. *A Global History of Christians*. Grand Rapids: Baker Academic, 2008.

"St. Ambrose, Recalling His Sister's Consecration." *Sponsa Christi* (blog), November 17, 2009. http://sponsa-christi.blogspot.com/2009/11/st-ambrose-recalling-his-sisters.html.

Stanley, John E. "Reclaiming the Church of God Heritage of Women Pastors." Paper presented at the Doctrinal Dialogue, Anderson University School of Theology, Anderson, IN, 2009.

Stanley, Susie C. *Holy Boldness: Women Preachers' Autobiographies and the Sanctified Self*. Knoxville: University of Tennessee Press, 2002.

Stasson, Anneke. "The Legacy of Irma Highbaugh." *International Bulletin of Missionary Research* 42, no. 3 (2018): 262–71.

———. *Walter and Ingrid Trobisch and the Globalization of Modern, Christian Sexual Ethics*. Eugene, OR: Wipf & Stock, forthcoming.

"St. Hildegard of Bingen." Franciscan Media. Accessed October 21, 2020. https://www.franciscanmedia.org/saint-hildegard-of-bingen/.

"St. Marcellina, Sister of St. Ambrose." Antiochian Orthodox Christian Archdiocese of North America. Accessed October 21, 2020. http://ww1.antiochian.org/node/19051.

"St. Radegund." Jesus College, Cambridge. Accessed October 21, 2020. https://www.jesus.cam.ac.uk/college/about-us/history/people-note/st-radegund.

Stubbs, W. "Bertha, Wife of Ethelbert, King of Kent." In *Dictionary of Christian Biography and Literature to the End of the Sixth Century A.D., with an Account of the Principal Sects and Heresies*, edited by Henry Wace. Christian Classics Ethereal Library. http://www.ccel.org/ccel/wace/biodict.html?term=Bertha,%20wife%20of%20Ethelbert,%20king%20of%20Kent.

Sutton, Matthew Avery. *Aimee Semple McPherson and the Resurrection of Christian America*. Cambridge, MA: Harvard University Press, 2007.

Swan, Laura. *The Forgotten Desert Mothers: Sayings, Lives, and Stories of Early Christian Women*. Mahwah, NJ: Paulist Press, 2001.

Temple, Liam Peter. "Mysticism and Identity among the English Poor Clares." *Church History* 88, no. 3 (2019): 645–71.

Tertullian. *Apology*. In vol. 3 of *The Ante-Nicene Fathers*, translated by S. Thelwall, edited by Alexander Roberts, James Donaldson, and A. Cleveland Coxe. Buffalo: Christian Literature, 1885. Revised for New Advent by Kevin Knight. https://www.newadvent.org/fathers/0301.htm.

Thérèse of Lisieux. *The Story of a Soul*. Translated by John Beevers. New York: Doubleday, 2001.

Thompson, Sally. *Women Religious: The Founding of English Nunneries after the Norman Conquest*. New York: Oxford University Press, 1991.

Thurston, Lucy G. *Life and Times of Mrs. Lucy G. Thurston, Wife of Rev. Asa Thurston, Pioneer Missionary to the Sandwich Islands, Gathered from Letters and Journals Extending over a Period of More than Fifty Years*. 2nd ed. Ann Arbor, MI: Andrews, 1882.

Tucker, Ruth A. *Extraordinary Women of Christian History: What We Can Learn from Their Struggles and Triumphs*. Grand Rapids: Baker Books, 2016.

———. *Guardians of the Great Commission: The Story of Women in Modern Missions*. Grand Rapids: Academie Books, 1988.

———. "The Role of Bible Women in World Evangelism." *Missiology: An International Review* 13, no. 2 (1985): 133–46.

Tucker, Ruth A., and Walter Liefeld. *Daughters of the Church: Women and Ministry from New Testament Times to the Present*. Grand Rapids: Academie Books, 1987.

Turpin, Andrea L. "Whose Stories We Tell and How We Tell Them: Honoring Christ in Choosing Topics and Analytical Lenses." *Fides et Historia* 51, no. 1 (2019): 94–99.

Van Engen, John. "The Voices of Women in Twelfth-Century Europe." In *Voices in Dialogue: Reading Women in the Middle Ages*, edited by Linda Olson and Kathryn Kerby-Fulton, 199–212. Notre Dame, IN: University of Notre Dame Press, 2005.

Vasilopoulos, Georgia. "Inheritance of Holiness: The Mothers of the Three Holy Hierarchs and the Teachings of the Three Holy Hierarchs on Family Therapeutics." Lecture at St. John the Baptist Greek Orthodox Church, Des Plaines, IL, 2019.

Venarde, Bruce L. *Women's Monasticism and Medieval Society: Nunneries in France and England, 890–1215.* Ithaca, NY: Cornell University Press, 1997.

Wall, Barbra Mann. *Into Africa: A Transnational History of Catholic Medical Missions and Social Change.* New Brunswick, NJ: Rutgers University Press, 2015.

Walls, Andrew. "Converts or Proselytes? The Crisis over Conversion in the Early Church." *International Bulletin of Missionary Research* 28, no. 1 (2004): 2–6.

———. *The Missionary Movement in Christian History.* Maryknoll, NY: Orbis Books, 2002.

Ward, Benedicta. "Apophthegmata Matrem." In *Studia Patristica.* Vol. 16, part 2, *Papers Presented to the Seventh International Conference on Patristic Studies Held in Oxford 1975*, edited by Elizabeth A. Livingstone, 62–66. Berlin: Akademi-Verlag, 1985.

———. *Harlots of the Desert: A Study of Repentance in Early Monastic Sources.* Kalamazoo, MI: Cistercian Publications, 1987.

Ward, Haruko Nawata. *Women Religious Leaders in Japan's Christian Century, 1549–1650.* New York: Ashgate, 2009.

Wasson, Donald. "Constantine I." *Ancient History Encyclopedia.* April 19, 2013. https://www.ancient.eu/Constantine_I/.

Wellesley, Mary. "The Life of the Anchoress." British Library, March 13, 2018. https://www.bl.uk/medieval-literature/articles/the-life-of-the-anchoress.

Wells, Ida B. *Crusade for Justice: The Autobiography of Ida B. Wells.* Edited by Alfreda M. Duster. Chicago: University of Chicago Press, 1970.

Wesley, John. *The Works of John Wesley.* Vol. 1. Grand Rapids: Baker, 1996.

"What Is Hildegard's Viriditas?" Healthy Hildegard. Accessed October 21, 2020. https://healthyhildegard.com/hildegards-viriditas/.

Wheatley, Richard. *The Life and Letters of Mrs. Phoebe Palmer.* New York: Palmer, 1876.

White, James. "Hungering for Maleness: Catherine of Siena and the Medieval Public Sphere." *Religious Studies and Theology* 33, no. 2 (2014): 157–71.

Wijngaards, John. *The Ordained Women Deacons of the Church's First Millennium.* Norwich, UK: Canterbury Press, 2011.

Wilson, Dorothy Clarke. "Scudder, Ida Sophia." In G. Anderson, *Biographical Dictionary of Christian Missions*, 609–10. https://www.bu.edu/missiology/missionary-biography/r-s/scudder-ida-sophia-1870-1960/.

———. "Swain, Clara." In G. Anderson, *Biographical Dictionary of Christian Missions*, 652.

Wirba, Kenyuyfoon Gloria. *Women and Inculturated Evangelization in Africa*. Nairobi, Kenya: Catholic University of Eastern Africa, 2012.

Witherington, Ben. *The Acts of the Apostles: A Socio-Rhetorical Commentary*. Grand Rapids: Eerdmans, 2009.

———. *Priscilla: The Life of an Early Christian*. Downers Grove, IL: IVP Academic, 2019.

———. *Women and the Genesis of Christianity*. Cambridge: Cambridge University Press, 1990.

Wood, Ian N. "Gregory of Tours and Clovis." *Revue belge de Philologie et d'Histoire* 63, no. 2 (1985): 249–72. https://www.persee.fr/doc/rbph_0035-0818_1985_num _63_2_3503.

Wu, Silas H. L. "Dora Yu (1873–1931): Foremost Female Evangelist in Twentieth-Century Chinese Revivalism." In Robert, *Gospel Bearers, Gender Barriers*, 85–99.

———. *Dora Yu and Christian Revival in 20th Century China*. Boston: Pishon River Publications, 2002.

Zahirsky, Valerie G. "Deaconess Olympias: A Sister in the Faith." In *Encountering Women of Faith: St. Catherine's Vision*, edited by Kyriaki Karidovanes Fitzgerald, 45–62. Brookline, MA: Holy Cross Orthodox Press, 2009.

INDEX